Creating a Culture for Learning

Paula Rutherford

with

Brenda Kaylor

Heather Clayton Kwit

Julie McVicker

Bruce Oliver

Sherri Stephens-Carter

Theresa West

 Just ASK Publications & Professional Development

Creating a Culture for Learning

Published by Just ASK Publications & Professional Development
2214 King Street
Alexandria, Virginia 22301
Toll Free 1-800-940-5434
FAX 1-703-535-8502
email info@justaskpublications.com
www.justaskpublications.com

To access tools and templates introduced in **Creating a Culture for Learning**, go to www.justaskpublications.com/CCLtemplates.

All Web links in this book were correct as of the publication date but may have become inactive or been changed. The publisher will check the accuracy of links at the time of each subsequent printing. Should you find a link that is changed or no longer available, please send an email to info@justaskpublications.com with updated information. Please include the link, the book title, and the page number.

Printed in the United States of America
ISBN 978-0-9830756-0-8
Library of Congress Control Number 2011934723
10 9 8 7 6 5 4 3 2 1

Table of Contents

Table of Contents

Tools and Templates Table of Contents

Go to www.justaskpublications.com/CCLtemplates to access these templates.
Thumbnails of these tools can be found on pages 289-307

Tools and Templates Table of Contents

Introduction
Creating a Culture for Learning

In high achieving environments, there exists a unified belief system that has been carefully crafted after extensive discussion and input from all stakeholders. There is no need to debate or argue about whether or not to act on these beliefs; put succinctly, all stakeholders accept the beliefs as pivotal to the success of the organization. They represent practices that are so much a part of the culture that outside observers are impressed by their efficacy and insiders do not even give them a second thought. We call these practices non-negotiables.

As you read through the descriptions of **Just ASK's Non-Negotiables for Creating a Culture for Learning**, reflect on your school's current status and ask yourself: How do these non-negotiables reflect our current practice and how might we use these non-negotiables to advance the learning of adults and students in our school?

We act on our belief that <u>all</u> students can learn!

This, the most important non-negotiable, appears first on our list. Readers will note that there is extra punctuation for emphasis. The word all is underlined because we cannot disregard the learning needs of any individual. Every child we face in our classroom deserves our attention as well as our relentless effort to find the key to his success. The exclamation point at the end of the sentence denotes the passion with which we embrace the belief that all children will show clear evidence of learning. We know that it is not acceptable to simply believe in the ability of all youngsters to learn; it must be identifiable in our words and actions and the responses of the students. Without exception, we must see each child as a capable individual who can grow in knowledge and skills.

We accept learning as the fundamental principle of the school and examine all practices in light of their impact on learning.

When student learning is the lens through which we examine our practices, the tenets of standards-based education developed by the SBE Design Team of Centennial BOCES, Longmont, Colorado, and listed below serve us well.

- Standards guide all classroom decisions.
- The focus is always on student learning.
- Expectations for learning are the same for all students, even those who have traditionally performed at low levels.
- The final determination of the effectiveness of instructional practices is whether or not they result in higher levels of achievement for students.
- Assessment results are used to inform teachers, individually and collectively, about the effectiveness of curricular and instructional decisions.

Introduction

In order to accomplish this, we know that we must be open-minded, lifelong learners who keep abreast of, share, and use research-based practices, who seek ways to scaffold and extend learning, and who are willing to forego practices that do not help students learn.

We engage in and assume leadership for promoting collaborative practice.

Noted educator Roland Barth wrote, "The relationship among the adults in the building has more impact on the quality and character of the school and the accomplishments of its youngsters than any other factor." In our meetings, including collaborative team meetings, hallway conversations, and other chance encounters, a spirit of collaboration is palatable. In fact, administrators, classroom teachers, specialists, parents, and community members work together, sharing leadership roles, to promote student learning. This requires explicit knowledge and skill, and perhaps additional training, in areas such as planning and facilitating productive meetings, adult learning theory, building consensus, and providing growth-producing feedback to one another.

We believe that all students belong to all of us.

In high-performing cultures, there is clear, enduring evidence that all stakeholders accept and act on the belief that all students belong to all adults. Inclusive pronouns such as "our" and "we" are used instead of "your," "my," and "I." The notion that one grade or content area does not have a standardized test is nonexistent because all stakeholders feel responsible for the learning of all students. General educators do not leave the education of students with special needs, accelerated learners, second language learners, etc. to the specialists who are present to support the learning of those students. Those specialists, in turn, extend their expertise to all students. As teachers work together for the success of all students, there is no evidence of blaming or finger pointing when things do not go well but instead a resolute commitment to seek solutions to problems or setbacks in the interest of each and every student's achievement.

We collectively develop and adhere to clearly articulated norms.

Working together is the guiding principle that enables us to reach our desired outcomes. At the outset of our collaborative efforts, we establish standard procedures we would follow in our work together. We work collectively to devise a list of the norms we would follow and view adherence to these norms as instrumental to our success. Norms range from establishing meeting times, decision-making processes, a respect for a variety of opinions, and that participation is both a right and a responsibility. Most importantly, we accept the premise that the primary purpose of our work together is to make a difference in

Introduction

student achievement. We agree to follow a pre-determined meeting agenda and stick to the topic under discussion so that we can move toward making decisions that will improve our practice. We believe that in cultures where norms are not established, goals are harder to reach, collaborative efforts are less structured, off-task behavior can more readily occur, and participants can become disenchanted about the potential work the team can accomplish.

We establish and maintain an atmosphere of mutual respect and trust.

Words like trust and respect are often seen in the vision or mission statements. It is all well and good to include these words in our belief statements, but they must also be reflected in our day-to-day practice. When our actions match our words, we treat each other as valuable, contributing members of the team. Visible signs of trust and respect include:

- New territory is explored and disagreements are treated with respect and opportunities to offer alternative ways of thinking are the norm.
- Each individual is given equal time to express an opinion or share an idea.
- Differences of opinion are encouraged and seen as potential solutions to problems.
- Ideas which lead to increased student learning are recognized and praised by peers.
- Interactions are characterized by honesty presented in a positive manner.
- Individuals feel comfortable exposing their vulnerability with one another because they know they will not be judged.
- The interest of the school as a whole is put first as educators share their best ideas.

Such an atmosphere of trust and respect leads to an unspoken comfort level that can lead to extraordinary results.

Isolation is not an option! Collaboration is a right and a responsibility.

In this age of accountability, schools are often judged on the results they achieve. Studies have repeatedly shown that the schools with the highest achievement are places where structures for collaboration are established and maintained over time. No longer can we work in an environment where we close our classroom doors and carry out our lessons in isolation, rarely if ever interacting with our fellow teachers. When we do not operate as individual entities and instead work in true cooperative ventures, we can expect the following results:

- Gains in student achievement
- Unforeseen solutions to problems
- Increased confidence among staff members
- A desire to test new ideas

Introduction

- More support for new teachers
- An expanded repertoire of strategies, materials, and teaching approaches

Numerous studies have concluded that a major source of discontent among professional educators is a feeling of isolation. We talk openly about the importance of working together, and organize our work environment so that collaboration will occur in a natural and fluid manner.

All adults are committed to the success of all other adults.

When we propose this non-negotiable in our workshops, there is almost always a collective gasp as participants grapple with the potential power of this construct. We interpret this reaction to mean that, for most educators, this is not a norm in their schools. If, however, we want all students to achieve at the highest levels, then all of us must also perform at the highest levels. Great care must be taken to make sure that each one of us has all the necessary information to design and carry out the best possible learning experiences for students. We avoid blaming previous teachers or parents for student learning gaps. We instead see the learning of our colleagues and the parents of our students as important components of our professional responsibility.

We focus on results.

This means that we analyze assessment results together, hold data-driven discussions, make data-driven decisions, establish SMART goals for specific measurable skills and knowledge, identify improvement strategies, and adapt instruction to meet student needs. Our definition of data extends far beyond standardized test results to creating a body of evidence that includes formative assessment data from classroom assignments and interactions with students as well as multiple other sources.

Some of the questions we continuously ask ourselves are the following:
- What data should we gather and analyze?
- What data do we have to inform our daily practice?
- How can we use data to inform long-term curricular and instructional decisions?
- How do we determine the significance of the data?
- How should the data be analyzed so that it is useful to all members of the school community, including students and parents?
- And most importantly, what action do we take after we have analyzed the data?

When these non-negotiables are in place, the way we engage in our practice almost seems seamless and uncomplicated because we no longer have to debate or discuss the way we do business. Negotiations about how to proceed are a thing

Introduction

of the past. The ultimate indicators of success can be seen in the ways these adult commitments result in more learning for more students more of the time.

We believe that it is also essential to align all the processes in our school communities so that as Terry Deal said, "We are all headed roughly West." That means for our work to make a significant difference, we must align the:

- Strategic plan
- Interviewing and hiring process
- Induction and mentoring program
- Professional development at the district, school, and team levels
- Faculty, department, and team meeting areas of focus
- Supervision and evaluation criteria and process
- Professional growth plans for individuals and teams
- School improvement plans

What does that look like? A strong example is West Irondequoit Central School District, Rochester, New York, where the Board of Education has established three focus areas in its strategic framework: Learning and Achievement, Culture and Climate, and Transitions. Pat McCue, Principal of Irondequoit High School, reports that each year, using data from standardized assessments, classroom data, and student work, each school planning team establishes or updates goals within these three focus areas, including specific targets and benchmarks to measure student progress. Each department (secondary) or grade level team (elementary) then uses these goals to guide their development of team and individual action plans and professional goals. In terms of professional learning, all faculty, department and grade level meetings are devoted to analysis of student work and other activities that promote collaborative inquiry to inform planning and improve instruction.

He wrote that at Irondequoit High School, a series of faculty meetings engaged teachers in discussions related to learning and achievement that focused on ways to strengthen students' ability to justify a claim or argument using text evidence. For example, teachers worked in interdisciplinary groups at faculty meetings to jigsaw research articles to gain understanding of effective strategies without focusing on specific content. Then, in subsequent department meetings, each department worked in teams to adapt or apply strategies in their content areas. At a follow-up faculty meeting, the interdisciplinary groups then debriefed on the effectiveness of strategies tried in their subjects knowing that writing for justification looks different in math than it does in social studies, but learning from each other's experiences and gaining new ideas.

Introduction

With those non-negotiables and the necessity of alignment in mind, this book is designed to assist educators in answering the following essential questions:

- What do schools look like when they organize around a commitment to the achievement of high standards by all students?
- What do schools look like when all the adults in the school are committed to the success of all the other adults?
- What do schools look like when they are results oriented?
- What do schools look like when all the stakeholders are committed to continuous improvement no matter how well they are already doing?

More specifically, resources for answering the focus questions listed below are provided throughout the book:

- What are the characteristics of a culture for learning?
- What are structures that promote and support a culture for learning?
- What is the role of individuals and groups in creating a culture for learning?
- What knowledge, skills, and attitudes are needed to create, implement, and maintain a culture for learning?
- What is the role of data in a school with a culture for learning?
  - How do we use data to inform daily practice?
  - How do we use data to inform long-term curricular and instructional decisions?
  - What data should we gather and analyze?
  - How do we determine the significance of the data?
  - How should the data be analyzed so that it is useful to all members of the school community, including students and parents?
- What does a review of the literature tell us about creating cultures for learning?
- What is best practice in teaching, learning, and leading in a standards-based environment?

Throughout the book, you will find self-assessments, reviews of the literature, points to ponder, practitioner exemplars, and tools and templates. The tools and templates can be accessed on the Just ASK website. Thumbnails of the tools and templates can be found on pages 289-307. The availability of these templates online is noted throughout the book and in the index with a "T" in the entry so indicating.

Also embedded throughout the text is a case study of the culture for learning that exists at McNair Elementary School located in Herndon, Virginia. The staff at McNair, a Fairfax County Public School, has demonstrated a relentless focus and commitment that has resulted in the kind of student achievement that can occur in many more places if we put our hearts, heads, and hands together and make it happen.

Introduction

This text represents our collected experiences and expertise up to this point. We look forward to continuing to learn from all the educators we are fortunate enough to work with in the future.

Paula, Brenda, Heather, Julie, Bruce, Sherri, and Theresa
September 2011

Acknowledgements

In July 2010 and again in July 2011, a team of Just ASK consultants led a **Creating a Culture for Learning Summit** in Las Cruces, New Mexico. Bruce Oliver delivered the keynote addresses and he, along with other authors of this book, Brenda Kaylor, Julie McVicker, Sherri Stephens-Carter, and Theresa West, designed and led concurrent sessions. Their personal practical experiences and expertise contributed not only to the success of those summits, but also to the ideas and exemplars that are an integral part of this book.

Additionally, Heather Clayton Kwit, a practicing principal in Pittsford Central School District, New York, consented to having components of her previously unpublished manuscript incorporated into this book. Her wisdom and voice add much to the richness of the information included here.

Other contributors include Katherine Ruh and Sarah Wolfe Hartman, ASK Group Consultants; Marcia Baldanza, Director of Federal Programs for The School District of Palm Beach, Florida; Maria Eck, Principal, McNair Elementary School, Fairfax County Public Schools (FCPS), Virginia; Richard Green, 4th Grade Teacher, Glen Forest Elementary School, FCPS, Virginia; Jay McClain, Principal, Bailey's Elementary School, FCPS, Virginia; Jeanne Spiller, Director of Professional Learning, Kildeer Countryside K-8 School District, Illinois; Barbara Walker, Educational Specialist, FCPS, Virginia; Pat McCue, Principal, Irondequoit High School, West Irondequoit Central School District, New York; Tina Grayson, High School English Teacher, Prince William Public Schools, Virginia; Chris Bryan, Instructional Improvement Group; Jason Cianfrance, Math Teacher, Legacy High School, Adams 12 School District, Colorado; and Bud Hunt, Instructional Technologist, St. Vrain Valley School District, Colorado.

Historical Perspectives
The Connections between Culture, Collaboration, and Student Learning

Faculty members, administrators, and others in successful schools have established norms of collegiality for discussing and debating the big questions about how to constantly renew and improve the educational environment for all students.

Successful schools seek, produce, and consume information, and they see educational renewal as a continuing process, not as an event.

Carl Glickman, 1984

It is not, as we commonly believe...that the past plus the present form our vision of the future.

Rather, the past plus our vision of the future form the present.

Phillip Schlechty, 1990

While it may be easier to imagine how to restructure schools rather than change their culture, the latter is the key to successful reform.

Louis, Marks, and Kruse, 1994

There is abundant research linking higher levels of student achievement to educators who work in the collaborative culture of a professional learning community.

Rick DuFour, 2011

1

Cultures for Learning

A learning community has at its heart a culture for learning by leadership, students, and staff. This learning community may be a district, school, department, team, or other groups of educators who continuously seek and share learning and then act on what they learn. The unwavering goal of their learning and actions is to enhance their effectiveness as professionals so that students learn and achieve at higher levels.

A "who's who" listing of researchers and authors on the connections between culture, collaboration, and student learning would take at least ten pages. Several significant contributions are discussed here and throughout the book. Other, no any less significant, are cited in the **Resources and References** section.

In 1985, ASCD published an article by **Jon Saphier** and **Matthew King** titled: "Good Seeds Grow in Strong Cultures." In that article they described 12 Norms of a Healthy School Culture which have withstood the test of time. That article combined with the Judith Warren Little's landmark work: "Norms of Collegiality and Experimentation: Workplace Conditions for School Success" published in 1982 in the **American Education Research Journal** are two of the writings that most strongly influence our work. The key ideas from each of those can be found on page 5.

Other important contributions to the literature on learning cultures include the work of **Susan Rosenholtz** who in 1989 wrote that teachers who felt supported as ongoing learners were more committed and effective as teachers than teachers who did not receive such support. She described that support as cooperation among colleagues and expanded roles as professionals. According to Rosenholtz, this increased teacher sense of self-efficacy resulted in teachers meeting students' needs more effectively. Finally, she concluded that teachers with a high sense of efficacy were more likely to experiment with new classroom practices and were more likely to remain in the profession. **Milbery McLaughlin** and **Joan Talbert** reached similar conclusions in research published in 1993. They discovered that when teachers were given opportunities to collaborate with one another, they were able to more frequently and productively adapt their instruction to meet the needs of learners and subsequently share their learning and wisdom with one another. In 1996, **Linda Darling-Hammond** pointed out that shared decision making had a significant positive influence on curriculum reform and the transformation of the roles of teachers in schools. She found that schools were more effective when teachers were provided time to work together to plan, to observe one another in the classroom, and to share feedback with one another.

Peter Senge wrote in his 1990 book, ***The Fifth Discipline***, that learning organizations are "organizations where people continually expand their capacity

Cultures for Learning

to create the results they truly desire, where new and expansive patterns of thinking are nurtured, where collective aspiration is set free, and where people are continually learning to see the whole."

Rick DuFour and **Robert Eaker** in their book *Professional Learning Communities at Work: Best Practices for Enhancing Student Achievement* offer practical and comprehensive applications of the research on learning organizations. Many schools and school districts are working hard to establish and sustain professional learning communities (PLCs) as described by DuFour and Eaker.

This book is designed to help readers explore a wide array of collaborative practices that result in higher student achievement and greater teacher satisfaction. It also delves into how this array of practices can be combined and used in a comprehensive way. The desired state is one in which each school is a PLC and each department or team is a collaborate team. There are, however, many actions that educators can take along the way to that desired state. Providing that they result in action, collegial collaboration, professional inquiry, and data-driven discussions in the interest of student learning are always worthwhile endeavors.

Driving Forces for
Creating a Culture for Learning

Jon Saphier and Matt King's
Norms of School Culture

- Collegiality
- Experimentation
- High expectations
- Trust and confidence
- Tangible support
- Reaching out to knowledge base
- Appreciation and recognition
- Caring, celebration, and humor
- Involvement in decision making
- Protection of what's important
- Traditions
- Honest, open communication

Judith Warren Little's
Norms of Collegiality and Experimentation

- Frequent concrete talk about teaching and learning
- Common vocabulary and concept system
- Continuous improvement (experimentation)
- Frequent observation of one another in our practice
- Asking for and providing one another assistance

Driving Forces for
Creating a Culture for Learning

Terry Deal and Kent Peterson's
Essential Culture Attributes

- The staff has a shared sense of purpose.
- The underlying norms are collegiality, improvement, and hard work.
- The rituals and traditions celebrate student accomplishment, teacher innovation, and parental commitment.
- The informal network of storytellers, heroes, and heroines provides a social web of information, support, and history.
- Success, joy, and humor abound.

Culture influences everything that goes on in schools: how staffs dress, what they talk about, their willingness to change, the practice of instruction, and the emphasis given to faculty and student learning.

Rick DuFour and Robert Eaker's
Four Key Questions

- What is it we want our students to learn?
- How will we know if each student has learned it?
- How will we respond when some students do not learn it?
- How can we extend and enrich the learning for students who have demonstrated proficiency?

We respectfully wish to modify the second question to read: **How will we and they know when they have learned it?** Additionally, we would insert as the third bullet: **How will they learn it?**

Driving Forces for
Creating a Culture for Learning

Bruce Joyce and Beverly Showers'
Impact of Professional Development on Classroom Practice

Impact / Training Components	Understanding Knowledge and Skills	Actually Learn Skills	Actually Apply Skills in Classroom
Presentation of Theory	85%	15%	10-15%
Modeling	85%	18%	10-15%
Practice and Low- Risk Feedback	85%	80%	10-15%
Coaching Feedback/Peer Visits	85%	90%	**80-90%**

This legendary research clearly indicates the necessity of collaboration in the form of coaching and feedback, collaborative planning, peer observations, lesson study, and learning walks. Best practice in 21st century professional development does not negate the power of attending conferences and workshops; it however, is clear, that such attendance is not enough. Public teaching, holding one another accountable, and making data-driven decisions must also be part of the equation.

Creating a Culture for Learning

The essential question for our work is: **What do schools look like when they are organized around a commitment to the achievement of high standards by all students?** This question has many different answers but some constants hold true. In such a school, learning is not a goal just for students; it is also a goal for all staff members. In such a school, all educators are committed not only to the achievement of high standards by all students but to the achievement of high standards by all educators. In such a school, the answer to a query of what are we going to do to make that happen is, whatever it takes!

In such a school, professional development is not an event; it is a way of life. In fact, in such a school, it is the norm for all to seek frequent opportunities to learn from and teach each other.

In such a school, student success is the most important criterion for measuring the success of teachers and administrators collectively and individually. It is the norm for all to examine student work and use what is learned from that examination to make decisions about instruction. In such a school, general education teachers, special education teachers, and administrators study and learn together.

In such a school, there is little turnover of staff. Richard Ingersoll notes that while teacher retirement creates many job openings, the "revolving door" significantly increases the number of new teachers needed. We must create cultures in which new teachers are supported in becoming fully-qualified and feel welcomed as contributing members of the staff. In such a school, new staff members are given equal status and are not subjected to hazing-like conditions such as the least desirable schedule, multiple preparations and teaching locations, and leftover materials and furniture.

In such a school, all staff members epitomize professionalism by mentoring new staff formally and informally, and by willingly and productively learning to co-teach in inclusive classrooms without turf wars or a me/my mentality. In such a school, value is placed on shared leadership, responsibility, and decision making in recognition of individual and collective commitment to student learning.

In such a school, there are commonly held, clearly articulated, and acted upon beliefs. Those beliefs place high value on student learning and professional growth of staff. Acting on those beliefs means that in such a school, teachers gather and analyze data, and use the disaggregated data to make instructional and curricular decisions. In such a school, people make internal rather than external attributions, and therefore, constantly and honestly monitor the effectiveness of their efforts. In such a school, there is a sense of interdependence and continuous improvement rather than a focus on autonomy and maintaining the status quo.

Points to Ponder
Building Strong School Cultures: Signs of Progress
Bruce Oliver

Educators all across the nation and world are searching for answers that will help improve student achievement and overall learning in their schools. In their search, many schools are going through a restructuring process as they try to determine what is working in their buildings and what needs to be revised or changed completely. As they seek new and better ideas, they develop improvement plans, extensively analyze achievement data, and examine their overall school culture. Almost universally, they are making sincere, good-hearted attempts to make a positive difference in their schools.

In schools where educators are achieving their goals, there are certain behaviors that are indicative of strong school cultures. A closer examination of the attitudes and actions in these schools provides vivid clues about why some schools are successful while others seem to struggle. Three questions that may lead to some answers are:

- **What makes a school culture stronger?**
- **What are the indicators that the culture has strengthened?**
- **What do administrators and teachers do that results in exceptional student achievement?**

The following practices offer insights into the signs that the culture of the school is moving in the right direction.

Unified Vision
All adults in the school are involved in the establishment of the school's mission and vision. As a result, the words contained in the mission statement are not pat phrases or empty rhetoric, but true representations of the views of the adults who will be charged with bringing life to the words in the vision. The staff members also fully understand that there is no one formula or recipe to reach projected goals. They begin by adapting a conceptual framework which is fluid and which can be altered and adjusted as the vision is pursued.

Collaborative Decisions
In great school cultures, all stakeholders know that they not only have a voice in decisions but that they will be truly heard. Leaders do not provide answers but instead ask questions that not only inspire but also provoke. As author Jim Collins notes, in strong cultures, leaders "encourage debate and dialogue, not coercion." They establish a system whereby "red flags" expose data and information that can no longer be ignored. The leaders also understand that top-down mandates do not work. There are no pronouncements or decisions made in isolation. The leaders build alliances with teachers, parents, and students recognizing that everyone must be included in establishing the school's direction.

Points to Ponder
Building Strong School Cultures: Signs of Progress

Guaranteed Curriculum
In cultures dedicated to student learning, all students are guaranteed and have access to the same rich curriculum, knowledge, and skills as all other students. No students are ever left behind. Data are continually used to identify students who need additional support for learning. Students are not made to feel that they are burdens or "losers" but individuals who may need more time and support to master the identified curriculum. Adults devise a system of supports for student learning that enables all students to be successful.

True Collaboration
When schools reach a stage of true collaboration in all arenas of the school, there is no competition, no distrust, and no disharmony. Teacher teams fully understand that their mission is to increase student learning. They are willing to bring any and all issues related to improved instruction to a team meeting or to a table discussion with no hesitation or reservation. As Rick DuFour describes it, the adults move from "collaboration lite" to honest, purposeful professional interactions.

Deep Discussions
Discussions at team meetings have depth, explore new territory, and expand on ways to take student learning to higher levels of thinking and problem solving. Bloom's Taxonomy is ever-present at team meetings. The adults understand that teaching is not simply a march through benchmarks but the execution of exciting, student-centered learning experiences based on research-based strategies. In addition, the team members establish pacing guides which guarantee that each team member will be able to teach the essential content for which the teachers are responsible. The teammates fully understand and believe that collaboration is the most effective method that will enable each member to deliver the best instruction possible.

Rigorous Instruction
There is extensive evidence of rigor throughout all curricular areas since the adults understand that their mission is to stretch each student to his or her fullest potential. To motivate students to tackle a rigorous curriculum, teachers build close relationships with students and provide encouragement and reinforcement to keep students intrinsically motivated and totally immersed in their learning. Researchers Linda Darling-Hammond and Diane Friedlaender examined the practices of five urban California high schools that had the same low-income populations as surrounding schools with similar demographics. They found that the five schools graduated and sent students to college at levels far above the state average. The reason for the difference in achievement, they concluded, was the "rigorous courses led by teachers who build close bonds

Points to Ponder
Building Strong School Cultures: Signs of Progress

with students and who collaborate professionally."

Data-Driven Analyses

Teachers make decisions that are based on student achievement data. As they collaborate, they examine both formative and summative data to determine next steps in instructional delivery. They firmly believe that there must be a way to improve student learning. Likewise, they are not defensive about data; they don't make excuses if data results are not good. They analyze, reflect, and, in some cases, decide which students need second chances on an assessment or which students may require reteaching. As Robert Marzano has written, confident educators use "disappointing results as implementation challenges to inspire hope and resilience."

Caring Attitudes

As problems arise and school wide decisions are made, strong cultures do not respond with more rules and harsher punishments. Instead there is a renewed emphasis on high expectations and a caring attitude toward individual students. The adults clearly understand and accept that it is the student/teacher relationships that can make the greatest difference in student growth.

Responsive Leaders

In his work in professional learning communities, Rick DuFour has written that "Hosts of researchers...have concluded that substantive change inevitably creates discomfort and dissonance as people are asked to act in new ways." It is often a conflict that cannot be ignored or avoided. A diligent leader also understands the human dynamics of the change process and anticipates that change may result in a certain amount of fear, insecurity, and, in some instances, stonewalling on the part of the teaching staff. The leader must persevere with a sense of calm and establish a tone of persistent effort over time by making the vision statement a living document and by being responsive to the concerns of teachers, parents, and students.

Ongoing Support

In healthy school cultures, the leader is tuned in to the day-to-day climate of the school and responds to needs in a timely manner. He or she is able to distinguish when individual teachers are going through the motions instead of having an emotional investment in the school's vision. This leader does not judge, neglect, or abandon struggling staff members but instead determines what type of support an individual might need in order to establish a stronger commitment to the school's goals. The leader also has a clear plan to involve new staff members in becoming acclimated to the school's vision. Stated another way, the competent leader looks for ways to revitalize not demoralize.

Points to Ponder
Building Strong School Cultures: Signs of Progress

Fierce Resolve

Participants in establishing and maintaining an enduring school culture realize, in the words of writer Jim Collins, that there is "no single defining moment." It is a "cumulative process, step by step, action by action, discussion by discussion, and pushing in a constant direction over an extensive period of time" that makes an unquestionable difference. To achieve legitimate success, there are no shortcuts but a fierce resolve to maintain a coherent and constant work ethic over the long haul.

Educational Politics

Calling upon my background as a social studies teacher, another way to determine if the school culture is moving in the right direction is to use political terminology in an analogous comparison to the culture of schools. If schools are to become truly invigorated, there must be a sense of **bipartisanship** in which all participants work toward a collective goal. The culture needs to include **constructive dialogue and negotiations** in order to **form a more perfect union**. Once the vision is established, participants must agree to eliminate the "**pork**" from every curriculum area and concentrate on consistent standards from classroom to classroom. The leader must periodically apprise the staff of the **state of the union** in order to encourage honest dialogue and, where appropriate, introduce a **stimulus package** to promote ongoing progress. And finally, when all is said and done, the culture of the school can be summed up in just a few words: **We can do it!**

These remarks, written by Bruce Oliver, were originally published in the March 2009 issue of *Just for the ASKing!* Over eighty issues of *Just for the ASKing!* are archived and available at no charge at www.justaskpublications.com.

Waving Your Priorities from the Flagpole
Heather Clayton Kwit

Establishing a Set of Common Beliefs That Support Your Focus

After a school has spent time learning about best practices in a specific area and embedded these practices into a school improvement plan, it is important to make your beliefs concrete. Every staff member in the building needs to know what the vision is and demonstrate practices that lead the school towards achieving that vision.

The following process was followed in a school that had established literacy as its focus for several years. After the first year of this focus, staff gathered together to review all that they had learned and to combine that into a concrete set of beliefs that all staff would commit to supporting.

For this activity, staff was broken into mixed groups. Each group included teachers from various grade levels, special area teacher(s), special education teachers or service providers from related areas such as speech teacher, a reading specialist, or English as a Second Language teacher, and paraprofessional. At each table was a collection of the articles that had been read by staff over the previous year, along with any book excerpts, or entire books that were read by the staff. In addition, any videos that had been viewed were available.

An essential question given to each group read: *What do we believe our students need in order to be proficient literacy learners?*

Each group used their background knowledge along with the professional resources they had previously read to record on chart paper a list of ideas to support the essential question. After the lists were posted, each group shared its list. Statements that appeared on more than one chart, most of the time appearing on several charts, were recorded on a separate chart. At the end of the activity, the common ideas that had been recorded on the summary chart formed a core set of beliefs about literacy. The staff was invited at that time to make additional revisions to the list.

Waving Your Priorities from the Flagpole

Our Belief Statement on Literacy Learning

Our classroom practice is based on our beliefs about what children need to be proficient literacy learners. The following statements help us to design our reading and writing workshops for students. You will find evidence of these beliefs as you visit our classrooms.

In order to be proficient literacy learners, we believe our children need:
- Confidence in their abilities as readers and writers.
- Large blocks of predictable time to read appropriate materials and to write each day.
- Physically appealing and organized environments that are print rich.
- Access to rich collections of texts, varying by level, topic, and genre.
- Opportunities to read, write, listen, and speak for authentic purposes across all curricular areas.
- Explicit teaching of strategies and opportunities to flexibly apply these strategies in the context of their reading, writing and content area studies.
- Instruction in a variety of formats (small guided groups, individual conferences, whole group mini-lessons, and share sessions).
- An understanding that reading is a meaning-making process.
- To dialogue about their reading and writing and reflect on their growth as readers and writers.
- An understanding of the reading-writing connection and how words work.
- Models for life-long literacy and demonstrations of fluent reading behavior.

Once this document was developed, it became a source of common language and practices across the building. Not only should belief statements be posted, but they should be put in the hands of parents and should be evident to anyone visiting the school, but especially to the children.

Waving Your Priorities from the Flagpole

Measure Your Beliefs Against Your Everyday Practice

Once you have consensus on a core set of beliefs that drive the practices in your building, it is an excellent time to measure what people believe and what practices are used on a consistent basis to strengthen those beliefs.

Prior to meeting with staff, create a common beliefs inventory and **Common Practices Inventory**. The common beliefs you list would be those generated previously with staff. The **Common Practices Inventory** consists of practices that correlate with each belief. For example, practice #1 would match belief #1. First, distribute the **Common Beliefs Inventory** to each member of your staff and have them read the statement, then circle the percentage that indicates their degree of agreement with 100 percent being the highest level of agreement to 10 percent showing the lowest level of agreement. Hanging on the wall should be charts with one belief listed on each one. After completing the inventory, staff members should place a colored sticky note next to the percentage they answered for each belief statement.

Belief Statement Listed Across Top

100%   Place small sticky notes next to the
         percentage given for listed statement.
90%

80%

70%

60%

50%

40%

30%

20%

10%

Waving Your Priorities from the Flagpole

Next, distribute the **Common Practice Inventory** to each member of the staff and have them read the statement, then circle the percentage that indicates their degree of agreement with 100 percent being the highest level of agreement to 10 percent showing the lowest level of agreement. Hanging on the wall next to the chart for each belief statement should be a chart listing the practice that correlates with that belief statement. There should be a chart **for each practice** listed. After completing the inventory, staff members should place a colored sticky note next to the percentage they answered for each belief statement.

Practice Statement Listed Across Top

100%   Place small sticky notes next to the
         percentage given for statement listed.

90%

80%

70%

60%

50%

40%

30%

20%

10%

Once each pair of charts has been displayed, staff can look at the data to see if there is a disconnect between what they believe and what they actually practice. This presents a great opportunity to have some discussion about which practices should be built into the everyday life of the school.

Waving Your Priorities from the Flagpole

Our Common Beliefs Inventory on Literacy Learning

I. Directions: For each statement below, circle the percentage that indicates your degree of agreement, 100 percent (highest level of agreement) to 10 percent (lowest level of agreement). Use your own personal experience and observations to mark each statement.

In order to be proficient literacy learners, I believe that my students need

1.   A physically appealing and organized environment that is rich in print.

    100   90   80   70   60   50   40   30   20   10

2.   Opportunities to read, write, listen and speak for authentic purposes across all curricular areas.

    100   90   80   70   60   50   40   30   20   10

3.   Explicit teaching of strategies and opportunities to flexibly apply strategies in the context of their reading and writing.

    100   90   80   70   60   50   40   30   20   10

4.   Instruction in a variety of formats (small guided groups, individual conferences, whole group mini-lessons and share sessions).

    100   90   80   70   60   50   40   30   20   10

5.   An understanding that reading is a meaning-making process.

    100   90   80   70   60   50   40   30   20   10

6.   To dialogue about their reading and writing and reflect on their growth as readers and writers.

    100   90   80   70   60   50   40   30   20   10

II. Directions: When you have completed your ratings, use the colored sticky notes to record your responses (percentages) on the wall charts for each topic.

Waving Your Priorities from the Flagpole

Our Common Practices Inventory on Literacy Learning

I. Directions: For each statement below, circle the percentage that indicates your degree of application, 100 percent (highest level of application) to 10 percent (lowest level of application). Be sure that you respond according to what actually is, not what should be in your classroom.

1. In our classroom, I have prominently displayed student work, literacy-based resources, and essential vocabulary. The environment is organized and clutter-free with all materials readily accessible to students.

    100   90   80   70   60   50   40   30   20   10

2. In our classroom, students are expected to read and write for a variety of real-world audiences and purposes. Students frequently send their work out into the world of the school, their families or the wider community.

    100   90   80   70   60   50   40   30   20   10

3. In our classroom, rather than telling my students what to do as readers, I explicitly show learners how I think and apply strategies when I read by modeling and thinking aloud, guiding students in small groups, and providing large blocks of time for students to read and practice using and applying strategies.

    100   90   80   70   60   50   40   30   20   10

4. My literacy instruction is driven by my students' needs. I confer with students daily, record the data and use that information to plan varied instructional groups, mini-lessons, guided reading and writing lessons and opportunities for sharing.

    100   90   80   70   60   50   40   30   20   10

5. I have devoted time to exploring my own processes as a reader. Frequently reading adult texts, I practice metacognition and apply comprehension strategies to build a foundation for understanding how to teach comprehension.

    100   90   80   70   60   50   40   30   20   10

Waving Your Priorities from the Flagpole

6.   In our classroom, all students know their independent and instructional reading levels, as well as their writing levels as they relate to a 4 pt. or 6 pt. rubric. All students use their current levels of academic performance to set goals for improvement and reflect on those goals in writing at regular intervals.

      100   90   80   70   60   50   40   30   20   10

II. Directions: When you have completed your ratings, use the colored sticky notes to record your responses (percentages) on the wall charts for each topic.

Our Common Beliefs Inventory on Literacy Learning and
Our Common Practices Inventory on Literacy Learning are available online.

The Saga of Gemini Junior High School Math

Katherine Ruh

Year	AYP % Required (Students meeting or exceeding standard)	AYP Status
03-04	40.0	No
04-05	47.5	No
05-06	47.5	Yes
06-07	55.0	Yes
07-08	62.5	Yes

This is a historical documentation of what changed at Gemini Junior High School, East Maine School District #63, Des Plaines, Illinois, to cause the scores to rise at a rate that exceeded the increase in AYP status percentage.

Standards guide all classroom decisions.

The math team, under the guidance of the curriculum department, carefully reviewed the Illinois State Standards and the Math Assessment Frameworks. This resulted in significant changes in the district's benchmarks for math. As a result, new math instructional materials were purchased. The team then carefully reviewed every book and identified:
- which chapters covered the benchmarks
- what order the chapters should be taught
- what parts of each chapter should be taught
- what additional materials needed to be used to teach the benchmarks

The focus is always on student learning.

In addition to continually revising and refining instruction, the principal, school leadership team, and teachers took the following actions:
- The principal and school leadership team set forth a goal requiring a lesson in math to be taught weekly in every subject. Teachers in all subject areas were expected to structure a math lesson tied to the subject at hand, showing real-world connections.
- The course schedule offerings were changed to include an additional hour of math instruction (called Math Enrichment) for students in need of additional support in math.
- Math teachers volunteered to run lunchtime tutoring sessions for students. There was an expectation that students who were not succeeding would attend.

The Saga of Gemini Junior High School Math

Additionally, **Skills Tutor**, an online math instruction program, was used after school. Math teachers were paid to work with students. Each student in need of this program had a conference with the principal, and parents were informed that their student "must" attend. There was a very high rate of attendance.

Expectations for learning are the same for all students, even those who traditionally performed at low levels.

The team recognized that there were different expectations for students in the area of math. Before making changes there were two tracks for math:

- Lower performing students took 7th grade math and then 8th grade math (both courses were watered down, with low expectations).
- Average or above average performing students took Pre-Algebra in 7th and Algebra in 8th.

The team determined that all students would leave 8th grade having successfully taken at least Pre-Algebra. As a result, the course sequence was changed. Lower performing students took a 7th grade course (with changes in content) and then Pre-Algebra as 8th graders and the remaining students followed the previous sequence.

The final determination of the effectiveness of instructional practices is whether or not they result in high levels of achievement for students.

The chart on the previous page says it all. Currently more than 85% of all students meet or exceed standards, and every subgroup also met or exceeded the 62.5% state requirement.

Assessment results are used to inform the teacher about the effectiveness of curricular and instructional decisions.

All students were given the MAP (Measure of Academic Progress) online math test three times per year. This data was used to determine placement in the math courses and to determine what areas of instructional need existed for individual students. There is a high correlation between MAP test scores and probable success on the Illinois State Achievement Test (ISAT): this was used to identify students who needed to attend Skills Tutor programming.

The Saga of Gemini Junior High School Math

The entire math team regularly examined MAP and other assessment results and made changes in curricular focus and instructional strategies as needed.

Other notable points
- All math teachers had taken **Instruction For All Students I** and most had taken **Instruction for All Students II**, both led by the Executive Director of Curriculum and Instruction.
- The principal, along with all other district administrators, completed both **Instruction for All Students I** and **Leading the Learning**.
- The curriculum department supported the changes with funding and time.

Good schools are places that recognize the powerful relationship between the learning and achievement of students and the development and expression of teachers.

Sara Lawrence-Lightfoot
Harvard Professor of Education

Our Professional Learning Community
McNair Elementary Case Study
Theresa West and Maria Eck

This is the first of many artifacts of the **McNair Elementary Case Study**. Theresa West, Principal, and Maria Eck, Assistant Principal, of McNair Elementary School, Fairfax County Public Schools, Virginia, wrote this overview as part of their work in Just ASK's **Leading the Learning** workshop series.

What we tried to do:

Our goal was to create a school that is organized around a commitment to achievement of high standards by all students. We began this journey by:

- Creating a master schedule to support collaborative teams and set aside two days a week to meet specifically to discuss math and language arts.
- Supporting teachers with the development of common assessments and the practice of reviewing them together.
- Facilitating the creation/use of pacing guides to support instruction at each grade level.
- Analyzing student achievement data in order to determine how to proceed with our teaching.
- Providing a variety of staff development opportunities to improve and extend teachers' instructional repertoire.
- Providing teachers the opportunity to observe high functioning teams in action.

Why we chose the actions we did:

- We did not have common structures or organization in place to support student learning.
- Although people met as teams, they did not have effective meetings that focused on teaching and student learning.
- We had never made AYP at McNair.
- Teaching strategies were not matched to the needs of our students.
- We needed a common structure and a common language to support learning at McNair; our students deserved consistency.

How what we intended to do matched what we actually did:

- We intended to create an effective schoolwide PLC, it matched very well, but was a two-year and an ongoing process.

How the outcomes matched what we wanted:

- The teachers have the tools and support to be more thoughtful and reflective practitioners.
- The teachers have expanded their repertoires and have new instructional strategies to use with their students.
- Even the lowest functioning teams successfully incorporated the basic tenets of PLC.

Our Professional Learning Community
McNair Elementary Case Study

- High functioning teams have really taken off and shown increased student achievement as demonstrated by assessments results.

What we will do differently:
- Change the level of supervision to provide more structure for low functioning teams.
- Differentiate structures for teams based on identified needs.
- Create a larger focus on unit plans vs. pacing guides and request that they be submitted as part of the team notebook.

What we want to do as a result of the actions we took:
- Participate in continuous improvement by revisiting our team planning practices.
- Use "Examining the Current Status" assessment, and continue to build and improve upon what has been developed.
- Have our teachers become experts and be able to share with others.

The connection of this work to student achievement:
- Students are being taught what is being measured.
- Common assessments are showing strong results; when the results show an extra need, teachers are working to meet the needs.

The Connections between Culture, Collaboration, and Student Learning

Prior to implementing this plan, McNair Elementary had never made AYP. Following this process, McNair made AYP for the first time in 2008-2009 and made it again in 2009-2010.

Look for multiple artifacts from the **McNair Elementary Case Study** in each chapter of this book.

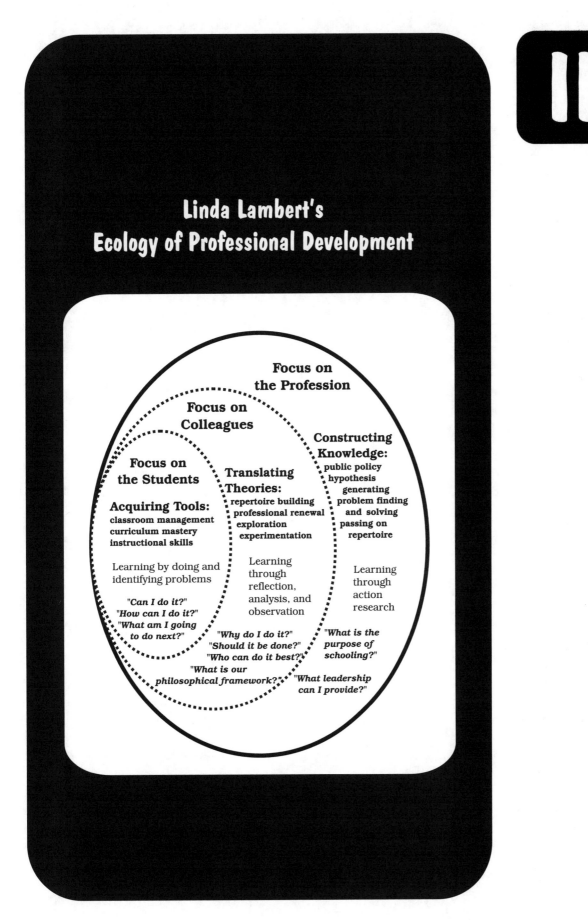

Linda Lambert's
Ecology of Professional Development

Focus on
the Profession

Focus on
Colleagues

**Constructing
Knowledge:**
public policy
hypothesis
generating
problem finding
and solving
passing on
repertoire

Focus on
the Students

**Translating
Theories:**
repertoire building
professional renewal
exploration
experimentation

Acquiring Tools:
classroom management
curriculum mastery
instructional skills

Learning by doing and
identifying problems

Learning
through
reflection,
analysis, and
observation

Learning
through
action
research

"Can I do it?"
"How can I do it?"
*"What am I going
to do next?"*

"Why do I do it?"
"Should it be done?"
"Who can do it best?"

*"What is the
purpose of
schooling?"*

*"What is our
philosophical framework?"*

*"What leadership
can I provide?"*

Communication Skills for Collaboration

Communication Skills
Respecting Differences and Building on Commonalities

It is essential that we make deposits in our relationships checking accounts and there is no better way to do that than through exquisite communication skills. How we listen, how we speak, how we read non-verbal cues and many more communication skills greatly impact our capacity to make those deposits. For starters, while we bring different life experiences to our professional work, we can certainly build on our commonalities. As Bruce Oliver wrote in the February 2007 issue of *Just for the ASKing!*, "It is all about relationships." With that perspective in mind, three chunks from the research base on who we are as individuals and adults need to be explored.

We learned from Judy-Arin Krupp that we all want:
- Personal worth
- Well-launched children
- Ability to handle adversity
- Health
- Success by our own definition
- Meaningful relationships
- Independence for as long as possible

Jennifer Deal wrote in her recent book that:
- All generations have similar values; they just express them differently.
- Everyone wants respect. They just don't define it the same way.
- Trust matters to all of us.
- Loyalty depends on the context, not on the generation.
- People want leaders who are credible and trustworthy.
- Organizational politics is a problem - No matter how old (or young) you are.
- Everyone wants to learn - More than just about anything else.

The extensive body of research on adult learning reveals that our colleagues:
- Need to be validated
- Experience a dip in self-efficacy with new initiatives
- Spend all day with children so they need adult socialization
- Need choice of how they learn
- Internalize and use strategies that they experience
- Respond to humor
- Want feedback on work they do
- Need examples that match their realities

This chapter explores some of the commonalities, complexities, and contrasts we encounter as we seek to fine tune our communications skills and move toward more and more interdependence and collaboration in our professional lives.

Communication Skills

Everyday Listening 101
- Stop talking and listen.
- Concentrate. Do not plan your response while the other person is still talking or you will miss part of what is said.
- Do not interrupt.
- React to the ideas being expressed not to the person.
- Listen for what is not said.
- Listen for how something is said.
- Listen for external and internal attributions and use attribution retraining to help reframe external attributions.
- Try to identify the underlying cause of any concerns and then match your response to your best guess as to the cause of the concern.
- Monitor your own filters.

If You Want to Signal That You Are Ready to Listen...
- Have calls held and cell phone off.
- Have related papers and materials where you can access them immediately.
- Put away all other papers that might be a distraction.
- Make eye contact.
- Nod affirmatively and make minimal encouraging responses like "I see," "Hmmm," and "Interesting."
- Paraphrase what is said.
- Ask clarifying questions.
- Avoid communication stoppers like "If I were you, I would have tried...," "Based on my experience, I feel that the best thing to do is...," "I told you that wouldn't work."
- In conference situations, be prepared with notes analyzed, connections to past experiences clarified, and questions and discussion points ready.

If You Want to Signal That You Want to Work Collaboratively...
Do all of the above and...
- Sit side-by-side rather than on the other side of a table or desk
- Explicitly learn and use the six-step problem solving process and follow the steps in working together.
- Prepare copies of any materials you are going to refer to during the meeting or conference

Communication Skills

If You Want to Signal...

- That the professional conversation is over... digress to personal topics, look at your watch, begin to check your calendar, stand up, and head toward the door.
- That you are just going through the paces... follow only your own script and do not respond to colleagues' silences, emotions, questions, and concerns; take phone calls, leave your cell phone on, have difficulty finding your notes from the last meeting or other necessary papers.
- That you are taking a position of authority and/or superiority...sit behind a desk and control the flow of the conversation
- That you have better things to do... flip through your calendar, make notes about unrelated issues.
- That you do not believe these collaborative team meetings or other interactions provide valuable opportunities for professional dialogue... cancel appointments, be late for meetings, always be in a hurry, or forget to bring materials you promised to bring.

Avoid killer statements such as...

- "Don't you believe... ."
- "Wouldn't you agree...?"
- "Where did you get that idea?"
- "Everyone ought to... ."
- "People should... ."
- "Everyone knows that... ."
- "That will not work... ."
- "The best solution is... ."

Do You Hear What I Say?
Do I Hear What You Say?

Our own personal experiences combined with our natural tendencies to process information in certain ways makes understanding or influencing another's thinking a complex endeavor. We should never underestimate the power of understanding how others view the world and the lens through which they process events, information, and authority. If we can predict, or at least consider, why people react and respond the way they do to us, to new initiatives, to new directions, to conflicting information, to financial and political realities, and to data, we can better plan our collaborative interactions.

No way of processing information is better than any other way. We all have preferences or default behaviors. Handedness is an example of a strongly held preference. We automatically write with either our left or right hand, but when necessary we can write with our other hand. It would be harder, slower, and messier, but we could do it. It would definitely require practice to build skill in using the non-preferred hand. The same is true with information processing styles.

The communication challenge comes with the need to step out of our own comfort zone to establish cognitive empathy, recognize another's view of the world, and respond accordingly. Use the **Information Processing Style Survey** on the following pages to assess your own tendencies and then read through it again trying to see the world the way you think those with whom you are collaborating do. Once you identify potential differences, you can plan how to accommodate them. On the other hand, it may be that all those working on a task view the world the same way; in that case, you may need to assume a different stance and question rapidly made decisions. This information on information processing styles can be valuable not only in your interactions with colleagues, but also with students and parents.

Information Processing Styles Survey
Do you hear what I say? Do I hear what you say?

Complete the survey below by identifying your own preferences. Then compare your choices with a partner. Discuss how the similarities and differences you identify could impact the effectiveness and efficiency of your interactions as you work together in a collegial relationship.

Me You Preferences in Processing Information

___ ___ **Are you more introverted or extroverted?** Do you prefer to respond to new information immediately and do your thinking out loud (extroverted) or do you prefer information in advance so that you have time to think about the issues before you have to respond (introverted)?

___ ___ **Are you more global or analytical?** Do you tend to see the big picture and like to have scaffolding on which to hang details (global) or do you prefer to see the bits and pieces and then put them into the whole (analytical)?

___ ___ **Are you more random or sequential?** Do you prefer to work through steps in sequence (sequential) or are you more inclined to jump around and deal with what interests you in the moment (random)?

___ ___ **Are you more concrete or abstract?** Do you want to see the real thing (concrete) rather than hear about the theory or the possibilities (abstract)?

___ ___ **Do you live more in the moment, in the past, or in the future?** Is what happened in the past, what is happening right now, or what the future will bring that matters most?

___ ___ **Are you inclined to be more decisive or open-ended?** Do you tend to make quick decisions and stand by them (decisive) or do you prefer to continue to gather information and have several options (open-ended)?

___ ___ **Do you lead with your heart or your head?** Do you most often say, "I think" (head) or are you more likely to say "I feel" (heart)?

Information Processing Styles Survey

___ ___ **Do you ask why or how?** Which question is the first to come to your mind when someone presents information. Do you ask "Why is that a good idea?" (why) or do you more often ask "How would that look?" (how)?

___ ___ **Do you learn by observing or are you a hands-on active learner?** Do you learn best by observing from a distance (observer) or do you need to get into the action and mess around with the new ideas and processes (hands-on)?

___ ___ **Are you inclined to seek out research or focus on personal practical experience?** Are you interested in what the experts have to say about the information or strategy (research-based) or do you tend to rely more on what you have used in the past (personal practical experience)?

___ ___ **Do you prefer to plan ahead or wait until the last minute?** Do you finish projects well in advance and put them away until needed (plan ahead) or are you inclined to fill all available time no matter when you start (last minute)?

___ ___ **Do you make internal or external attributions?** Do you tend to question the effectiveness of your own efforts (internal) or do you attribute success or failure to variables that are beyond your control (external)?

___ ___ **Do you consider yourself more positive or pessimistic?** Do you view the world through a rose-colored lens (positive) or are you more likely to see problems just around the corner (pessimistic)?

___ ___ **Are you more logical or intuitive?** Do you prefer to measure and quantify things (logical) or are you comfortable knowing without knowing how you know (intuitive)?

___ ___ **Do you consider yourself a systems thinker or do you have more of a focused personal view?** Do you think more about how actions and information impact the complex organization around you (systems) or do you focus on the world right around you (personal view)?

___ ___ **Do you see power as based in position power or personal power?** Do you define authority primarily by the titles people hold (position)? or by the respect they have earned (personal)?

Information Processing Styles Survey template is available online.

Using Knowledge of Self to
Develop Interpersonal Skills
Based on the Myers-Briggs Type Indicator

So you want to make things happen! You want to get things done! You want to convince someone else to walk beside you on a new or different adventure. Use your intrapersonal knowledge to be more interpersonally effective! Identify the three approaches you find most challenging.

_____ **Stop, look, and listen**. Extraverts always think they can talk their way through... and out of... most conflicts. The very thing they find most difficult is what may be needed most: listening to the other person's point of view. (Extraverts)

_____ **Express yourself**. As difficult as it often is, and sometimes seemingly redundant, it still is imperative to tell your side of the story... and maybe even tell it again until the other person has heard it. When conflict is concerned, a little overkill can help. Make sure you get a hearing. (Introverts)

_____ **There's more to conflicts than just the facts**. Sometimes, though it seems a waste of energy and may appear to cloud the issue, it is important to look at extenuating circumstances. If someone always disagrees with you no matter what you say, there may be issues involved that need attention other than just the situation of the moment. (Sensors)

_____ **Stick to the issues**. When conflict arises, intuitives want to relate it to the total picture. That's not always appropriate or helpful. It clouds the specifics and complicates resolution. Sometimes it helps just to gather the facts you need for the moment. (Intuitives)

_____ **Allow some genuine expression of emotions**. Thinkers become unglued when others cry at work; they act similarly when people hug or express warmth. But these emotions... at work or anywhere else... are integral with conflict resolution. Even if you're unable to express these things yourself, you should allow others the freedom to do so. (Thinkers)

Using Knowledge of Self to
Develop Interpersonal Skills

____ **Be direct and confrontive**. The world won't come to an end if you say something you really mean, even if it's negative. What sounds harsh to you as you say it probably won't be received as harshly by other types; if you are given to expressing a lot of emotion, don't apologize or feel guilty for doing so. Being upfront about your feelings facilitates moving to constructive resolution. (Feelers)

____ **You're not always right**. It may be difficult to believe this, but you must if you want a conflict ever to be resolved. Judgers see the world as black and white, right and wrong, and have difficulty accepting opposing points of view. It's hard to negotiate with someone who thinks he or she is always right. (Judgers)

____ **Take a clear position**. Perceivers can often argue both sides because they truly see both sides of an argument. Sometimes it comes in the form of playing devil's advocate. While flexible and adaptive, that's not always helpful to resolving a problem. It may even intensify the dispute. If you really feel strongly about something, better to take a stand and defend it. (Perceivers)

Develop Interpersonal Skills template is available online.

Generational Differences

Generational differences, as well as age differences, need to be considered in communicating with one another and in establishing professional relationships. Some of our values and actions are transitory and, therefore, change as we age. It is important to note that while not all people of the same age have the same outlook, there are patterns and trends that are often associated with those in their twenties, thirties, forties, and so on. Values and actions are also shaped by personal and world events that occurred at a given point in our lives.

Generational differences influence thinking about family life, selection of jobs or careers, balance of work and family, gender roles, organizations, politics, culture, lifestyle, and outlook about the future. We need to study these differences and their impact on the lives of colleagues so that we have an awareness, develop an understanding, accept the differences, and then interact in appropriate and productive ways.

Today there are four generations in the workplace. Why is that so? The Baby Boomers just don't want to quit! They retire and then they "un-retire" because they are bored or because their finances don't support the lifestyle they want to continue. They may retire from one school district and go to work in another. They may retire from a business, medical, military, or other government services job and become educators. In addition to these rotating retirees, one third of "new teachers" are educators who are returning to teaching after an absence of 10 or more years. Career switchers, the folks who decide in mid-stride that their current career is not what they want, join the teaching ranks as new teachers. Add in those twenty-somethings who have taken a traditional preparation path and the range of life experiences is phenomenal.

Impact on Work Environments
- When one of the four generations is much larger in number than the other three, the environment is greatly influenced and perhaps even controlled by that generation.
- Given that people are working longer and often move on to new jobs after their retirement from another, there is a possibility that an educator from an older generation can be working with or being supervised by someone quite a bit younger.
- Possible misunderstandings and missed opportunities can occur because of issues of formality and informality, definitions of autonomy, interdependence, and chain of command.

Generational Differences

- Three areas related to our collaborative practice impacted by generational differences are:
  - communication channels (especially the use of technology)
  - feedback
  - appreciation and recognition

Focus on Communication Channels

Traditionalists grew up with and still like
- face-to-face interactions
- letters
- proper thank you notes
- Baby Boomers tend to prefer
  - face-to face-interactions
  - letters
  - long distance calling plans
  - emails... but they may only check them once a week!
  - cell phones... but, they may not turn them on except in the case of an emergency or to play a game, and most likely do not carry them around in their hand
- Gen Xers and Millenials are happy with
  - cell phones... they may not even have a "land line"
  - email... they will often send an email to someone down the hall or even across the room rather than getting up and chatting with the person face-to-face
  - texting
  - social media

Focus on Technology

- Technology is the biggest generational divide we face today. We are a nation, in fact a world, of Digital Natives and Digital Immigrants. Those of us who are 45 and younger are Digital Natives. We teethed on technology! Those of us older than 45 are Digital Immigrants and have all the assimilation issues any immigrants face. That is, some parts of technology are easy for us; others we try to ignore. We adopt some of the customs and others don't seem to fit. Go to marcprensky.com for more information on this issue.
- It is clear that this variable may cause more communication and relationship problems than any other.
- Those who do not regularly check their email may miss requests for information or assistance or important information from colleagues.
- While there is no minimizing the power of face-to-face interaction, there are

Generational Differences

not enough hours in the day for all the face-to-face professional interactions we would like to have.

- Technology allows all parties to access and request information and assistance at their convenience.

Focus on Feedback

- Traditionalists generally believe that no news is good news. They are very comfortable with the chain of command and respectful of seniority and expect others to be as well.
- Baby Boomers are also quite comfortable with the chain of command. Cooperative learning as an instructional strategy and "works well with others" as an entry on report cards were introduced after these Baby Boomers left school as students. That may be why some older teachers are reticent about professional learning communities, serving on committees for strategic planning, and may think that lecture or "chalk and talk" are the best, if not the only, instructional strategies that really work.
- Our youngest colleagues, the Gen Xers and Millenials, have grown up getting instant feedback via video games and instant messaging. They want to know immediately and frequently how they are doing. Gen Xers and Millenials who teethed on cooperative learning are into collaboration. They respect authority without being awed by it. Millenials have no problem interacting with principals or superintendents or even school board members and telling them exactly what they are thinking. They have, after all, had the capacity to email the president of the United States since they were in elementary school.

Focus on Appreciation and Recognition

- The values and characteristics of each generation listed on following pages offer a starting point for recognizing and appreciating the efforts of your colleagues.
- Needs assessments and goal setting offer other sources of information about how to match interactions, comments, and suggestions to their lens on the world.

Maximizing the Power of Multiple Generations

Traditionalists' Values and Characteristics (born before 1942)

- Privacy
- Hard work
- Trust
- Formality
- Respect authority
- Loyal to institutions
- Believe in law and order
- Follow the rules
- Material possessions

Building on Traditionalists' Strengths and Life Experiences

- Acknowledge and ask about their experiences.
- Be explicit about the ways they have made a difference.
- Let them know that they are the historians of the changes in education.
- Use retired teachers as mentors who will share their institutional history and their belief that hard work is the right thing to do.
- May expect "perks" given their age so provide them when possible and explain rationale for alternative decisions.

Baby Boomers' Values and Characteristics (born 1942-1960)

- Competition
- Change
- Hard work
- Success
- Personal gratification
- Teamwork
- Inclusion
- Involvement
- Health and wellness
- Optimism
- Independence

Building on Baby Boomers' Strengths and Life Experiences

- Offer them opportunities to be involved in school life beyond the classroom
- Watch out for overcommitment and burn-out. They can be "workaholics."
- They are process-oriented so may need guidance to keep an eye on desired results.

Maximizing the Power of Multiple Generations

Gen Xers' Values and Characteristics (born 1960-1980)

- Entrepreneurial spirit
- Global thinking
- Independence
- Self-Reliance
- Informality and fun
- Feedback
- Quality of work life
- Diversity
- Balance of personal and professional lives

Building on Gen Xers' Strengths and Life Experiences

- Gen Xers prefer action to talk so have them "do" rather than listen and watch. Honor that preference but monitor work because often the focus is on getting the task done rather than thinking through alternatives, considering pros and cons, cause and effect, and identifying the best course of action.
- Use their technology skills to enhance the work of the organization.
- Because they value relationships over organizations, earn their respect with personal power rather than with position power.
- Let them know that they are on the right track and give them space to work as independently as possible.
- Given that they value patience and trust, do not micro-manage them.
- Recognize their productivity and results.

Millenials' Values and Characteristics (born 1980-2011)

- Time with family
- Autonomy
- Confidence
- Positive outlook
- Diversity
- Optimism
- Money
- Technology

Building on Millenials' Strengths and Life Experiences

- Use cutting-edge technology whenever possible
- Use email to communicate
- Make the work environment a fun place
- Use humor
- Understand that they can multi-task
- Let them know that they are the future and that you believe in them
- Millennials want feedback and may view silence as disapproval

Stages of Development

When we listen and observe behavior carefully, we can identify the mindset of our colleagues. You will probably be able to see yourself and each of your colleagues functioning in one of the four phases described below.

Just Tell Me What To Do!
- Know one way and, for the moment, want to know only one way to do something
- Seek the cookbook that provides strategies guaranteed to work all the time
- Make good faith effort to do as told and may feel inadequate if it does not work
- Give up and quickly abandon new strategies when they do not work perfectly
- Focus on the classroom and the learners assigned to them
- Little interest in or energy for departmental and school initiatives
- Want a supervisor and colleagues who are willing to tell them what to do, when it should be done, how to do it, and who recognize that they are giving their best effort

Are You Sure? I Think That...
- Begin to ask more questions
- Are hearing about and becoming more interested in different points of view
- May begin to resist direction from authority figures
- Prefer to be engaged in collaborative efforts where options are put forth and they can decide which to try and which to ignore
- Want colleagues who appreciate that they are finding their own voices, celebrates and encourages that, and can change approaches in mid-sentence

Let's Talk!
- Want to be active participants in identifying the focus of their learning
- Want a role in deciding how things are done in their own classroom and perhaps in the school
- Want colleagues who are knowledgeable about teaching and learning and are skilled at collaboration and coaching

I Think I've Figured Out A New Way To...
- Review alternatives and make rapid decisions about what to do
- May need help in finding resources to implement new initiatives
- View supervisor as a colleague also working to increase student learning
- Wants colleagues who are respectful of their knowledge and skills, who listen well, who ask hard questions, and provide resources through coaching or access to materials and ideas

Change Happens!

According to Michael Fullan, "**The very first place to change is within ourselves.**" To that end the discussion of the change process is included here because it is an important variable to consider in our quest to understand and work with one another productively. Where we are in dealing with any change greatly influences how we speak, what we hear when others speak, and how we respond to new programs, products, and processes.

The Realities of the Change Process

- Change happens... it either happens to you or you make it happen!
- Some experts say that we fear change. Others say that we can deal just fine with change; we just cannot give up what we already know and do, so we try to do it all.
- Change takes place in a context. Too much change at once can cause, at least momentarily, chaos or paralysis.
- Organizations do not change; individuals change.
- Changes takes place at different speeds depending on how much else is changing and how different the change is from current practice or knowledge.

When change in the form of new approaches, new programs, new standards, new administrators, and certainly, new accountability measures are introduced, there is often a sense of anxiety and even resistance. This may be caused by our tendency to have an endless series of new initiatives annually instead of engaging in long-term sustained and integrated initiatives. A young teacher recently expressed his frustration that his district seemed to embrace every new program or initiative as the solution to all its current problems. While talking recently with Bruce Oliver, he spoke with great passion. He noted that it appeared that decision makers rarely evaluated the effectiveness of the current approach before embarking on another new endeavor.

The anxiety and what looks like resistance may be caused by the fact that people who enter the field of public education often are more comfortable maintaining the status quo than in charting new courses. Another variable may be that changes are often announced without any effort to explain the rationale or assess the readiness levels of the people who have to implement the change.

Leadership for Change

A focus on learners and learning should be the lens through which all change is considered, initiated, and supported. When new ideas are put forth always ask, "How will this help students learn?" When we frame change in the interest of student learning, it is more difficult for anyone to resist.

From a Principal's Perspective
Leadership for Change
Julie McVicker

Six Key Actions to Take

- Say it
- Teach and model it
- Organize for it
- Analyze it
- Protect it
- Reward it

The greatest cause of unmet expectations is unclear expectations. Don't leave anything to chance. The following is a strong example of how one principal clearly communicated expectations for staff and for herself.

What I Expect of You

- Keep what's best for children as your most important focus
- Treat children with respect
- Have high standards for yourself, the children, and me
- Be willing to take risks in order to become better
- Keep grounded in the values you hold dear
- Appreciate the wonder of children and learning
- Share what's important to you with all of us
- Listen with an open heart to what others have to say
- Value and model professionalism
- Believe that all of us together are better than any one of us alone
- Celebrate how great our school is and commit to making it even better
- Reflect on our practices and their effectiveness
- Help evaluate my performance
- Respect and value your own expertise and that of others

What You Can Expect of Me

- Decisions and actions that contribute to children's achievement and sense of self-efficacy
- Commitment to a safe and productive learning environment
- Value and respect for each person
- Willingness to listen to a variety of viewpoints
- Work with you as a team member
- Forward thinking of how we might become better
- Commitment to supporting your work
- Sense of humor and fun
- Accountability for my actions
- My best thinking, skills, and energy
- Actions that reflect my beliefs

Points to Ponder
The Change Process

Ten Assumptions About Change

- Do not assume that your version of what the change should be is the one that should be implemented.
- Assume that any significant innovation, if it is to result in change, requires individual implementers to work out their own meaning.
- Assume that conflict and disagreement are not only inevitable, but fundamental to successful change.
- Assume that people need pressure to change (even in directions that they desire). But, it will only be effective under conditions that allow them to react, to form their own position, to interact with other implementers, to obtain technical assistance, etc.
- Assume that effective change takes time; 3-5 years for specific innovations, greater than 5 years for institutional reform.
- We should not assume that the reason for lack of implementation is outright rejection of the values embodied in the change, or hard core resistance to all change. There are a number of possible reasons: value rejection, inadequate resources to support implementation, insufficient time elapsed.
- We should not expect all or even most people or groups to change. Progress occurs when we take steps that increase the number of people. Our reach should exceed our grasps...but not by such a margin that we fall flat on our face.
- Assume that you will need a plan that is based on the above assumptions.
- Assume that no amount of knowledge will ever make it totally clear what action should be taken.
- We should assume that changing the culture of institutions is the real agenda, not implementing single innovations.

Michael Fullan, 1990

It must be remembered that change is not synonymous with progress.

Bruce Oliver, 2004

Change, even if predictable, is almost always perceived as threatening. Even small changes are sources of tension. When I began teaching myself to use a computer, I put a kitchen timer nearby and set it to go off at fifteen minute intervals. The idea was to hold down the panic.

Jennifer James, *Thinking in the Future Tense*

Michael Fullan's
Three-Step Process for Change

Step One: Analyze the Gap
- Figure out where you want to go. As Lewis Carroll wrote in **Alice in Wonderland**, "If you don't know where you are going, it doesn't matter which road you take."
- List the main differences between where you are now and where you want to be

Step Two: Plan the Route
- Identify what is in place to help you.
- Identify the barriers and what can and should be done about them.
- Identify what steps need to be taken to move forward.

Step Three: Manage the Journey
- Provide resources
- Support and train
- Monitor progress
- Analyze the new gaps

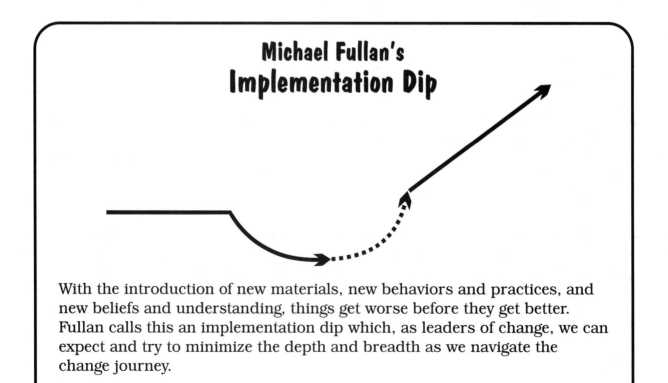

Michael Fullan's
Implementation Dip

With the introduction of new materials, new behaviors and practices, and new beliefs and understanding, things get worse before they get better. Fullan calls this an implementation dip which, as leaders of change, we can expect and try to minimize the depth and breadth as we navigate the change journey.

Dealing with Change

Potential Human Barriers to Change

Why People Don't Do What We Want Them to Do!
- They don't know what to do.
- They don't know how to do it.
- They don't know why they should do it.
- They don't want to do it.

What We Might Do
- If they don't know what to do, we need to clearly articulate expectations and provide or facilitate the acquisition of the necessary knowledge.
- If they don't know how to do it, we have to teach the necessary skills or create the conditions that promote the acquiring of those skills.
- If they don't want to do it, we need to find out how to create the desire. Madeline Hunter responded to the statement "You can lead a horse to water, but you can't make it drink," by saying, "That may be true, but you can put a little salt in its oats."

©Just ASK Publications

Concerns-Based Adoption Model (CBAM)

The Concerns-Based Adoption Model (CBAM) was designed at the University of Texas Research and Development Center to study how people responded to educational innovations. It has been used by researchers and practitioners for over 30 years. CBAM measures Stages of Concern, Levels of Use, and Innovation Configurations. Only the Stages of Concern component is explored here.

Assumptions of CBAM

Change is:
- **A process**, not an event
- Made by **individuals** first, then institutions
- A highly **personal** experience
- Entails **developmental** growth in feelings and skills

Responses and interventions must be related to:
- People first
- The innovation (new programs, products, or processes) second

Typical Expressions of Concern about an Innovation

		Stages of Concern	Expressions of Concern
Impact	6	Refocusing	I have some ideas about something that would work even better.
	5	Collaboration	How can I relate what I am doing to what others are doing?
	4	Consequence	How is my use affecting learners? How can I refine it to have more impact?
Task	3	Management	I seem to be spending all my time getting materials ready.
Self	2	Personal	How will using it affect me?
	1	Informational	I would like to know more about it.
	0	Awareness	I am not concerned about it.

Adapted from: Shirley Hord, William Rutherford, Leslie Huling-Austin, and Gene Hall, *Taking Charge of Change*, and SEDL.

Concerns-Based Adoption Model (CBAM)
Responding to Stages of Concern

To help bring about change, we need to first know an individual's concerns. Then we need to address those concerns. While there are no set formulas, below are some suggestions for intervening in a way that addresses the apparent stage of concern.

Focus on Self

In general, people who are at one of the three stages focused on self are gathering data about the innovation and preparing to decide whether to commit to the change based on how it will affect them personally. During these three stages, people will not be "sold" on making a change because it will help someone else. They will want to know how the change is going to make their life easier. The change has not actually taken place yet, so these stages represent a pre-implementation phase of the change process.

Awareness Stage Typical Expressions of Concern

People at this stage know little or nothing about the innovation. If asked what they think, they might say:
- "I've never heard of that."
- "Oh that, I'm really not interested."
- "I'm afraid I can't help you on that one!"

The lack of enthusiasm that is typical at this stage should not be perceived as a negative response. Quite often the person who does not seem to be interested will become a strong proponent of the change once she/he has a chance to learn more.

Addressing Awareness Stage Concerns
- If possible, involve teachers in discussions and decisions about the innovation and its implementation.
- Share enough information to arouse interest, but not so much that it overwhelms.
- Acknowledge that a lack of awareness is expected and reasonable, and that there are no foolish questions.

Responses to Stages of Concern
Focus on Self

Informational Stage Expressions of Concern

At this stage, the individual will be actively seeking more information about the innovation in question. Some typical comments at this stage are:

- "Where can I get a book on the subject?"
- "I am taking a class to learn more about it."
- "I've been talking to some people from other offices/schools to find out more about it."

Addressing Informational Stage Concerns

- Provide clear and accurate information about the innovation.
- Use several ways to share information verbally, in writing, and through available media. Communicate with large and small groups, and individuals.
- Help teachers see how the innovation relates to their current practices. People at this stage will be asking questions to get a clear definition of the innovation in question. They will want to know what the long-term benefits of the change are, but, they will not decide to participate until they know what the short-term costs are going to be for them personally.

Personal Stage Typical Expressions of Concern

This is a critical stage for those leading the change. People involved in the change are becoming aware of how much time and energy is going to be expended in order to implement the change and an aura of stress can surface. People at this stage might say:

- "I'm not at all sure I can commit to this!"
- "This is going to be a lot of work!"
- "I'm not sure this will work in my office/classroom."

Addressing Personal Stage Concerns

- Legitimize the existence and expression of personal concerns.
- Use personal notes and conversations to provide encouragement and reinforce personal adequacy.
- Connect these teachers with others whose personal concerns have diminished and who will be supportive.

Responses to Stages of Concern
Focus on Task

Management Stage Typical Expressions of Concern

This is the earliest stage of implementation. People at this stage will very quickly recognize the tremendous amount of time and energy involved in making a change. People at this stage might say:

- "I'm taking work home every night!"
- "There doesn't seem to be enough hours in the day since we made that change."
- "I just don't have the time to get all this done."

Management concerns will usually be specific in nature, and may be a serious cause of stress and overload. Personal concerns (Stage 2) will quite often become very prevalent again after people reach Stage 3.

Addressing Management Stage Concerns

- Clarify the steps and components of the innovation.
- Provide answers that address the small specific "how-to" issues.
- Demonstrate exact and practical solutions to the logistical problems that contribute to these concerns.

Responses to Stages of Concern
Focus on Task and Impact

Consequences Stage Typical Expressions of Concern*

People at this stage are beginning to consider the impact of the innovation on their students/clients. At this point, individuals have moved away from the "self" related concerns typical of the earlier stages. Some typical comments from people at this stage are:

- "I would like to excite my colleagues/students about their part in this program."
- "I am concerned about my students' attitude about this program."
- "We are really doing well with this, but I'm beginning to wonder about the long-range impact for my students."

People are comfortable with their ability to deliver the program. Quite often, people at this stage are gathering data on the effectiveness of the innovation in order to make minor changes to improve student outcomes.

Addressing Consequence Stage Concerns

- Provide individuals with opportunities to visit other settings where the innovation is in use and to attend conferences on the topic.
- Make sure these teachers are not overlooked. Give positive feedback and needed support.
- Find opportunities for these teachers to share their skills with others.

*In the original model the **Consequence Stage** was placed in the task category. Given the typical expressions of concern found in the literature, Brenda Kaylor suggests that there is an overlap onto the impact category.

Responses to Stages of Concern
Focus on Impact

Collaboration Stage Typical Expressions of Concern

People at this stage are very eager to get together with others who are involved in the same innovation. They want to share ideas, thoughts, and experiences in order to increase the impact on student learning. Common statements from people at this stage are:
- "We need to coordinate a bit better on our delivery."
- "I think we should have more opportunities to share ideas on this."
- "This would work better if we could 'team' it."

Addressing Collaboration Stage Concerns
- Provide opportunities to develop skills for working collaboratively.
- Bring together, from inside and outside the school, those who are interested in working collaboratively.
- Use these teachers to assist others.

Refocusing Stage Typical Expressions of Concern

People at this stage are ready for a major change. At this stage, the innovation has been in place for several years and individuals have integrated the "new" behaviors into their repertoire. Consequently, they are open to new programs or major revisions of the program. People at this stage often might say:
- "I know of some other approaches that might work better."
- "I am interested in looking at alternatives to our current system."
- "I really believe we are ready to move on to something new.

Addressing Refocusing Stage Concerns
- Respect and encourage the interest these individuals have for finding a better way.
- Help these teachers channel their ideas and energies productively.
- Help these teachers access the resources they need to refine their ideas and put them into practice.

Adapted from ***Taking Charge of Change*** by Shirley Hord, William Rutherford, Leslie Huling-Austin, and Gene Hall

CBAM Practice

Read the statements below and determine the level of concern of each statement.

1. _____ I am very concerned about the time it's taking me to do all of this.

2. _____ It sounds like a good idea, but I don't know much about it.

3. _____ My class is just fine the way it is; I don't need or want any new ideas now.

4. _____ This is a great idea and my kids seem to be handling it well, but I wonder what the long-range impact will be on my student's achievement.

5. _____ I would like to do more team teaching with other people in my grade level because I think we could do a better job with this.

6. _____ Well, this is certainly a revolutionary idea! What can I read to find out more?

7. _____ I'm going crazy trying to keep all this record keeping straight. I have to work two hours at home after school every night.

8. _____ I think this approach was a good start, but now we need to make some changes to make it work smoother. I have read about another program that we could adapt and that would be a logical extension of our program.

9. _____ Can we have more grade level meetings to share ideas? I know we can do a better job if we share more.

10. _____ Oh, yeah, that! Well, I'm not concerned about it. Things like this pass almost as quickly as they come.

CBAM Practice template is available online.

CBAM Case Study
Timberline Middle School
Brenda Kaylor

Background Information

As a result of studying current data on both school culture and student achievement, Timberline Middle School has begun to implement learning community structures of collaboration across grade levels and content areas. A leadership team made up of two teacher representatives from each grade level, a special education teacher, the principal, and several interested parents in guiding the work.

The key responsibilities of the leadership team are:
- prioritize the academic focus for the school
- study and model effective practices of collaboration and instruction
- support development of grade level/content area teams that focus on improved student achievement

The student data that the leadership team studied indicated a need to focus their collaborative work on student writing across the content areas. The data also indicated that many staff members in the school are accustomed to working in isolation rather than in collaborative teams with shared goals.

Year One

During the first year, the leadership team worked with their school and community to build knowledge about effective practices in data-driven collaboration. During this year, the leadership team attended conferences to further their background knowledge, led book studies with staff, and created general awareness of the concepts embedded in the work of collaborative cultures. The team also analyzed their own student performance data in the area of writing. They, then, helped others in their grade level begin to study their own data in writing.

The team was also authorized to select a program in writing to address the needs of their students across all grade levels. They brought in two well-respected consultants to conduct a two-day awareness workshop in March. At the workshop, the teachers examined student data collaboratively to identify specific grade level needs, received materials and worked together to learn how to use the new program with students. There seemed to be a lot of enthusiasm for working together to improve student writing.

Year Two

Expectations for implementing learning community teams increased. Grade level teams were asked to work collaboratively to determine a minimum number of

CBAM Case Study
Timberline Middle School

essential learnings in writing for the first quarter. They were also asked to begin writing a common assessment to measure student progress.

In late October, a second series of training sessions on the new writing program were held. A week before the training, the teachers were asked to complete an open-ended statement: **When you think about working collaboratively to implement the new writing program, what are your concerns?**

The Leadership Team studied the data from this question. They identified five responses to the open-ended concerns statement that represented a broad spectrum of response.

Practice Using the Model

Read and identify the **Stage(s) of Concern** reflected in each statement. On the chart, note each statement's predominant **Stage(s) of Concern**, the specific issues around which the teacher indicates concerns, and possible actions to take.

Teacher A

I'm concerned about finding the time to teach writing in my content area. It takes much longer to set up a writing assignment with the students. I don't have a ready stash of mini-lessons. I could use some help with those. So far, the students don't seem to be responding well. Some haven't completed a good piece of writing yet. I don't think this program works.

Additionally, the program is too open-ended. I would rather have concise directions that are easy to follow. Besides that, I don't have enough time to devote to writing. After all, I teach math and science.

Teacher B

Not only do we have a new writing program in our school but we are supposed to implement it collaboratively. I find it much slower to work with my colleagues than it is for me to just figure it all out on my own. We can't agree on what good writing looks like. We haven't agreed on the essential learnings within writing yet, either. I do notice that two of our team members bring higher quality writing samples that are significantly different than what the rest of us are getting from our students. I do wonder what they are doing instructionally that I am not.

Teacher C

Being a new teacher this year, I am feeling overwhelmed. When you ask me to list my concerns about this new writing program, I don't know where to start. I

CBAM Case Study
Timberline Middle School

missed the earlier training the other teachers had last spring. Someone just handed me the materials and disappeared. I don't understand most of what we talk about at our grade level collaborative team meetings.

Teacher D

I can see many possibilities for this writing program. My team is very willing to work together and we meet weekly to talk about student work in writing. We do have essential learnings in writing for this quarter and are beginning to write some common assessments. I am wondering how we can best use the data from both the upcoming assessments and our student work samples to modify practice. I would love to see my colleagues in action teaching writing.

Teacher E

This program is really a change for me. I have always emphasized editing grammar, spelling, etc. It makes me now realize how little background knowledge I actually have in the area of teaching writing. I don't really like to write myself so how can I inspire my students? This is a little embarrassing for me.

Teacher	Specific Issues	Stage of Concern	Strategies to Use
Teacher A			
Teacher B			
Teacher C			
Teacher D			
Teacher E			

Reflections on Timberline Middle School

1. What **Stages of Concern** seem to be most common at Timberline?
2. If you were designing professional development in support of this change, what are some actions you might take?
3. Who else might you involve in the follow-up work? What support would you recommend be made available to them?

The ASK Construct
Attitudes, Skills, and Knowledge

Our **attitudes, skills, and knowledge (ASK)** influence every decision we make. Individually, or in combination, they cause us to place a high priority on one task and to procrastinate about another. Sometimes we know something, but are not skilled at using that knowledge in appropriate or productive ways. Sometimes we are both knowledgeable and skilled, but our attitudes about the situation cause us to avoid action. We need to self-assess our own attitudes, skills, and knowledge and then learn to analyze the decision making and actions of others through the same lens.

For educators there are three components embedded in each of the three variables, **A S K**. That is, educators must consider their **knowledge** about content, learners and learning theory, and repertoire for connecting the learners and the content. Lack of knowledge about one or more of those components can cause problems. Even when one has knowledge about content, learners and learning theory, and has a rich repertoire of instructional strategies, issues surface if there is a lack of **skill** in applying that knowledge in a given situation. For instance, a teacher could have considerable knowledge of and skills with the curriculum at the fifth grade level and really enjoy, understand and work well with fifth graders. When that teacher is assigned to teach second grade he may have to revise or develop a new repertoire of strategies for working with students of that age and may struggle with chunking the content in ways so that it is accessible to second graders. The same is true for administrators. Our response to a new teaching or leadership assignment or a hesitant or negative response to the expectation that all staff members will work in collaborative teams may look and sound like an **attitude** problem when, in fact, it is an expression of fear caused by concerns about the lack of knowledge and skill to be successful in these new situations. Consequently, when working collaboratively, we may encounter colleagues who have managed in the past to hide insecurities or a lack of knowledge or skills by closing the doors to their classrooms or offices and working in isolation. We need to be skillful diagnosticians, get beyond what appears to be an attitude problem, and interact with colleagues in ways that uncover the real issues. The more closely we can identify whether a colleague's behavior is rooted in issues of knowledge, skills, or attitudes, the better we can plan our interactions.

It is important to remember that in addition to using the **ASK Construct** to determine why colleagues respond the way they do, we can use it to self-assess our own knowledge, skillfulness, and attitudes toward teaching, leading, and working collaboratively and recognize how each may impact our own decision making and actions.

Consulting, Collaborating, and Coaching

Collegial interactions involve a variety of approaches that fall along a continuum. When partners use consultation strategies, one partner is the expert giving advice to the other (learner). In collaboration, both partners share expert and learner roles. Coaching, through questioning, facilitates thinking, planning, and reflecting around classroom practice. There is a time and place for each approach.

Collegial Interaction Approaches	Consultation	Collaboration	Coaching
Purpose	Give advice to… • clarify goals • plan for, observe, and provide feedback about teaching practice • improve practice • create resources • provide follow-up	Plan, observe, provide feedback, and refine instructional strategies to… • improve practice and student learning results • share resources and expertise • develop collegial, professional relationships and diminish professional isolation • data analysis	Use strategies to help a colleague think about and reflect on professional work as the individual shapes and reshapes his or her teaching practices and solves related problems.
Roles	A teacher or administrator who… • provides formal or informal opportunities to observe professional practice • clarifies problems and successes • gives advice regarding solutions, resources, or changes in practice when needed	Colleagues who… • work in collaborative teams targeting areas of their practices for examination and then providing and receiving feedback • collaborate as critical friends to improve teaching, student learning, and leading	A teacher or administrator who… • asks insightful questions to coach a partner's decision-making and reflective process • helps a colleague examine the relationship between perceptions, attitudes, thinking, and behaviors that will affect student learning
Knowledge and Skills Required	The colleague… • is a skillful teacher or administrator • is able to describe or demonstrate effective teaching/administrative strategies • has a thorough understanding of the curriculum being taught • practices good listening and communication skills • is sensitive to the needs of others • is effective in establishing rapport	The collaborative partners… • plan for and focus on developing skills and/or improving practice • practice good listening and communication strategies • are sensitive to each other's needs • are open to observation of and feedback on their teaching practice • are effective in establishing rapport	The supervisor, coach, or mentor… • is a good role model • is effective in establishing rapport • practices good listening and communication strategies • asks appropriate questions

Adapted from Results-Based Professional Development Models, St. Vrain Valley School District, Longmont, CO

Coaching Approach

Outcomes

Your colleague becomes more reflective, more aware of the cause and effect of behaviors, and more conscious of the decision-making process used.

Coaching Behaviors

- pause, paraphrase, and probe*
- actively listen (See **Communication Strategies for Coaching** on the next page.)
- be non-judgmental
- encourage self-awareness
- encourage self-reflection
- use data, as appropriate
- See question stems on page 193.

When Used

- Your colleague has the knowledge, skills, and attitudes to think through the decision-making process, and, with coaching, arrives at own conclusions about what needs to be done.
- Your colleague asks you to coach rather than give suggestions or tell you what to do.
- This is the default approach! Start with coaching and return to coaching whenever possible!

* Costa and Garmston identify pause, paraphrase, and probe as the three essential skills of cognitive coaching.

Communication Strategies for Coaching

Attentive Silence

This adult wait time allows both parties to process what has been said, to collect their thoughts, to review notes, and to figure out and formulate next points of discussion.

Acknowledgment Responses

These responses are given to indicate that you are paying attention to what is being said. They are accompanied by head nodding, eye contact, and a posture matched to that of the teacher. When talking with a very reflective teacher, the vast majority of your responses may be acknowledgment responses. Interestingly enough, when the conversation or conference is over, the teacher may well say, "Thank you for your help," because what she needed to do was think out loud. Examples of acknowledgment responses are: "I see." "That's interesting." "Hmmm."

Paraphrasing and Summarizing

When paraphrasing, you check for understanding and summarize what the teacher said. You attempt to capture the essence of the feelings and content of the statement and paraphrase them in an abbreviated form. You make no inferences. In order to avoid adding your own voice, think of paraphrasing and summarizing as a parallel to the way you paraphrase to be sure you have the correct directions to a party.

Reflecting Meaning and Feelings

With this strategy, you add inferences about what you think the teacher is saying. For example, a teacher might say, "That lesson was a big success. The learners really got it!" You might respond, "You are feeling pretty good about the learning results you got!" If you are on the mark, the teacher response might be, "Yes! They did so much better than they have before!" If you are off the mark, the teacher might respond, "No, but they at least knew what to do." You make an effort to ensure you are interpreting the right emotion and that the words you heard conveyed the meaning the person meant to send.

Questions That Promote Teacher Thinking

Costa and Garmston write that when you coach, you attempt to move the teacher with whom you are working to a new place. Carefully crafted questions can help you do that. Examples of such questions which are likely to promote teacher thinking are found on the next page.

©Just ASK Publications

Getting Started with
Questions That Promote Our Thinking

Questions that promote our thinking are open-ended; there is not one correct answer. They are not leading, accusatory, or nosy. We ask these questions to:
- initiate a discussion and keep discussions on track
- focus on new concepts or a different aspect of a concept
- facilitate flexible thinking
- challenge the obvious
- break down complex tasks and issues
- consolidate previous discussions and experiences
- explore possible next steps

Questions/Question Starters
- Why do you think that is so?
- What do you need to do next?
- Based on what you know, what can you predict about...?
- Does what... said make you think differently about...?
- How do you decide...?
- How does... tie in with what we have discussed before?
- Suppose..., what then?
- How does this match what you thought you knew?
- What might happen if...?
- When have you done something like this before?
- What sort of impact do you think...?
- How would you feel if...?
- How did you come to that conclusion?
- How about...? What if...?
- Tell me what you mean when you...
- What do you think causes...?
- When is another time you need to...?
- What do you think the variables/issues/problems are?
- What were you thinking when...?
- Can you think of another way you could do this?
- Why is this one better than that one?
- How can you find out?
- How is... different (like)...?
- What have you heard about...?
- Can you tell me more?
- What else do you see?
- How does that compare with...?

Post-Observation Conference Menus
Marcia Baldanza

When Marcia Baldanza was principal of Patrick Henry Elementary School, Alexandria, Virginia, she created menus of questions for the post-observation conferences she held with teachers. She shares the questions with teachers in advance so that they know the level of thinking they will be asked to do. These questions are appropriate for conferences following peer observations.

By design, the questions included in Conference A begin quite analytically and move to more reflective thinking. Conference B is more reflective and begins to focus on asking for data to support opinions. Conference C is more data-driven, and Conference D is designed to be used at the end of the year.

Conference A
- How did you decide what to teach today?
- How does what you and your students worked on today fit in with the context of the unit on which you are working?
- How did you go about finding out if your students had the background knowledge and skills required to be successful on this lesson?
- How did you decide what instructional strategies to use today?
- What are the variables, beyond completion of assignments, that you consider in determining whether or not the students have learned what you wanted them to learn?
- What do you think worked and did not work in this lesson? Why do you say that?
- When you teach this lesson again, what will you do differently?

Conference B
- As you look back on this lesson, how did it help students learn? What happened to make you think this way?
- What do you remember about your actions during the lesson? How did what you actually did match what you had planned? What caused you to make those changes?
- What do you remember about student work and behavior during the lesson? How did their actions and work match what you hoped/expected would happen?
- How successful were the students in moving toward competency with the standard? What is your data?
- What do you think caused some students to not "get it"?
- What did you take from this conversation that may influence your future thinking and planning?

Post-Observation Conference Menus

Conference C

- From your perspective, was the learning objective clear and significant? What evidence can you provide?
- What percentage of the students mastered the objective? What evidence can you provide?
- What work did the students do to achieve the objective, and did that work add up to a quality learning experience? How do you measure that?
- To what extent were the students actively involved in the construction of meaning? What evidence can you provide?
- How do you explain students' success or lack of success?
- How will your practice change as a result of our reflection together?

Conference D

- As you examine data and look for trends, do your students typically have difficulty with the same areas or experience success in the same areas? In what areas? Why do you think that is so?
- Where would you like to see improvement?
- How closely did the students' products/performances match your expectations?
- What do you do to keep growing professionally?
- What do you need to do more of to keep growing professionally?
- How have you engaged in learning within the school?
- What strengths do you see in your practice?
- What areas for improvement can you identify?
- What experiences shape you as an educator?
- In what situations do you feel most/least competent?

Reflective Questioning
Brenda Kaylor

Reflective questions are a key component in creating cultures of learning. Coaching conversations should include pauses, paraphrases, probing questions, and reflective questions. As described below, reflective questions should be questions for the commute home; questions that recipients still wonder about at the end of the day.

Characteristics of Reflective Questions
- Invite reflection
- Are open-ended
- Include plurals (criteria, thought processes, hunches, etc.)
- Include a positive presupposition when appropriate
- Have a single focus
- Are honest
- Contain non-judgmental language
- Use present or future tense
- Are presented with an approachable voice
- Use exploratory language

Examples of Reflective Questions
- What influences your thinking when deciding on the lesson focus for your struggling learners?
- What criteria do you use when grouping students for instruction?
- How do you ensure that the Common Core Standards are now the targets for your instruction?
- What data do you collect to show that all students are engaged at high levels?
- As you plan with your colleagues, what criteria do you use to detemine essential understandings?
- What are the ways you ensure that students are able to self-assess their own work?
- What are some specific patterns or trends that seem to be emerging with your students during reading instruction?
- As you plan with your colleagues, what criteria do you use to determine essential understandings of a unit?
- What are ways you will influence the culture of your grade level team?

Writing a reflective question is different from asking one in a coaching conversation. When the question is presented in a written format, it needs to include contextual clues as a reminder about what was going on at the time. For example: When I visited your class today, the students were reading a variety of materials with partners. What are the ways you ensure students are reading materials at their individual instructional levels?

Collaborative Approach

Outcome
Mutually agree on the next steps in learning or refining new teaching or collaboration skills, identify problems, and develop solutions for problems

Collaborative Behaviors
- focus on the team's agenda
- guide problem-solving process
- explore pros and cons of solutions
- keep discussion focused on problem solving

When Used
All parties are equally engaged in determining the next steps.

Essential Components of the Collaborative Approach
- Identify the problem, issue, or concern from the teacher's perspective through sharing of data and questioning
- Check for understanding of the issues
- Brainstorm possible solutions
- Weigh alternatives
- Agree on a plan and a follow-up meeting to assess if solution is working and plan next steps

See the next page for a description of the **Six-Step Problem Solving Process** that is widely used for individual and group problem solving.

Skills for Collaborative Problem Solving
- Pausing, paraphrasing, and probing
- Active listening
- "I-messages" or assertive messages
- Brainstorming
- Consensus building

For information on these prerequisite skills, see *People Skills* by Robert Bolton.

The Six-Step Problem Solving Process

Step One: Identify the Problem

A great deal of time is spent solving the wrong problem. Often people try to "fix" a symptom rather than getting to the problem. Once the problem can be written in a problem statement that says, "The problem is that...," write a goal statement describing what a successful remedy would accomplish. It may be that the problem is so big and complex that the components of the problem may need to be tackled one at a time.

Step Two: Generate Potential Solutions

This step calls for divergent thinking and brainstorming. The goal is to generate as many potential solutions as possible. Consider doing individual brainstorming before you share ideas. Do not judge solutions as they are generated, but jot them down for later consideration as a solution or as a component of the solution. Do not stop too soon. Often the best ideas come toward the end of the brainstorming because ideas begin to be integrated.

Step Three: Evaluate the Solutions

Some suggested solutions may need to be eliminated because of the time, energy, or money they would require. Others may be eliminated because of policies and rules. After those have been eliminated, examine the remaining possibilities and rank order them by criteria you design. Identify the two or three solutions that have the best potential and analyze them further as to how feasible it would be to implement them and the possible impact each might have.

Step Four: Select a Solution to Try

In this step the teacher decides which solution to try. If the solution involves the assistance of other people, they will need to be consulted about their willingness to participate. Once a solution is identified, decide on the criteria to be used to evaluate the effectiveness of the solution after the implementation.

Step Five: Make a Plan and Implement It

Using the description of the ideal situation, the solution selected to try, the time frame for implementation, and the criteria to be used to evaluate the effectiveness of the solution, make an action plan and implement it.

Step Six: Evaluate the Solution

Use the criteria established in step five to decide whether or not the solution is working and determine if the plan should be modified. Use the problem-solving process to plan any needed modifications.

The Collaborative Conference

Attendees_____

Date _____ **Time** _____

Purpose of Conference _____

How will we create a congenial beginning?

How will we identify the problem or issue? What data will be used?

How will we check for understanding and/or agreement on the area of focus?

What criteria will we use to weigh the alternatives?

What questions might we ask to facilitate the consideration of the alternatives?

The Collaborative Conference

How will we identify the acceptable action?

What data will be used to determine the success of the action?

When will a follow-up meeting be held to determine how the solution is working?

The Action Plan:

The Collaborative Conference template is available online.

Consulting Approach

Outcomes
- colleagues learn new techniques
- perfects a technique
- changes a behavior
- develops a plan for change
- determines next steps

Consultant Behaviors
- pause, paraphrase, and probe
- inform
- direct
- model
- give advice
- critique
- make suggestions
- give instruction for change

When Used
The colleague or team has agreed that he/they need expert direction. It may be that the colleague or team:
- does not have knowledge about the topic under discussion
- wants to learn from others who have been successful in similar situations
- has been directed to participate in professional development on a new initiative

---

Laura Lipton and Bruce Wellman's
Strategies for Learning-Focused Consulting

- Offer a Menu of Choices
- Think Aloud
- Share the What, Why, and How
- State a Principle of Practice
- Generate Categories
- Name Causal Factors
- Consider an Alternative Point of View
- Reframe the Problem or Issue

This chapter provides points to ponder, self-assessments, practitioner examples, and tools and templates to support you in:
- building collaborative teams in a variety of formats
- establishing norms
- reaching consensus
- dealing with conflict
- orchestrating celebrations
- finding the time
- making meetings matter
- making collaborative teams work
- creating a school-wide professional learning community

Collective Commitment To Creating a Culture for Learning

We will...
- teach the essential learning of the course and provide evidence of the extent of each student's proficiency
- be positive contributing members of our team and our school as we work together interdependently to achieve common goals
- provide timely feedback to students, parents, and designated staff regarding student achievement
- continually look for ways to help each other help all students achieve success

The staff of Thoreau Middle School, Fairfax County Public Schools, Fairfax, Virginia

Does Your School Have a Culture for Learning?

Which set of attributes best describes your school?

Conventional

- autonomy for the individual teacher
- small cliques of teachers within the school who befriend one another
- lack of dialogue about teaching across classrooms, departments, and grade levels
- school site seen as a physical place of work

Congenial

- characterized by open, social climate for adults
- communications are friendly
- people easily socialize with one another
- good refreshments at meetings
- great parties

Collegial

- purposeful, adult-level interactions focused on teaching and learning experiences and successes of students
- people do not necessarily socialize with one another
- people respect differences of opinion about education
- everyone has the students' interests in mind
- people believe that differences will be resolved and that students will benefit
- people have moved beyond the social facade of communication and discuss conflicting ideas and issues with candor, sensitivity, and respect

Carl Glickman, *Renewing America's Schools*, 1994

Hopefully you are able to say that the descriptors Glickman listed under collegial best describe your school. The survey on the next page is framed by the work of Judith Warren Little and provides you an opportunity to dig deeper into what a culture for learning looks like over 15 years after the publishing of Glickman's book. Complete the survey individually, and then compare your assessment with colleagues. You may want to gather data about the perceptions of staff throughout the building.

Collegial Collaboration
Practices That Promote School Success

We use our knowledge, skills, and energy to...	Frequently	Sometimes	Rarely
• analyze standards, and design instruction and assessments to match those standards			
• design and prepare instructional materials together			
• design and evaluate units together...especially those based on clearly articulated national, state, or local standards			
• research materials, instructional strategies, content-specific methodologies and curriculum ideas to both experiment with and share with colleagues			
• design lesson plans together (both within and across grade levels and disciplines)			
• discuss/reflect on lesson plans prior to and following the lesson			
• examine student work together to check match to high standards and to refine assignments			
• agree to experiment with an idea or approach, to debrief about how it worked, and to analyze the results and make adaptations and adjustments for future instruction			
• observe and be observed by other teachers			
• analyze practices and their productivity			
• promote the concepts of repertoire and reflection			
• teach each other in informal settings and in focus groups			
• use meeting time for discussions about teaching and learning rather than administrivia			
• talk openly and often about what we are learning or would like to learn			
• concentrate efforts and dialogue on quality and quantity of student learning, rather than on how many chapters have been covered in the text			

Self Assessment: Collegial Collaboration template is available online.

Collaborative Teams on Parade
Brenda Kaylor

Leadership Teams

The Leadership Team of West Irondequoit Central School District in Rochester, New York, meets monthly to focus on teaching, learning, and leading. This team is made up of all district and school-based administrators and curriculum area leaders. At least 75 percent of meeting time is devoted to the professional growth of those educators. Facilitation and leadership of the learning rotates among team members. Data is used to drive discussions and decisions. This unwavering focus on student learning and the leaders' collaborative approach yields results. A Manhattan Institute Report based on 2006-2007 data identifies West Irondequoit, as the only Monroe County school district to deliver higher than expected academic achievement results. The distinction is based on higher than expected NYS test scores when per pupil expenditures, size, income, and demographic characteristics were taken into account.

Mesa County Valley School District #51 in Grand Junction, Colorado has modeled leadership development and support through their collaborative work in elementary cohorts. The elementary principals are divided into cohorts of small teams. Teams are balanced in terms of experience and background. The administrators collectively determine who will lead their cohorts. The teams work collaboratively to support each other in the implementation of instructional improvement efforts, understanding of new research, and facilitation of strategies to increase the use of data across the schools. The facilitators also meet regularly as a small team to create agendas that will focus common conversations across the district.

Departmental Teams

The common course teams at Legacy High School in Broomfield, Colorado meet 3 out of every 4 Wednesdays during early release time. This early release is a 2-hour block of time devoted to collaborative learning teams. The department sets their own schedule as to how to use this time. The math department, for instance, splits this time into three 40-minute blocks. The facilitator is responsible for sending an agenda to the team in advance and also typically takes care of the minutes as well. The teams usually spend most of their time addressing issues that can be categorized into six topics.

The group agrees to focus their time together on the "big six topics."
1) Pacing/planning/sharing of materials.
2) Formative assessment sharing.
3) Summative assessment preparation (all summative assessments are common.)

©Just ASK Publications

Collaborative Teams on Parade

4) Summative assessment grading rubrics and guidelines.

5) Data analysis

6) Policy discussions (how will we all deal with _____?)

For more information contact Jason Cianfrance at Jason.Cianfrance@adams12.org

Vertical Teams

How does a district create a culture of continuous learning and collaboration while building district-wide curriculum and growing teacher leaders? Mesa County School District in Grand Junction, Colorado developed district Vertical Alignment Teams (VAT's) that represented major content areas and included representation from all schools. Elementary, middle, and high school levels each had their own content teams that met 4-6 days per year, and were led by district content specialists. These district/school teams created instructional supports, such as essential learnings, interim assessments, pacing guides and overviews. Throughout the year, a cycle of teaching and learning ensued: gather data, build curriculum, share with school-based PLC's, pilot in the classroom, gather feedback, and return to the vertical team to revise. Throughout this model there is a continuous flow of ideas between district to schools and schools to district.

Beyond the development of instructional supports, vertical teams offer input on professional development needs and its design. Because school-based teacher leaders are continually being developed within the vertical team, many members become school and district-wide professional development facilitators resulting in continuous growth and development for all.

Content Area/Job-Alike Teams

Job-alike teams in the Kildeer Countryside K-8 School District in Buffalo Grove, Illinois provide clarity and focus for the district. The teams come together six times per year for two hours each time. They focus on the questions of collaborative learning communities paying especially close attention to the questions in SBE Planning Ovals (see page 203) one and two: What is it students should know and be able to do? How will we and they know when they have learned it?

Every elementary classroom teacher has a spot on one of the content teams: reading, writing, math, and science/social studies. Special education, English language learning, media, and other specialists make up a fifth team working in an integrated fashion.

Collaborative Teams on Parade

Middle school job-alike teams are also structured by content. Teachers are part of the team that matches the primary content that they teach. However, middle school teachers are also responsible for understanding and using the curricular work completed by another job-alike team in their secondary content emphasis. All agendas, minutes, goals and working templates are public and housed in an electronic "Team Room."

The job-alike teams are now experienced and becoming self-directed. They know the processes and protocols to get the work done. Focusing on the Common Core Standards, they clarify SBE Planning Ovals 1 and 2, analyzing the intent of each standard, determining the essential outcomes, writing aligned assessments, and creating a pacing guide for the use and analysis of the assessments. The job-alike teams also lead the work in their curricular area at their own schools. They help their colleagues use the standards and revised assessments, collecting feedback and data to bring back to the next job-alike meeting. It is a continuous cycle of improvement around standards and assessment.

Jeanne Spiller, Director of Professional Learning, explains the power of the job-alike teams in creating their culture for learning. "It used to be that the meetings of grade level and vertical teams lacked focus. They were more like opportunities for complaining or spinning wheels. We hadn't provided expectations for the work. Results were minimal. Today the work of the job-alike teams is what gives our district its focus and clarity. The teams have tight agendas and expectations for every meeting. Every team has a facilitator who is clear about district expectations for their role. The facilitators communicate regularly with each other and with district leadership staff. All work agendas, minutes, revisions, and data become public tools."

Data Teams

Data teams can also be grade level teams, leadership teams, vertical teams or content area teams. There really are many structural formats but student work is the consistent tool that guides the work of a data team. Data teams learn to use protocols that lead them through a cycle of continuous improvement. Teacher leaders often lead the work of the data team. They facilitate data dialogues focused on data that includes results from state assessments, common formative and summative assessments and day-to-day student work. Data teams also examine the effects of newly implemented instructional practices. Action research is a part of the work of some data teams.

Chris Bryan, Instructional Improvement Group, formerly with Adams 12 Five Star School District, Colorado, says that the steps in setting up the data team

Collaborative Teams on Parade

process are:
- Create a culture of inquiry
- Build teams (schoolwide leadership, grade level, vertical, core) that are focused on using data to inform their work.
- The leadership teams create the school goals based on areas of need identified through examination of data.
- Each team then uses a data analysis process

In order to create a culture of inquiry, one in which teachers seek to understand their system versus blame others for the results they are getting, there needs to be a schoolwide focus on learning, teachers collaborate in order to best meet the needs of students, data dialogues are an expected school-wide practice and as a result, teachers engage in data driven collaborative inquiry they feel a sense of responsibility to their students versus because someone is "making them" do it.

The data analysis process we use follows these steps:
- Collect and disaggregate data
- Identify patterns in the data
- Generate theories of causation and identify root causes
- Write goal(s)
- Identify appropriate interventions
- Identify what/how the adults need to learn in order to best instruct students
- Implement/measure results/revise goals and interventions

For more information contact Chris at lcrsbryan@msn.com.

Mentoring Teams

In order to accomplish all that we want, each of us should always have a mentor and be mentoring others. At the very least, we need to hold ourselves accountable for supporting and mentoring new teachers. The **Mentoring Culture Survey** on pages 81-82 is an excellent tool for starting conversations about the practices in schools that call themselves a professional learning community.

In many schools the model of assigning one mentor to each new teacher and having all other staff members excused from that responsibility has morphed into a model where some staff members are designed as lead mentors, but everyone in the school is considered to have responsibility for mentoring and supporting new staff members. **The Mentoring Team** tool on page 83 was

Collaborative Teams on Parade

developed by lead mentors in Alexandria City Public Schools, Virginia. It serves as a way to ask staff members to step up and say that they are willing and available to provide assistance in one or two areas of expertise and interest.

Leaders need mentors too. In the St. Vrain Valley School District, Longmont Colorado, induction coaches new to their positions receive rigorous mentoring. The novice coaches meet monthly with the lead induction coach to problem solve and hone their skills in coaching. Each novice coach also has a formal mentor who is an experienced coach. The novices observe their mentor in action with beginning teachers at least six times per year. In turn, the mentor observes the beginning coach regularly. Each observation is followed by a reflective coaching conversation and an opportunity for growth-producing feedback. Professional growth goals are data-driven and based on the needs of both the induction coach and also the teachers whom they support. The novice coaches are part of a larger collaborative team. They meet two mornings per month with the full coaching team. The time is focused on new learning, practice, and examination of data.

Grade Level Teams

See the examples of grade level collaborative teams from the **McNair Elementary Case Study** throughout this book.

Co-Teaching Teams

See what works in inclusive classrooms, fundamentals of co-teaching, and approaches to co-teaching on pages 78-80.

Co-Teaching Teams
What Works in Inclusive Classrooms

Teachers working in inclusive classrooms in Honeoye Falls-Lima School District, New York, provide the following suggestions for successful co-teaching:

- Establish common goals.
- Discuss roles and methods before school begins...and then revisit your decisions and adjust as necessary.
- Be flexible! Be focused but not limiting!
- Communicate constantly. Be specific. Be positive.
- Keep your sense of humor.
- Demystify special education.
- Accept responsibility! Always do at least your share and a little more.
- Think "our" students, not yours and mine.
- Remember one size doesn't fit all!
- Differentiate learning and enrich the environment with 3x3 tactics.
- Become familiar with all learning styles and alter teaching styles to suit.
- Incorporate activities that reach the different intelligences.
- Allow for divergent thinking by students and teachers.
- Practice wait time in the classroom and with each other.
- Do informal task analyses.
- Don't make assumptions.
- Incorporate active learning into the fabric of the classroom life.
- Don't differentiate between special needs students and others in public.
- Demonstrate utmost respect for all colleagues, students, and parents.
- Have special education teachers work with all students.
- Tap into students' interests.
- Take the risk to give up or set aside the tried and true and try something new.
- Schedule time together throughout the year to work on goals and skills.
- Seek out professional development opportunities.

Fundamentals of Co-Teaching

Successful co-teaching relies on effective communication. Simple matters, if not clarified, can lead to misunderstandings that interfere with the co-teaching success. Before you co-teach, and throughout the process, be sure to discuss these and any other fundamental issues you identify.

Instruction and Assessment: When you are working together in a standards-based classroom there must be a clear understanding of what standard(s) is the focus of the instruction and what mastery looks like. Adaptations around assessment for students with special needs may require much discussion. Will rubrics or performance task lists be used? What flexibility is built in and what might be areas of contention?

Co-Teaching Teams
What Works in Inclusive Classrooms

Planning: Who is going to take responsibility for which parts of the planning? When does planning get done? Does it happen one year, one month, one week, or one day in advance? Who designs the tasks, the assessment, and the criteria for demonstrating competency?

Instructional Format: How will the lesson be delivered and who will deliver it? What will be acceptable additions or clarifications? Which option for co-teaching will you use? How will a wide array of resources be assembled and organized? Who will take the lead for which tasks?

Teacher Status: How will it be clear to you and the students that you hold **equal status**? For example, think about how to do introductions to students, parents, and others, titles to be used, which names are on the report cards, who calls parents, and classroom allocation of adult space (such as desks and chairs).

Noise: How will the sound level in the classroom be monitored and adapted? Noise includes teacher voices, instructional activities, noise of machines or equipment, student voices, movement, and environmental sounds.

Procedures and Routines: What expectations does each teacher have for how classes should operate? This includes everything from headings on student papers to permission to use the pencil sharpener or restroom.

Discipline: What are the acceptable standards for student classroom behavior? What is absolutely intolerable for each teacher and what is okay some of the time in some situations?

Feedback: When will you meet to assess how the co-teaching arrangement is operating and how you will discuss both successes and problems? Identify timelines for feedback and the format of the feedback in advance.

Grading: What will be the basis for grades and who will assign them? Be sure to discuss the effect of instructional/assessment adaptations on grades.

Data Gathering and Analysis: What data will you need to gather to make future instructional decisions? How will this data about the effectiveness of instructional decisions and about student learning be gathered and analyzed?

Teaching Chores: Who duplicates materials, contacts speakers, arranges field trips, corrects papers, records grades, and so on?

Pet Peeves: What other aspects of classroom life are critical to you? The issue for you could be the extent of organization of materials, the ways students address teachers, or the fact that it really bothers you when someone opens your desk drawer without asking. Try to identify as many as possible in advance.

Co-Teaching Teams
What Works in Inclusive Classrooms

Approaches to Co-Teaching

Co-teaching teaming situations are most often collaborative efforts of general education and special education teachers or general education and teachers of second language learners. In either collaboration there are several approaches to working together. They include:

Co-Planning: If the schedules of members of a co-teaching team do not allow for teaching together on a regular basis, the team members can plan together either face-to-face or electronically.

One Instructor, One Observer: One teacher has primary instructional responsibility, while the other observes and gathers data on students, their performance, their interactions, and their behavior in general; each teacher can assume either role.

One Instructor, One "Floater": One teacher has primary instructional responsibility, while the other assists students with their work, monitors behavior, corrects assignments, etc. Each teacher can assume either role.

Station Teaching: Teachers divide instructional content into two parts (e.g., vocabulary and content, or new concepts and review). Each teacher instructs half the class in one area. Both groups rotate through instruction with each teacher.

Parallel Teaching: Each teacher instructs half the student group; the same content is taught simultaneously to all students though the instructional methods may vary.

Remedial Teaching: One teacher instructs students who have mastered the material to be learned, while the other works with students who have not mastered the key concepts or skills.

Supplemental Teaching: One teacher presents the lesson in standard format. The other works with students who have difficulty mastering the material, simplifying, and otherwise adapting instruction to meet their needs, or works with students who have already mastered the material to provide enrichment and extension. This option is often used when special education teachers and regular education teachers first work together.

Team Teaching: In this model, the most sophisticated form of co-teaching, the teachers collaborate to present the lesson to all students. In fully developed team teaching situations, the teachers are so comfortable with their roles, the content, and the students that they are able to pick up on nuances and read each other's signals so well that they essentially teach as one.

Mentoring Culture Survey

Use this survey to analyze the mentoring culture at your school. It can help you determine to what degree your school prepares for, welcomes, befriends, supports, develops, and retains new teachers and to then plan next steps.

Reflective Questions	My View My Data	My Colleagues' View Their Data
• How are new teachers perceived? Are they eagerly anticipated as new resources and a source of energy to the school? • Is there an existing, ongoing committee or group that annually plans and coordinates activities and experiences to bring new staff on board? • Do you regularly question new staff in order to ascertain needs and interests to help you plan? • Does the staff at large feel interest in or responsibility for the success of new teachers, or is that to be taken care of only by mentors? • Are there known ways for a veteran teacher to express his or her interest in mentoring or being involved in the school's induction of new teachers? • In allocating professional development resources, is consideration given to the needs of new teachers and their mentors in meeting the induction requirements?		

Mentoring Culture Survey

Reflective Questions	My View My Data	My Colleagues' View Their Data
• Is the administrative staff visible and vocal supporters of mentors and new teachers?		
• How do teachers feel about the mentoring roles and responsibilities? Do they volunteer or accept invitations to serve? Do they follow through on commitments?		
• Are collaborative team, grade-level, and departmental meetings structured and conducted to help a new teacher make good use of the time and learn the purpose and value of the meetings?		
• Are new teachers allowed to settle in, "learn the ropes," and focus on learning to teach, or do they have multiple committee assignments and extra duties?		
• When classes are scheduled, is consideration given to providing common planning time for mentors and new teachers?		
• To what degree do all staff members regularly observe each other teaching and engage in collegial, reflective conversation and instruction?		
• To what degree is continuous professional development to improve instruction modeled by senior staff?		

Mentoring Culture Survey template is available online.

The Mentoring Team

Please sign up for the area(s) in which you would be willing to support new teachers. That means you might have them observe in your classroom, observe them, share resources, and answer their questions.

SBE Lesson and Unit Planning	Assessment	Instructional Repertoire
Active/Engaged Learning	Special Needs Students	Second Language Learners
Essential Understandings and Concept-Based Instruction	Looking at Student Work	Rigor and Relevance
Instructional Technology	Data Analysis	Differentiation
Communicating with Parents	Organizational Systems	Co-Teaching
Resistant Learners	Professional Responsibilities	Other

The Mentoring Team template available online.

83

Points to Ponder
The Power of the Team

School leaders need to create an environment for learning and promote the attitude and belief that all students can achieve at high levels. As a strong culture is created, it is important to establish structures that support that culture so that beliefs and attitudes can be translated into actions and results.

One structure that has a positive impact on student learning as well as the relationship of adults in the workplace is teaming. Middle schools got it right when they adopted the philosophical belief that the interests of students could best be served when teachers meet regularly to discuss student learning and the unique needs of early adolescents. Time and again in team meetings I saw the positive impact of collective inquiry and problem solving on student achievement. Noted educational scholar Roland Barth expressed it this way: "The relationship among the adults in the building has more impact on the quality and character of the school and the accomplishments of its youngsters than any other factor."

When we established collaborative teams as part the professional learning community work in our school, good became great. While middle school interdisciplinary teams focus on the students that the teachers had in common, the addition of collaborative teams allows teachers to meet in curriculum teams and confer about the common content they taught. Adults have the time during their work day to address the needs of children as well as opportunities to talk with peers about the best instructional practices to use to achieve greater student learning. Many schools, including my former school, Thoreau Middle School in Fairfax County Public Schools, Virginia, have master schedules that enable teachers who teach the same grade level (elementary schools) or the same subjects (middle or high schools) to meet regularly within the school day. When collaborative teams in these schools meet and follow established protocols for effective collaboration, the teachers are pleased with the results of their collegial discussions, become better analyzers of student achievement data, and generally feel more empowered as professionals.

Putting in place a team structure and the development of a master schedule that will allow professional collaboration to occur is not enough. In order for teams to function at their optimum, team members need to establish norms of behavior for their work together. Variables such as confidentiality, participation by all members of the team, respect for differing opinions, and decision making by consensus must be discussed and agreed upon when the team begins to meet. It is also critical that the workload of the team be distributed equitably. This can be accomplished by setting up specific roles for team members such as team leader or facilitator, recorder, time keeper, liaison to the administration, and technology expert.

Points to Ponder
The Power of the Team

The team structure, a master schedule that builds in time for collaboration, and clearly articulated norms for teams is still not sufficient. In some instances teaming is mandated by a school leader without the necessary guidance or support. In these instances, although teams are established on paper, there is no definitive change in student achievement because teams are left on their own to determine how they should function. Team members must understand the purpose of their collaboration and be given guidelines that ensure that their conversations will directly impact their classroom practice. When teams meet, the focus of their work must consistently center on student learning. When the team leader or facilitator publishes a meeting agenda prior to the team meeting all team members know how their time will be spent. Unless it is clearly established that the purpose of teaming is professional collaboration, team meetings can quickly degenerate into complaint sessions, times for socialization, or discussions about administrivia. Meredith Casper, Principal of Pine Crest Elementary School, Montgomery County Public Schools, Maryland, uses the 80/20 rule for the teams at Pine Crest. When teams meet, 80% of their time is to be devoted to collaborative work around teaching and learning; a maximum of 20% can be used for other issues or congenial interactions.

When best practices become the focus of team discussions, it is important to remember that all discussions must center on specific actions to increase student achievement. Topics may include ways to engage students at the beginning of a lesson, strategies to help students process their learning throughout the lesson, the use of formative assessments to make instructional decisions, summarizing strategies, ways to meet the needs of diverse learners, and ideas to promote higher level thinking. Best practice areas of focus should be based on what an analysis of the data reveals about student learning needs.

The use of the team structure to analyze data, solve problems collaboratively, and investigate best practices can have powerful results. Teachers should return to their classrooms with the mindset that they are equipped with strategies they can use to help every child learn and experience success.

These remarks, written by Bruce Oliver, were originally published in the September 2006 issue of *Just for the ASKing!* All eighty issues of *Just for the ASKing!* are available at no charge at www.justaskpublications.com.

Isolation is Not an Option!
Building Collaborative Teams

In schools that have collaborative cultures, teams are the norm, and everyone is expected to be on a team or teams. Unfortunately, these teams are not always as productive as they might be. The reasons that many teams are ineffective, or even dysfunctional, include the lack of clearly articulated and agreed upon goals or the fact that team members lack the communication and collaboration skills for working together in the interest of student learning. The success of teams requires attention to the following variables:

School Culture: The study of culture is important because it, as well as the individual belief systems of team members, will have direct bearing on team effectiveness and team activities at each school.

Change Process: Because team development does not happen quickly or in a linear fashion, team members need to understand the change process. See pages 40-55.

Effective Meetings: Team members must become experts in planning, leading, and participating in meetings. See pages 115-120.

Diversity of Team Members: Team members should complement each other; that is, they should learn to recognize, seek out, appreciate, and capitalize on differences in styles, skills, talents, and interests. See pages 27 and 30-39.

Communication Systems: Teams and team members need to constantly assess and improve communication skills. See pages 28-29 and 57-68.

Group Process Skills: Teams, early in the development process, should work diligently to develop expertise in establishing norms, communication skills, and consensus building. They also need to put in place systems for dealing with differences of opinions and for making necessary adjustments in plans and procedures. See pages 87-97.

Individual Needs: Team success depends on the degree to which members' needs for influence and parity as well as a sense of competence and confidence are met. See pages 35-40 and 45-56.

Interdependence: Team members must take the initiative to share ideas and practices they value and believe that these will strengthen their efforts. They must also be willing to give up some autonomy to accomplish actions based on common visions and agreements. See pages 121-131.

Maintaining the Momentum: The high levels of commitment, energy, and enthusiasm typical at the beginning of the teaming experience can be maintained only with reflective practice, a balance of autonomy and interdependence, guidance, training, and support. See pages 135-194.

Norms of Collaboration
Establishing Norms
Brenda Kaylor and Stevie Quate

Norms, ground rules, or agreements are important for a group that intends to work together on difficult issues or will be working together over time. The norms may be added to or condensed, as the group progresses. Starting with the basic norms builds trust, clarifies group expectations of one another, and establishes points of reflection to see how the group is doing regarding process.

Steps in Establishing Norms

- Each person in small groups of 4 to 6 write for 1 to 2 minutes in response to the first question.
- Then, each person shares his/her ideas (1 minute per person).
- Next, each person writes for 1 to 2 minutes in response to the next question.
- Each person shares his/her responses (1 minute per person).
- Continue through all the questions.
- All the groups come back together to discuss their proposed norms.
- Work for consensus on the final set of norms.

Questions

When I think about groups that have worked exceptionally well, I realize that in those groups we...

When I think about groups that worked exceptionally poorly, I realize that in those groups we...

Therefore, I think that for us to work together we need to...

Establishing Norms template is available online.

Sample Team Norms

Special Education Department Team Norms

- All team members will meet Tuesdays from 8:30 to 9:00.
- All members are expected to be on time, every time.
- We will stay on task during the meeting.
- We will encourage active participation by all and listen respectfully.
- We will make decisions by consensus.
- We will confidentially discuss children's issues and concerns.
- We will arrive prepared and with any necessary materials.
- We will use data to guide our work.
- We will openly share thoughts, ideas, or concerns.
- We will define and clarify everybody's expectations and roles as special educators and instructional assistants.

Elementary Grade Level Team Norms

We will
- begin meetings on time and end meetings on time.
- deal with one topic or piece of team business at a time, and stick to the topic under discussion.
- act on the belief that participation is a right... and a responsibility.
- disagree or challenge in a constructive way.
- encourage the opinions of everyone in the group. Silence does not always mean agreement.
- on a regular basis, continue to develop conditions that promote respect, trust and caring.
- devise a problem-solving method to deal with disagreements.

Biology Department Norms

- The biology department will meet on Tuesdays at 12:45 pm in the science workroom. Everyone is expected to attend and be a full participant.
- We will keep our discussions private and professional.
- We will keep our minds open to new ideas.
- We will create quarterly assessments. Each department member will bring assessment items to a planning meeting where the final quarterly assessment will be developed.
- All decisions will have student learning as the goal. We will remain flexible in our thinking as we continue to find ways to support students.

Decision-Making Norms

During decision making, it is should be safe to differ; in fact, surfacing differences of opinion are encouraged so that the group can reach a decision that ultimately addresses multiple perspectives and needs.

- Decisions will be made based upon the roles and responsibilities, vision, and SMART goals for improving student achievement.
- Decisions will be made by consensus with the promise to revisit them if a need arises and is deemed necessary by the members of the team.
- Strategies to make decisions may include:
  - Use of criteria
  - Pros/cons in writing
  - Use of feedback from staff members on the possible options
  - List of five and/or other agreed upon steps to reach consensus before the decision is made
  - Time limits and "air time" agreements to reach the decision
  - Other strategies as developed by the team
  - After a decision is made, all team members will support it until it is revisited

Courageous Collegial Conversations

Linda Lambert proposes in ***Building Leadership Capacity in Schools*** that we must put issues on the table and build skills at dealing with those issues even though disagreements and conflict will be part of the process. The following points are adapted from that work:

- Pose questions that hold up assumptions and beliefs for re-examination.
- Remain silent; create an environment where all voices surface.
- Raise a range of possibilities but avoid simplistic answers.
- Keep the value agenda on the table; remind one another what we have agreed on as important.
- Focus attention on student learning.
- Provide space and time for both teachers and administrators to struggle with tough issues about student learning and the effectiveness of practices in the classroom and beyond.
- Conduct data-driven discussions by confronting data and by subjecting one's own ideas to the challenge of evidence.
- Turn concerns into questions.
- Be wrong with grace, candor, and humility.
- Be explicit and public about strategies, since the purpose is to model, demonstrate, and teach them to others.

Points to Ponder
Norms of Collaboration

Robert Garmston and Bruce Wellman in **The Adaptive School**, William Baker, Group Dynamics Associates, Glenn Singleton, and Curtis Linton in **Courageous Conversations about Race: A Field Guide for Achieving Equity in Schools**, and others suggest the following norms of collaboration:

- Pausing
- Paraphrasing
- Probing for specificity
- Putting ideas on the table and pulling them off when needed
- Presuming positive intentions
- Balancing advocacy and inquiry
- Paying attention to self and others
- Staying engaged
- Speaking the truth
- Expecting and accepting non-closure

Learning Forward

Learning Forward, formerly known as the National Staff Development Council (NSDC), recommends that team norms be established around time, listening, confidentiality, the decision-making process, participation, expectations for productivity, and attendance. The exemplars on the previous pages include other variables to consider. You might also think about issues such as resourcefulness, self and group assessment, use of data, dealing with conflict, and responsibilities beyond the meeting times.

Access the Norm Planning Worksheet online. Use this worksheet to draft norms for your team. Some headings are suggested. Feel free to add others that are important to the efficient and effective functioning of your team.

Data Collection Tool
Use of Collaborative Norms

Behaviors	Participants						
Contributes ideas and opinions (puts ideas on the table)							
Models							
Presumes positive intent							
Clarifies/probes							
Paraphrases							
Summarizes							
Links							
Refocuses							
Checks perceptions							

Data Collection Tool: Use of Collaborative Norms template is available online.

Building Consensus

Consensus Means...
- You have a voice in the decision
- All points of view have been expressed, discussed, explored, and studied
- You can live with a decision... not necessarily 100%
- You can and will support the decision publicly
- The will of the group is evident, even to those most opposed

Consensus Is Not...
- A 100% vote in support
- Everyone gets their first choice
- Everyone likes the choice 100%

Reaching Consensus on Difficult Issues
After hearing background information and analyzing it through an exercise or protocol, use the following steps:
- Take an initial preference poll (individual, pair, or table). Record preferences on chart paper using small sticky notes (different colors for different groups such as classroom teachers and content specialists or by grade levels).
- Review charts for patterns.
- Identify where there appears to be agreement.
- Identify where there appears to be differences and why.
- Identify options for mutual gain.
- Ask tables to reach agreement on two "better options" for mutual gain. Record those for the whole group to see.
- Use patterns of commonality to reach consensus within the whole group.
- If there is still some dissension, focus on how to live with the decision.

Eight consensus building and group process tools are presented on the following pages.

Consensus Building Tools

The eight group process tools presented here are multiple purpose and can be used to build consensus, surface issues, and conduct needs assessments.

Facts in Five

- Have staff members individually generate a personal list of the five most important variables, issues, concerns, or data sets related to the topic under discussion.
- Have participants then move into groups of five.
- Have the group of five reach consensus on the five most important facts or concepts and clarify their rationale for selecting each.
- Have each group create a chart listing their consensus decision.
- Have each group present their selections and the rationale for each selection to the larger group.
- If time is short, post the choices on the bulletin board for later examination.

1-3-6

- Have participants follow the same sequence used in **Facts in Five**, but after they work individually, have them move to groups of three and then to groups of six.
- This format takes longer, but may be most effective if participants have little experience or success with building consensus. It also provides more opportunity for dialogue and debate.

Spend a Buck

If further consensus is needed, after the charts are posted, provide each participant with sticker dots "to spend."
- Give each one 10 dots worth 10 cents each and explain that they can spend all their dots on one point or they can divide them however they choose to include 10 cents on 10 different points.
- Have participants place their dots on the charts next to the points most important to them.
- When all have "spent their bucks," group priorities will be graphically displayed on the charts.

Consensus Building Tools

Nominal Group Technique

- Identify a problem or issue to be addressed.
- Ask individuals to record ideas and responses on index cards, one idea to a card.
- Then ask individuals to report out each giving one idea at a time. Have participants continue to report out responses, one at a time until all ideas have been reported.
- Chart all responses.
- Ideas can be clarified as they are shared or clarified after all ideas are recorded.
- Ask each participant to list on cards the best four to six ideas listed.
- Record those votes beside the ideas listed on the charts.
- An alternative approach is to have participants rank in order the four to six best ideas and record the ratings beside each idea listed on the charts.
- The ideas with the most votes and/or the highest ratings move to the top of the list as having been identified by the group as having the greatest potential for success.

Affinity Diagram

- Establish a clear question that will generate multiple diverse responses.
- As a group, brainstorm **aloud** and record all ideas on sticky notes, one to a note. Brainstorming guidelines are:
  - No criticism
  - No explanations needed
  - Seek combinations and improvements
  - Seek quantity over quality
  - Respond spontaneously, in no predetermined order
- Randomly place the sticky notes on chart paper or a blank wall.
- Push for breakthrough thinking, and then end verbal brainstorming.
- **Silently** sort random ideas into columns or clusters by placing like ideas in the same cluster or column.
- Continue to move and remove sticky notes but do not use verbal or nonverbal communication.
- Consensus is reached when there is no further movement of sticky notes.
- Develop a category statement that describes the essence of the ideas in each cluster or column.

Consensus Building and Group Processing Tools

Sorting

- After brainstorming ways to accomplish a specific goal (using guidelines included in the **Affinity Diagram** description on the previous page), post three large pieces of chart paper.
- Ask the group to sort the ideas into three categories:
  - **Quick Fixes**: Those ideas that are important, but can be accomplished simply or by one individual
  - **Out of Our Hands**: Ideas that are not realistic given the present circumstances
  - **Definite Possibilities**: The remainder of the ideas
- Concentrate team effort on the **Definite Possibilities** and eliminate the **Out of Our Hands** list.
- Do not ignore the items on the **Quick Fix** chart because they may be the source of early and easy successes. Individuals may tackle those issues freeing the group to address more significant matters.

Fist to Five

Use this tool to take a poll of group members and overall group thinking or feelings at any point in a discussion.
When asked to show first to five, participants show:
- Fist to indicate absolutely not, or total disagreement
- Three fingers to indicate that the feeling is neutral about the topic or issue
- Five fingers to indicate total agreement or comfort with the topic or issue

Thanks to Lou Chicquette, Linda Dawson, and Martha Howard from Appleton Area School District, Wisconsin, for their contributions to the descriptions of these tools.

Consensus Building and Group Processing Tools

On My Mind

This process allows you to quickly gather information about what group members and the group as a whole see as the main issues about the topic under discussion.

Individual Reflection

- You will find on your tables a stack of index cards. Distribute at least three of the cards to each member of your table group.
- Use these cards to record questions which are **On Your Mind** related to the topic under discussion. Please focus your questions and concerns on the stated purposes and please put only one question on each card. If you have only one question or more than three, feel free to use the necessary number of cards.
- On each card you complete, write a question you would like to have answered, or at least addressed during this workshop series.

Round One

- When you have completed your cards, circulate them for two or three minutes at your own table. If, as you read the circulating cards, you find that you are also concerned or curious about the question posed on someone else's card, place a small dot on the card and put the card back in circulation. If the question listed is not one of your main issues, simply place the card back in circulation.
- Read through as many cards as you have time to read.

Rounds Two, Three, and More

- After three minutes your table group will, at a signal, exchange cards with another table.
- Repeat the circulation process with the new cards and attach dots to indicate a high level of interest in the question posed.
- At the end of three to five minutes you will, at a signal, exchange cards with yet another table and repeat the process.

Collection

- Upon completion of these rounds, place the cards in the center of the table so they can be collected.
- The facilitator will organize the data and provide the group feedback.

Dealing with Difficulties

What Do You Do If Norms Are Not Followed?

- Check with the group to see if the norm needs to be revised or eliminated.
- If the group continues to ignore the norm, ask them to monitor it.
- Test out any assumption you're making with the group around the norm. ("I want to see if my assumption is correct or not. When the group discussed side bar discussions, I promised to give us all time to process understanding through 'talk time.' I'm assuming that I'm not giving you enough of that reflective time. Is that accurate?"
- Have folks self-monitor by rating how well they are meeting the norm.

What Do You Do When Groups Are in Conflict?

- Be honest. Respectfully tell group members what you think and feel.
- Do not sit in silence. Share your opinions in the group conversation.
- Stick to the topic under discussion.
- Contribute to creative and constructive solutions.
- Treat every individual on the team as an equal.
- Listen to one another's viewpoints.
- Allow equal time for all participants to talk.
- Focus on the problem and not personalities.
- Use active listening, make eye contact, and speak directly to the person with whom you may have an issue.
- Problem solve in the meeting, not in the teachers' lounge or the parking lot.

When Reactions and Results Are Not What You Want, Consider These Possible Causes

- Beginning without having an end in mind!
- Absence of mutually agreed upon ways of dealing with each other.
- Unwillingness to, or lack of skills for how to, communicate thoughts and feelings about issues and ideas.
- The tendency to see what we want to see. If we are working from a negative perspective, we are far more likely to note negative actions or data.
- Differences in rate of change. Given that change does not happen in a vacuum, past experiences and current competing priorities greatly influence the rate of change. It is important to remember that people, not institutions, change.
- Differences about facts, goals, priorities, and/or methods
- Competition for seemingly scarce resources and turf
- Misunderstanding
- Unmet expectations...usually caused by unclear expectations!

Celebrations!

Faculty Meeting Kudos
Theresa West

We begin each faculty meeting with appreciation for each other. The administrative team kicked this off with animals which are passed from teacher to teacher. Now, teachers bring the animals to faculty meetings and pass them along to someone else!

Animals include:
- El Toro of Love, for someone who has shown a lot of caring.
- Thankful Turkey, for someone we are thankful for.
- Wise Owl, for someone who was wise about a decision.
- "Purrrfect" Cat, for someone who did something perfect.
- Dynomite Dinosaur, for someone who was just dynamite.
- "Beary Special" Three Little Bears, for folks who did something very special.
- Turtle, for "shellebrating" something good.
- Purple Monkey, because they did not "monkey around."

The Crystal Apple Award
Bruce Oliver

I wanted to create the norm that the adults in our school would come together regularly to celebrate the successes we created. In my efforts to expand my repertoire of strategies for supporting the development of that norm, I read about an award that could be presented to faculty members in recognition of good teaching practices. A clear, glass apple on a tiny pedestal was purchased and christened the "Crystal Apple Award." It was inscribed with the words, "Instructional Excellence." The faculty member who received the award would keep it for a month and display it in his or her room. To initiate this tradition, I began my recognizing a faculty member who had recently demonstrated excellence in the classroom. I readily acknowledged that any number of faculty members were worthy recipients but that in order to get the tradition started, one particular teacher was selected. It was the responsibility of each recipient to pass on the award and recognize a fellow faculty member at the next monthly faculty meeting. In order to make a valid decision, it was necessary for the current holder of the apple to visit classrooms around the building. That tradition, which began so long ago, still continues today. At each meeting, the Crystal Apple presentation is the last item on the agenda. Faculty members give this portion of the meeting their undivided attention, and when the new recipient's name is announced, there are always cheers and an enthusiastic round of applause. The award keeps a constant focus on the fact that teaching young people is our most important mission.

Celebrations!

The ROSE Award

A district-wide initiative to celebrate the efforts of all stakeholders in Appleton Area School District, Wisconsin, resulted in many ROSE Award certificates posted on bulletin boards in classrooms, front offices, cafeterias, custodial offices, and homes. As shown below ROSE stands for Recognition Of Superior Effort. This process, like many of the others described here, engaged staff members in celebrating one another rather than simply recognition from the administration.

Appleton Area School District

Recognition Of Superior Effort

This
ROSE AWARD
is issued to:

Katherine Ruh

In appreciation of the following effort to improve the quality of instruction or services to the Appleton Area School District

For all you have done to ensure that we have the resources we need to meet the diverse needs of our learners.

Presented by the staff of Roosevelt Middle School

©Just ASK Publications

Celebrations!
A McNair Elementary Case Study Artifact

A Letter to the Staff Following a State Visit

Dear Teachers,

I would like to thank all of you for making today an exceptional day.

We began the day in my office with our School Improvement Team. At that time we shared the binders that our team has worked so hard to collect. The binders included your team minutes, agendas, pacing guides, common planning, common assessments, and data collection. They included information regarding staff development activities, conferences, consultants, and included my emails, letters, and correspondence with faculty members. In essence, the binders were a collection of McNair's activities, and specifically the work which you have produced this year.

After listening to the team and asking clarifying questions, our visitors Dr. Maureen Hijar and Dr. Calanthia Tucker, spent time in my office reviewing the binders and time observing teachers and teams throughout the building. At 2:00 they met with the cluster director and me. I want to share their comments with you. **The comments in bold are my thoughts tacked on to comments made by Dr. Hijar and Dr. Tucker**.

- The School Improvement Team did an excellent job. They modeled the epitome of organization and the samples of evidence should be commended. (**Awesome job team!**)
- When observing classroom practices they noted that the professional development highlighted in our binders was carried into practice. (**This is what it is all about!**)
- They noted that the lesson plans collected in binders mirrored the lessons they saw in classrooms.
- They were very impressed with the use of technology. The SMART Boards (SB) were being appropriately used. They described one class where a teacher posted an eCart question on the SB and students were answering it on a white board. After the students said this was very easy, the teacher ended with a display of data showing the actual class data when responding to this question. Students spoke about distractors in their answers. (**This is great stuff!**)
- They were impressed with the level of differentiation used in classrooms, they described another lesson where after the warm-up there were four separate student activities depending on the needs of the students, including going to

Celebrations!

the blackboard, use of manipulatives, and a separate review group. (**The LEARN model and careful planning rule!**)

- They described a lesson with co-teaching and a lesson with instructional support being provided by a SUM teacher. (**Go team!**)
- In sixth grade, there was proper use of calculators. A teacher had laminated formula sheets for use with tests taped to student desks. The found this impressive! (**This continues to be so cool!**)
- One thing that particularly pleased them was that the amount of teacher talk was low. After describing the two classrooms above, they shared that other classes were equally impressive. (**Best practices are evident at McNair!**)
- Classroom management was a strength as our teachers demonstrated great classroom management and students behaved appropriately! (**Woo-hoo! Go PBS! Go Fred Jones! Way to go McNair teachers!**)
- They told us they could see just how smart our kids were. They were discussing variables/independent variables/graphs/test taking skills. (**Our kids are impressive; thanks for bringing out the best in them!**)
- They were impressed with the levels of thinking. They were impressed with all observed. In one classroom, when working on word problems a child asked the teacher, "What are the key words to use with multiplication problems?" The class brainstormed this and came up with some ideas. Then the teacher asked students to look at the word wall to see if they had any other ideas. Knowing that word walls were part of our school plan, they liked seeing it in action. (**I liked hearing about it in action; thanks so much for putting this into practice!**)
- A huge compliment was paid to McNair when they said that what they saw in writing, and then our School Improvement team verbalized with them, was seen in your practice. The paper translates to your work! (**In research, they could say there is triangulation of the data. I can't tell you how proud I was to hear this!**)
- The agendas and team norms showed that you still know how to have some fun and they appreciated this, too. Especially our kindergarten team who has 'bring chocolate' as a norm! (**I like chocolate!**)
- They made a comment saying that they could tell things at McNair were well in place. Students followed procedures, knew where to look, knew how to work in groups, and knew when to get to their work. Evidence of your work up to now was noted as this is not something that is pulled together in a day! (**Hard work pays off!**)
- The work that Nanette has done with new teachers was great and the agendas showed that she focused on instruction, but also other facets of life that affect

Celebrations!

new teachers. It was clear that we worked in conjunction with the PLT office and had a variety of support for new teachers. (**Thanks to Nanette for planning and our new teachers for participating!**)

Next Steps
- Keep up the good work!
- We will need to continue data collection of lesson plans, team minutes, team agendas, and pacing guides for final submission at the end of the year.
- Go home and sleep well tonight; you should all be very proud!

Final Comments
I can't think of anything more fitting during Teacher Appreciation Week than recognizing and applauding the work you do. They gave us very specific examples and I have to say that we are thrilled with what is going on in your classrooms. It has been emotional around this building lately. I have to tell you that I listened to this report with a deep thrill that so much of what teams at McNair have put into place has come to fruition and been recognized. Everyday you work so hard, and today, our visitors from the Virginia Department of Education have seen the fruits of your efforts. They eagerly await our SOL results. I know we will do well. Thanks for being so flexible, thanks for working so hard, and thanks, above all, for putting our kids first!

Happy Tuesday!

Theresa

Theresa West, Ed.D.
Principal
McNair Elementary School
Herndon, Virginia

The Principals' Perspective
Celebrations!

Treasure Hunt
Bruce Oliver

As teachers arrived at a faculty meeting, they were asked to draw the name of another faculty member from a container. I explained that during the next month, each teacher was to visit the classroom of the person whose name they had drawn, to spend time in that person's classroom and complete a short piece of writing that depicted the **"treasure"** that he or she had found in a fellow teacher's classroom. At the following month's faculty meeting, everyone brought their completed **Treasure Hunt** form. We filled the two bulletin boards in the faculty lounges with the **Treasure Hunt** forms so the entire staff could see the expansive repertoire of ideas, the caring attitudes, and the place of learning we had all collectively created.

Snapshot
Theresa West

To: Heather Whitis
From: Theresa West
Date: November 3, 2011

When I was in your room I noticed...

You left great substitute plans today. Your substitute was working with an interactive SMART Board activity. All of your students were engaged as she used the decimal/fraction lesson that the rest of the team was also teaching.

Thanks for making sure that learning was taking place even when you were out of the building. I hope you feel better soon.

cc: School File

Celebrations!
A McNair Elementary Case Study Artifact

McNair, McNair teachers, staff and great crew,
We love, just love the things that you do!

We love the fact that you are here,
And work so hard everyday, all year!

We love it when on the bright side you look,
And especially when reading your kids a fine book!

We love our teachers and how they choose,
Just right things for our kids to do!

We love our secretaries and IA's that's true,
When around them one can never feel blue!

We love all the people who make this place great,
From the cafeteria to tech, from SACC to our fine PTA!

We love our parent center people, now this is so,
Custodians, clinic, library all, you are dynamo!

We love our resource teachers, specialists too,
The stuff that you teach is very way cool!

We love our staff; you are the cream of the crop
We shout this daily from McNair's rooftop!

We love that you're great, at the jobs that you do,
We love, we love it, we love working with you!

We love, we just love, all the specialness here,
We love kids that you all hold so dear.

We love that you come back, day after day,
You're the greatest we have in this US of A!

We hope you enjoy this deserved time,
Take time to rest, it's the end of our rhyme!

Happy Holidays!
From your Admin Team
Theresa, Brian, Maria & Karen

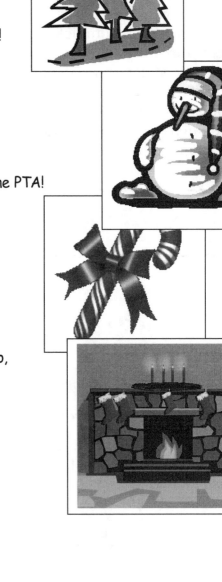

Celebrating Our Year!
Scavenger Hunt for Ten Great Ideas

This scavenger hunt was a part of the end-of-year celebrations held for new teachers in Alexandria City Public Schools, Virginia and for new teachers in Greece Central School District, New York. In each district senior district leadership, mentors, and student musical groups joined in the celebration of the accomplishments of the new teachers in their first year in the district. The inclusion of the instructionally focused scavenger hunt helped to remind all participants of the primacy of student learning.

Directions:

As we gather to celebrate the completion of your first year of teaching, let's celebrate the ways you have impacted student learning. Have the colleague who provides information on an item sign your sheet and then you write a brief summary of what that person tells you.

1. Find someone who has used several different ways to **check for student understanding** this year. Have him explain what he did, why he did it, and what the impact on learning was.
2. Find someone who can explain how she has integrated **literacy** across the curriculum.
3. Find someone who can name three **organizational systems** that she plans to put into place at the beginning of the next school year. Have her explain the systems and why she plans to use them.
4. Find someone to share a story of a **struggling student** who turned the corner. Have that person explain what happened and how he felt about it.
5. Find someone who can share a **parent communication system** that worked well and that she plans to use again next year. Get the details so you can use it too!
6. Find someone who can share a great **collegial relationship** that developed this year.
7. Find someone who used a new **active learning** strategy within the last month. Have her describe the activity and its impact on learning.
8. Find someone who can share three great ways to **put students into groups**.
9. Find someone who can tell you how she has successfully **integrated technology** as a learning tool for students.
10. Your own biggest accomplishment this year.

Scavenger Hunt for Ten Great Ideas template is available online.

Finding Time to Collaborate and Learn Together

Purnell and Hill (1991) identify six general approaches to creating time for collaboration and professional learning:
- Promote time outside the classroom during the school day
- Refocus the purpose of existing time commitments
- Reschedule the school day
- Increase the amount of available time
- Promote teachers volunteering some of their time
- Promote more efficient time use

In addition, Raywid (1993) cites a number of examples for creating collaboration and professional learning time:
- Use part or all of faculty, department, or team meetings.
- Lengthen the school day for 20 minutes four days per week.
- Use an early release on the fifth day to provide an extended period of time for collaborative work.
- One morning per week, engage students in alternative activities such as community service that are supervised by parents, community members, or non-instructional staff; use this time for professional development collaborative work.
- Provide a common scheduled lunch and planning period for teachers working on joint projects.

Brenda Kaylor and Stevi Quate added the following suggestions at the Mesa Valley School District Learning Community Institute in Grand Junction, Colorado:
- Design master schedule to create common time.
- Free teachers as much as possible from non-professional work.
- Have paraprofessionals and instructional aides cover classes at regular intervals.
- Use parents from a volunteer bank to lead activities and short lessons.
- Allocate professional development funds to planning time.
- Set up brown bag lunches.
- Bank time for late start days.

See examples on the following pages of master schedules and other scheduling information used by schools to find the time for collaboration.

Finding the Time in Middle Schools
Bruce Oliver

The essential core of a strong middle school is interdisciplinary teaming. The master schedule should provide time for teachers who teach the same students to have time during their day to discuss their content, teaching strategies and how to best meet individual student needs. These teachers comprise the **interdisciplinary team**. Additionally, teachers who teach the same subject/content should likewise be provided time for collaboration about methodology, the creation of common assessments and eventually data analysis to make future instructional decisions. These teachers comprise the **curriculum team**. The seven-period day master schedule we used at Thoreau Middle School, Fairfax County Public Schools, Virginia, during my tenure as principal provided both options. A recent master schedule is shown on the following pages. Teachers teach five out of the seven periods daily. Teachers in the core subjects of English, math, science and social studies are provided time for interdisciplinary teaming as well as subject and grade level teaming.

There are six core/interdisciplinary teams at Thoreau, three seventh grade teams (Dolphins, Trailblazers and Rockets). There are three eighth grade teams (Generators, Chili Peppers, and Tigers). Each of the core teams has a common time when all the teachers on that team can meet. For example, all Dolphin teachers meet during Period 4, all Trailblazer teachers meet during Period 3 and all Rocket teachers meet during Period 1. Additionally, all teachers who teach the same subject are provided a common time when they can meet. Note that all three seventh grade English teachers can meet during Period 7; all seventh grade science teachers can meet during Period 6; and all eighth grade civics teachers can meet during Period 3.

Every effort was made to allow teachers who teach special education classes to meet with their curriculum teams. For example, Barretta is able to meet when the seventh grade English curriculum team meet; Lowry is able to meet when the eighth grade English curriculum team meets. Including the special education teachers, whenever possible, during the curriculum team planning time is especially important since special education students should be taught the same curriculum as the regular education students.

In this schedule, there was no significant difference in class size. Because of the importance of collaboration, these teachers were not assigned any additional duties beyond their teaming responsibilities.

Thoreau Middle School Master Schedule

	Period 1	Period 2	Period 3	Period 4	Period 5	Period 6	Period 7
Dolphins Tarrant Furr Groz Loht	English 7 History 7 Math 7 Science 7**	English 7 History 7 Science 7	English 7 History 7** Math 7 Science 7		English 7** Math 7 Science 7	English 7 History 7 Math 7**	History 7 Math 7 Science 7
Trailblazers (2) Hurtling Clark Kamen Kozlowski	English 7* History 7* Math 7 Science 7	English 7** History 7 Science 7*		English 7 History 7* Math 7 Science 7**	English 7* Math 7** Science 7*	English 7 History 7* Math 7*	History 7** Math 7* Science 7*
Rockets (3) Muldoon Collins Welin Hutchinson		English 7 History 7 Science 7**	English 7 History 7 Math 7 Science 7	English 7 History 7 Math 7 Science 7	English 7** Math 7 Science 7	English 7 History 7** Math 7	History 7 Math 7** Science 7
Generators (4) Hepperle Carrington Theiss Mandell	English 8** Civics 8 Math 8* Science 8*		English 8 Math 8* Science 8*	English 8* Civics 8 Algebra Science 8	English 8* Civics 8** Science 8	Civics 8* Math 8 Science 8**	English 8 Civics 8* Algebra
Chili Peppers (5) Tedeschi Williams Gluck Lunger		English 8 Civics 8* Algebra Science 8	English 8** Math 8 Science 8	English 8 Civics 8 Algebra Science 8	English 8 Civics 8 Science 8**	Civics 8** Math 8 Science 8	English 8 Civics 8 Math 8
Tigers (6) Zeltner Fones Johnson Corcoran	English 8* Civics 8 Algebra Science 8	English 8 Civics 8* Math 8 Science 8	English 8 Math 8* Science 8**		English 8* Civics 8** Science 8	Civics 8 Algebra Science 8*	English 8** Civics 8 Math 8*

* Team Taught   ** Honors

	Period 1	Period 2	Period 3	Period 4	Period 5	Period 6	Period 7
Special Education							
Barretta	SC Eng 7	LD BSR 7	LD BSR 7		SC Eng 7	SC Eng 7	
Boyd		LD BSR 8			English 8*	History 7*	LD BSR 8
Brown, B	SC Autism 7/8		SC Autism 7/8	AUT BSR	SC Autism 7/8	SC Autism 7/8	SC Autism 7/8
Griffin			SC Math 7	SC Math 7	SC Math 7	Math 7*	Math 7*
Brown, M	English 8*	ED BSR 8	Math 8*	English 8*	English 8*	ED BSR 8	Math 8*
James	English 7*	Civics 8*	Math 8*		English 7*		
Kessler	Math 8*		Reading 8	Reading 7	SC Math 8	SC Math 8	SC Math 8
Lichtman		SC Eng 8	SC Eng 8	SC Eng 8		Reading 8	Reading 7
Lowry					ED BSR 7		ED BSR 7
McClanahan	SC Civics			SC Civics	SC Civics	Civics 8*	Civics 8*
Montagna		Science 7*	SC Sci 7		Science 7*	SC Sci 7	Science 7*
Ostenfeld	Science 8*	SC Sci 8	Science 8*	SC Sci 8		Science 8*	Tech Sys 8
Poll		History 7*	SC Hist 7	History 7*		SC Hist 7	SC Hist 7
Stars							
Art							
Gould	Art 8		Art 8	Art 7	Autistic Tues.	Art 7	Art 7
Music							
Sanger	Inter Band			Adv Band	Inter Band	Beg Band	Inter Band
Winder	Inter Orch	Adv Orch	Begin Orch				
Yacovissi	Adv Mixed	Chorus	Chorus	Beg Mixed	Chorus		
Harrison							
Foreign Language							
Safavi		French	IFL	IFL	IFL	ARI	French
Albright	Spanish 1	Spanish 1	Spanish 1		Spanish 1		Spanish 1
Speech & Drama							
Ryan		SP & DR	Th Arts	SP & DR	Th Arts	SP & DR	
ESOL							
McMillen	B1 LIT		SOC ST 8		A LIT	A LIT	SOC ST 7
Renfrew	A Sci	Fast Math	B2 LIT 7			A LIT	B2 LIT 8

* **Team Taught**   ** **Honors**

Thoreau Middle School Master Schedule

	Period 1	Period 2	Period 3	Period 4	Period 5	Period 6	Period 7
Unicorns							
Health & PE							
Frodigh	H/PE 8	H/PE 8		H/PE 8	H/PE 8	H/PE 8	
Stratton	Health 7	Health 7	Health 7	Health 7		Health 7	
Fisk	H/PE 7	Adapt PE	H/PE 7	H/PE 7	H/PE 7	Tech Sys 8	H/PE 7
Rowland	ARI	H/PE 7	H/PE 8	H/PE 8		H/PE 8	H/PE 8
McGowan			H/PE 8	H/PE 8	H/PE 7		H/PE 7
Technology							
Knotts	Tech Ed 7	Tech Ed 7	Tech Ed 7		Tech Sys 8	Tech Ed 7	Tech Ed 7
Teen Living							
Taylor	Wk/Fam 7	Wk/Fam 7			Wk/Fam 8	Wk/Fam 8	Wk/Fam 8
Resource							
Moses	Power Math	Power Math	Power Math	Power Lit 7		Power Lit 8	

McNair Elementary School Master Schedule

Time	Kindergarten	1st Grade	2nd Grade	3rd Grade	4th Grade	5th Grade	6th Grade
8:30 - 8:45	Morning Meeting	Morning Meeting	Morning Meeting	Morning Meeting	Morning Meeting	Morning Meeting	Morning Meeting
8:45 - 9:00	Morning Meeting	Morning Meeting	Morning Meeting	Morning Meeting	Morning Meeting	Morning Meeting	Morning Meeting
9:00 - 9:15	Language Arts	Language Arts	Language Arts	Language Arts	Math	Specials	Specials
9:15 - 9:30	Language Arts	Language Arts	Language Arts	Language Arts	Math	Specials	Specials
9:30 - 9:45	Language Arts	Language Arts	Language Arts	Language Arts	Math	Specials	Specials
10:00 - 10:15	Language Arts	Language Arts	Language Arts	Language Arts	Specials	Math	Math
10:15 - 10:30	Language Arts	Language Arts	Language Arts	Language Arts	Specials	Math	Math
10:30 - 10:45	Language Arts	Language Arts	Language Arts	Language Arts	Specials	Math	Math
10:45 - 11:00	Lunch	Language Arts	Language Arts	Language Arts	Specials	Math	Math
11:00 - 11:15	Lunch	Lunch	Language Arts	Specials	Recess 11:00 - 11:20	Math	Science/ Social Studies
11:15 - 11:30	Calendar/ Quiet Time	Lunch	Recess 11:10 - 11:30	Specials	Recess 11:00 - 11:20	Math	Science/ Social Studies
11:30 - 11:45	Calendar/ Quiet Time	Recess 11:30 - 11:50	Lunch	Specials	Lunch 11:20-11:50	Recess 11:20-11:40	Science/ Social Studies
11:45 - 12:00	Math	Math	Lunch	Specials	Lunch 11:20-11:50	Lunch 11:40- 12:10	Science/ Social Studies
12:00 - 12:15	Math	Math	Specials	Lunch	Science/ Social Studies	Lunch 11:40- 12:10	Science/ Social Studies
12:15 - 12:30	Math	Math	Specials	Recess 12:00 - 12:20	Science/ Social Studies	Language Arts	Lunch 12:10 - 12:40
12:30 - 12:45	Math	Math	Specials	Math	Science/ Social Studies	Language Arts	Lunch 12:10 - 12:40
12:45 - 1:00	Math	Specials	Specials	Math	Science/ Social Studies	Language Arts	Recess 12:40 - 1:00
1:00 - 1:15	Recess/Free Choice Classes to take turns in playground	Specials	Math	Math	Language Arts	Language Arts	Language Arts
1:15 - 1:30	Recess/Free Choice Classes to take turns in playground	Specials	Math	Math	Language Arts	Language Arts	Language Arts
1:30 - 1:45	Recess/Free Choice Classes to take turns in playground	Specials	Math	Science/ Social Studies	Language Arts	Language Arts	Language Arts
1:45 - 2:00	Specials	Science/ Social Studies	Math	Science/ Social Studies	Language Arts	Science/ Social Studies	Language Arts
2:00 - 2:15	Specials	Science/ Social Studies	Science/ Social Studies	Science/ Social Studies	Language Arts	Science/ Social Studies	Language Arts
2:15 - 2:30	Specials	Science/ Social Studies	Science/ Social Studies	Science/ Social Studies	Language Arts	Science/ Social Studies	Language Arts
2:30 - 2:45	Specials	Science/ Social Studies	Science/ Social Studies	Science/ Social Studies	Language Arts	Science/ Social Studies	Language Arts
2:45 - 3:00	Specials	Science/ Social Studies	Science/ Social Studies	Science/ Social Studies	Language Arts	Science/ Social Studies	Language Arts
3:00 - 3:15	Specials	Science/ Social Studies	Science/ Social Studies	Science/ Social Studies	Language Arts	Science/ Social Studies	Language Arts

111

Collaborative Teams Meeting Schedule
A McNair Elementary Case Study Artifact

	Collaborative Team Time	Tuesday	Wednesday	Thursday	Friday
Kindergarten	2:10 - 2:55	Language Arts Collaborative Team Meeting		Math Collaborative Team Meeting	
1st Grade	1:10 - 1:55	Language Arts Collaborative Team Meeting		Math Collaborative Team Meeting	
2nd Grade	12:10 - 12:55	Math Collaborative Team Meeting		Language Arts Collaborative Team Meeting	
3rd Grade	11:10 - 11:55	Math Collaborative Team Meeting	Language Arts Collaborative Team Meeting		
4th Grade	10:10 - 10:55		Math Collaborative Team Meeting	Language Arts Collaborative Team Meeting	
5th Grade	9:10 - 9:55		Math Collaborative Team Meeting	Language Arts Collaborative Team Meeting	
6th Grade	9:10 - 9:55		Language Arts Collaborative Team Meeting	Math Collaborative Team Meeting	

Finding Extended Time
A McNair Elementary Case Study Artifact

Half-Day Planning Sessions				
	November 12	**November 13**	**November 19**	**November 20**
7:40-11:10	Preschool FECEP 3 Substitutes	Second Grade 5 Substitutes & 1 Instructional Assistant	Kindergarten 3 Substitutes & 1 Instructional Assistant	First Grade 5 Substitutes & 3 Instructional Assistants
11:10-11:40	Lunch for Substitutes			
11:40-3:10	Third Grade 3 Substitutes & 3 Instructional Assistants	Sixth Grade 5 Substitutes	Fourth Grade 5 Substitutes	Sixth Grade 5 Substitutes

The schedule above displays how we scheduled half-day planning sessions for each Collaborative Team using three to five substitutes on each of four days or a total of 16 substitutes. We needed extra help at kiss and ride on those days as some staff members were in planning sessions.

Substitutes were not provided for ESOL and Special Education teachers; however, we expected all teachers to attend the planning sessions.

Finding the Time
Staff Meetings, Professional Learning, and Collaboration
Julie McVicker

At Indian Peaks Elementary School, Wednesdays were designated for total staff collaboration. Meetings were scheduled as follows:

- The first Wednesday: Building Focus Groups (BFGs)
- The second Wednesday: Staff development
- The third Wednesday: Nitty-gritty staff meeting with reports from the BFGs
- The fourth Wednesday: Book Club

Tuesdays were for grade level collaboration. The fourth Tuesday was for cross-grade level collaboration with the following schedule:

- September grade below
- October grade above
- November grade below
- January grade above
- February grade below
- April grade below
- May grade above

Building Leadership Team (BLT) met on Friday mornings twice a month on the 2nd and 4th Friday. One person from each BFG attended the BLT meeting.

The Building Leadership Team planned the staff development for the year using the results of the needs assessment to determine topics. For one school year the areas of focus were:

- Collaboration
- Effective Reading Strategies Research
- Data Analysis
- Technology
- Math
- Differentiation Strategies
- Literacy: 6 Traits

The Literacy Team went over data with 3rd, 4th, and 5th teachers in September. They went over data with K, 1st, and 2nd after the fall assessments.

Making Meetings Matter

Planning for faculty, department, team, or committee meetings involves the same process as planning instruction for the year, the unit, or the lesson. The questions to consider are essentially the same. As the meeting planner, ask:
- What do I want those at this meeting to know and be able to do as a result of attending and participating?
- How will we know when they/we are successful with those outcomes?
- What needs to occur at the meeting and following the meeting in order to move toward successful completion of the outcomes?
- How will we use data to determine next steps?

When these essential questions provide the focus for meetings, it is no longer possible to lead meetings that address primarily administrivia and/or a series of unrelated agenda items.

To assess how well-focused and organized the meetings you lead are, use the following guidelines to plan, to self-assess, and to get feedback from meeting attendees about the effectiveness of the meeting:
- The purposes of the meeting were clearly communicated.
- The activities at the meeting were aligned with the purposes.
- The meeting was structured so that all participants were meaningfully engaged.
- All the people who needed to hear the information and/or be involved in the decision-making process were in attendance.
- The topics under discussion needed face-to-face interaction and could not have been handled electronically or on paper.
- The decision-making process and ultimate decision makers were clearly identified.
- Essential data and rationales for action were used.
- The issues discussed, studied, and/or decided at previous meetings and addressed between meetings were discussed and integrated as appropriate.

Assessing Our Meetings

1. The purposes of the meeting were clearly communicated.

   ← 1   2   3   4   5 →

2. The activities at the meeting were aligned with the purposes.

   ← 1   2   3   4   5 →

3. The meeting was structured so that all participants were meaningfully engaged.

   ← 1   2   3   4   5 →

4. All the people who needed to hear the information and/or be involved in the decision-making process were in attendance.

   ← 1   2   3   4   5 →

5. The topics under discussion needed face-to-face interaction and could not have been handled electronically or on paper.

   ← 1   2   3   4   5 →

6. The decision-making process and ultimate decision makers were clearly identified.

   ← 1   2   3   4   5 →

7. Essential data and rationales for action were used.

   ← 1   2   3   4   5 →

8. The issues discussed, studied, and/or decided at previous meetings and addressed between meetings were discussed and integrated as appropriate.

   ← 1   2   3   4   5 →

Assessing Our Meetings template is available online.

A Principal's Perspective
Making Faculty Meetings Matter
Bruce Oliver

As a veteran principal, I clearly understand that a principal's typical day is unpredictable, and filled with multiple stops and starts. It is not uncommon for a principal to check the day's "to-do" list long after everyone has gone home only to find that most items on the list were never addressed. Student issues, stacks of memos and directives, surprise phone calls from the central office or a parent, test data, emails, teacher conferences, building problems - these responsibilities often take considerable time. Amid all the interruptions and demands, it is easy for a school leader to lose sight of his or her primary responsibility to be an instructional leader.

As the instructional leader of the school, it is essential for the principal to know as much as possible about what constitutes the best instruction, and to ensure the teaching staff is utilizing proven best practices. The principal must be seen by everyone as knowledgeable, competent, and well-informed.

As a principal, I was responsible for planning faculty meetings that were meaningful and valuable enough to take the time of the teaching staff. Gathering the teachers for a series of administrative announcements that could easily be conveyed in a memo or an email simply was not the best use of a teacher's time.

The challenge I found was to plan well, to model good instructional practices, and to structure meetings that allowed the staff members to actively engage in the learning strategy I was modeling. As I planned faculty meetings, the goal was to have the teachers transfer the learning activity I was modeling into their teaching.

My goal as a principal was always to be at the forefront of good instructional practices and to promote those practices among the staff. However, I frequently found the "urgent" (interruptions throughout the day) often took over the "important" (instructional leadership) I wanted to address.

I was pleasantly surprised one day to see a copy of Paula Rutherford's *Leading the Learning: A Field Guide for Supervision and Evaluation*. The shelves in my office were already filled with educational publications, so I was leery this would be one more book I might not get to, or that it would be so philosophical and impractical it would not provide me with any substantive ideas I could really use. When I opened Paula's book, I was pleasantly surprised to discover how user friendly it was. In the very first section of the book were two sections entitled **Collaboration and Job-Embedded Learning** and **Masterful and Meaningful Meetings**. What followed was a compendium of 18 ideas under the heading of **Strategies for Meaningful Meetings**. The purposes of the strategies were clearly stated, along with step-by-step directions as to how to address the topic. Each topic was transferable by the teachers to their classrooms.

A Principal's Perspective
Making Faculty Meetings Matter

One of my favorite strategies to get faculty members involved in a meeting was called **Graffiti** (see page 119.) I began by placing sheets of large chart paper around the meeting room with topics identified at the top of each page. I then divided the faculty into small groups of four to five. In their groups, they moved to a chart and responded to the topic by writing a response or two with a marker. After a few minutes, I asked each group to move to the next chart and record their thoughts. As each group moved to the next chart, they were able to read the responses from previous groups and then record their own ideas. After everyone had a chance to read and respond to all topics, they returned to their tables and processed the trends, patterns and implications they saw in the charts. Topics can be varied but may include such ideas as successful discipline strategies, getting students to complete homework, addressing varied learning styles of students, what to do when students do not learn content the first time, and ways to differentiate instruction.

Another strategy that can help to make meetings more meaningful is called **Stir the Faculty** (see page 120.) The purpose of the strategy is to access prior knowledge on a topic, to validate current best practices and to promote collegial collaboration. I started by distributing a data collection sheet to each faculty member. The sheet contained spaces for twenty responses. Each faculty member started by writing down three responses to the topic in the first three blanks on the data sheet. At a signal, everyone moved around the room collecting and giving ideas to other faculty members until their sheets are full. It is important to have participants move around the room and not simply remain in one place. After participants return to their tables, they can compare lists, prioritize the responses, or select two or three ideas they would like to try with their students. The topics for **Stir the Faculty** should be purposeful and add to the teachers' repertoire of teaching strategies. Topics may include such ideas as ways to assign/check homework, strategies for doing pre-assessments, ways to summarize at the end of a lesson, or ideas to promote inclusion of all students in the learning.

These remarks, written by Bruce Oliver, were originally published in the September 2006 issue of *Just for the ASKing!* All eighty issues of *Just for the ASKing!* are available at no charge at www.justaskpublications.com.

Strategies for Making Meetings Matter
Graffiti

Purposes
- To capture the thinking and reactions of the staff to multiple ideas or aspects of the same idea
- To have staff quickly see the opinions, reactions, or concerns of others
- To have staff process a great deal of information with movement

Process
- Write quotes, prompts, questions, or areas of concern (one to a chart) on large sheets of chart paper and post them around the room. Alternatively, you can tape 8½" x 11" sheets of paper to the middle of large sheets of chart paper.
- Have small groups of 4-5 begin work at different charts.
- Have them respond to the topic or title of the chart by writing responses or **Graffiti**, which can be short words, phrases, or graphics on the chart paper.
- After the allotted time period, have staff members move to the next chart.
- Repeat the process until all groups have reacted to all charts.
- Have staff members process the patterns, trends, and implications for their practice from what is written on the charts.

Possibilities
- Top Ten Questions for Secondary Teachers (See page 258 in *Instruction for All Students*). Place one statement on each chart and have staff members circulate to generate ideas of how they do or could do each.
- Top Ten Questions I Ask Myself When I Design Lessons (See page 36 in *Instruction for All Students*).
- See pages 158-159 for an example of how one school staff used **Graffiti** to generate **Look Fors** and **Listen Fors** in a Standards-Based Classroom.

Strategies for Making Meetings Matter
Stir the Faculty

Purposes

- To access prior knowledge and experiences
- To validate current best practice
- To promote collegial collaboration
- To generate comprehensive lists
- To set the stage for new learning

Process

- Provide each participant with a data collection sheet containing ten to twenty lines, or have them number their own sheets.
- Have each one write, as directed, three strategies, three reasons, three causes, three points of interest, etc., about the topic/concept to be studied. Ask them to make the third one on their list unique.
- At a signal, have them move around the room collecting/giving one idea from/to each participant. Ideas received from one person can be passed "through" to another person.
- After an appropriate amount of time, have them return to their seats. At this point, you can have them compare lists, prioritize, categorize, or select two or three they would like to try.
- At this point, they can continue with a format appropriate to the level of thinking you want them to do. They have had time to focus on the subject and to hear ideas from colleagues.
- As appropriate, create and distribute a master list of ideas.

Possibilities

- Ways we check homework
- Ways we pre-assess
- Ways we get students' attention
- Organizational systems for teacher, classroom, or students

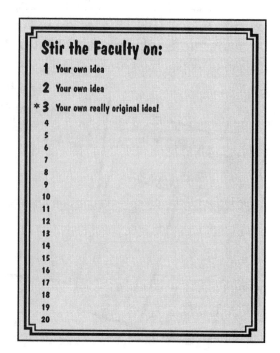

Stir the Faculty on:

1 Your own idea

2 Your own idea

*3 Your own really original idea!

4
5
6
7
8
9
10
11
12
13
14
15
16
17
18
19
20

Our Collaborative Team
Examining the Current Status

Directions:

As grade level or curriculum teams work in collaborative groups, it is important that they do periodic assessments of how well the team is functioning. Use the scale below to identify the current reality of their team. Teams members should first complete the assessment individually and then teams should come together to build consensus about the current status. This assessment can be administered multiple times throughout the year to track growth and progress.

1	2	3	4	5
We have not addressed or discussed this issue	This is true but only to a limited degree	Not Sure	We have talked about this issue	We have talked about this issue, are in agreement, and it is reflected in our practice

_____ 1. We ask for and provide one another assistance with planning, analysis, and reflection.

_____ 2. We have aligned the outcomes for our instructional program with the Common Core Standards, the state standards, and the learning outcomes for our district.

_____ 3. Each member of our team is clear about the standards we are to address in our instructional program as well as the outcomes for each unit.

_____ 4. We have identified the essential understandings, key concepts, and big ideas that are the foundation for our content at the unit and year-long levels.

_____ 5. We individually and collectively hold and select purposefully from a wide range of teaching strategies.

_____ 6. We use task analysis and pre-assessment data to determine how to teach each unit.

_____ 7. We have agreed on the criteria we will use to judge the quality of student work.

Our Collaborative Team
Examining the Current Status

_____8. We have developed a pacing guide with time built in to extend and reteach as needed.

_____9. We regularly inform students, prior to their beginning of tasks or assessments, the specific criteria to be used in measuring academic achievement, and when possible, we provide multiple exemplars of excellent work.

_____10. We use student work, classroom assessments, common assessments, data from standardized assessments, and all other available data to make decisions about the next steps in our instructional programs.

_____11. We collaboratively design or identify assessment tools to use with our students.

_____12. We provide feedback loops that give our students multiple opportunities to demonstrate their learning.

_____13. We share assessment results with students and help them develop learning goals and make action plans.

_____14. We regularly include an emphasis on strategies that expand the curriculum for students who need acceleration.

_____15. We enlist the support of instructional specialists and meet with them regularly.

_____16. Our collaborative team has established and uses norms that guide us as we work together.

Examining the Current Status template is available online.

McNair Elementry Case Study
Theresa West and Maria Eck

Theresa West, Principal of McNair from July 2008 to July 2011, and Maria Eck, Assistant Principal 2008-2011 and the newly appointed Principal of McNair, have shared the story of their efforts and accomplishments at McNair with multiple audiences. See index for a list of the other pages in this book that present additional information about McNair, located in Herndon Virginia; it is part of Fairfax County Public Schools. Before Theresa and Maria led McNair, the school had not made AYP. It has done so throughout their tenure.

The following text from the school's website (www.fcps.edu/McNairES/aboutmain.html) provides background information about the demographics and philosophy of the school:

> McNair Elementary School unites staff, families, and the community in working together to help academic and social goals, and develop the skills and dispositions to be responsible citizens and productive members of a global community.

> A hallmark of the McNair program is the staff's strong commitment to collaboration to help all students succeed. A large team of literacy, math, and English as Second Language specialists routinely plan and co-teach with classroom teachers. A range of special education services span preschool through grade six. Weekly team meetings allow staff to analyze student data, discuss best practice, and customize instruction to meet student needs.

> Recognizing the strengths and potential of the school population, McNair offers the full range of gifted/talented services, including school-based center classes beginning in third grade. A full-time gifted/talented specialist provides added support to all K-6 classrooms. A 30-unit computer lab, SmartBoard technology, four wireless 20-unit mobile labs, and computers in every classroom make state-of the-art applications available to all children. A grant-funded Design and Engineering Lab features robotics sets for student use, K'nex constructions, object-oriented computer programming, and architectural CAD programs.

> Located in a richly diverse community, McNair families represent over 50 countries and languages. McNair's own Parent Center, conveniently located next to the main office and staffed by a team of multilingual parent liaisons, offers parent coffees, informative workshops, and a welcoming introduction for new families. Working in partnership with the PTA, McNair Elementary School empowers parents to be proactive in supporting their children's achievement through participation in SOL information nights and other family events.

McNair Elementary Case Study

Opened in September 2001, the school was named for the McNair family, members of the Herndon community since 1904. McNair Elementary School continues a long tradition of civic pride through school-wide emphasis on positive citizenship, community service, and respect.

Below are some key talking points from Maria and Theresa about their work with interventions and extensions at McNair.

Our School as a Professional Learning Community
- Leading is our fundamental purpose
- We have a collaborative culture
- We focus on results

School Improvement Plan SMART Goal
We will implement a school-wide intervention block to meet AYP proficiency goals of 89% in reading and 87% in math and to increase the percentage of pass advanced students by 10% over 2009-2010 in each grade level.

Strong Collaborative Teams
- 2010-2011 was our third year with structured common assessments used on a monthly basis.
- It was also our third year using data to discuss results of common assessments.
- Teams meet two to three times a week to plan for instruction.
- Teams are very comfortable about sharing data with each other.
- The greatest success comes from teams who respect and like each other!

Other Development Initiatives
It all begins with our collaborative teams, but beyond that we:
- Consulted with other principals and learned about successful programs in place
- Discussed interventions at pyramids meetings
- Attended professional development sessions presented by other schools
- Talked with teachers about what works for them

Data We Use
- Math Reasoning Assessment K-2
- Reading Benchmark Assessments/DRA
- Common Assessments

McNair Elementary Case Study

- eCART
- Exit tickets
- Observation and anecdotal notes

Celebrations

- We integrate test-taking and study skills strategies.
- We make sure they really, really get it!
- The Advanced Academic Program specialist is a part of the whole team with interventions and enrichment.
- We are purposeful in our work.
- Our work as a professional learning community feels completely natural.
- We celebrate our efforts and accomplishments.
- Our parents are part of our learning community.

Challenges

- Being able to re-teach with a different perspective
- Figuring out how to group students
- Making lessons for specialists and instructional assistants
- Finding the time to plan meaninful interventions
- Following up with students who do not improve

McNair Elementary 5th Grade Collaborative Team Report

Why CTs are time well spent	• We believe that six brains in a room are better than one! • We make use of each of our strengths. • We collaborate and get the input of specialists so that we include instruction and materials for the wide range of students we have; that is, from level 1 ESOL students to our AA (GT) students. We are strong believers in divide and conquer! • Together we get the big picture and then break it down into manageable tasks. We are strong believers in divide and conquer! • Through our time together we have learned to trust each other. We know that each person will do her job. • Our math specialist attends our meetings as an integral part of our team. She provides support, materials, assessment data, and a "math brain" way of looking at the objectives.
How we organize the work	• We have an agenda, and we stick to it. The four main goals of the Collaborative Team are listed on each agenda, which is emailed to team members the day before the meeting. • We use the pacing guide that was set at the beginning of the year. We plan for the following week. • We look closely at the indicators so that we know exactly what must be covered. We then divide and conquer. • We assign each person a lesson to prepare. Lessons include: INB, Smartboard activity, stations, exit tickets, and homework. • Lessons are posted to the common server in our Grade 5 folder. • We know that once we leave, the meeting isn't over. We continue to share through emails, lunch chats, etc.
How we deconstruct the standards	• We feel that at times Standards or Learning wording can be vague. • We look closely at each benchmark and indicator to know exactly what the focus is. • We make note of the essential understandings, teacher notes, and essential new vocabulary to ensure we cover what we are supposed to cover. • We discuss what was done the previous year to see if we missed something and/or to find ways to improve our teaching.
What interventions are in place for struggling students	• We check the students' background knowledge so that we know if they are ready for upcoming objectives. • Exit tickets show us which students have or have not mastered the objective. • Stations allow the teacher to work in small groups, which gives the teacher more time to work directly with struggling students and allows the students to help each other. • We make use of early bird time to reinforce math skills. • We co-teach with the ESOL and special education teachers. • We use eCART data to design more effective lessons for our students' weak areas. We "teacher swap" if a teacher has a particularly successful approach to teaching an objective. • Our pacing guide includes spiraling. We also make use of buffer days for reviewing or re-teaching. If needed, we adjust our pacing guide if it's clear we need to back up or spend extra time on an objective.
How we challenge advanced learners	• We use flexible grouping in stations. • We give advanced students activities requiring higher-order creative and critical thinking. • We pull students gifted in math from the general education classrooms into the AA (GT) class for math.

McNair Elementary 3rd Grade Math CT Agenda

Team Norms
- Use data to drive instructional decisions
- Engage in respectful collaboration when sharing ideas
- Fulfill our professional obligations and be accountable to each other
- Honor the agenda
- Maintain confidentiality

Guiding Questions
- What do we want them to learn?
- How will we and they know when they've learned it?
- What will we do when they haven't learned it?
- What will we do when they already know it?

Topic, I/D/A*, and Time *Information/Discussion/Action	Desired Outcomes	Person Responsible	Notes
Roundtable celebrations (1-2 minutes)	• We will share any personal or professional celebrations	Entire Team	
ECART **Data discussion** (I/D/A-10 minutes)	• As a team, we will go look through our Number Sense assessment data in which we identify our areas of success as well as the concepts that we need to spend time re-teaching • We will generate some lesson ideas for focusing on the weaker SOL concepts identified throughout our discussion	Lynn Entire Team	• Lynn shared the beginning of the year eCART math data with us. • Fractions are a skill which was low on the data sheet so we need to really focus on fractions. • Lynn shared the excel sheets on the server to record math data (in math folder under data). • Lynn showed us the performance assessment for fractions located in our math folder.
Lesson planning for Fractions (I/D/A-30 minutes)	• We will form small breakout groups to plan math lessons and activities for the week of Oct. 13th -Oct. 16th • Jamie and Katie will focus on: Finishing up Name and Writing Fractions, and Comparing Fractions • Dia and Melissa will focus on: Equivalent Fractions, Comparing Fractions, and Ordering Fractions	Entire Team	**Next Week's Lessons** • **Tuesday:** Linear lesson-Jamie, Equivalence-Dia • **Wednesday:** Linear lesson-Jamie, Equivalence-Dia • **Thursday:** Comparing Fractions-Katie, Comparing and Ordering-Melissa • **Friday:** Comparing Fractions-Katie, Comparing and Ordering-Melissa
Parking lot items (1-1 minute)		Entire Team	
Set agenda items for next meeting (1-2 minutes)	• We will set agenda items to discuss at our next PLT Meeting	Entire Team	

Collaborative Team Agenda template is available online.

Events in the Parents' Center
A McNair Elementary Case Study Artifact

Parents Are Part of Our Collaborative Team!

January 11 - 9:30-10:30 a.m. **Supporting Young Readers** - Our reading teacher will share ideas for parents on helping your child as a young reader.

January 18 - 9:30-10:30 a.m. **African-American Health Issues** - Mrs. Smith, a nurse from Kaiser Permanente, will discuss health issues that are of particular concern for African-American families.

January 25 - No event - Teacher Workday.

February 1 - 9:30-10:30 a.m. **Ways to Help Your Child with Math Homework** - Our math resource teacher will share tips parents can use to assist with math homework assignments.

February 8 - 9:30-10:30 a.m. **Ask a Kindergarten Teacher** - McNair teacher, Mrs. Beach, will share information about kindergarten curriculum and answer questions about reading and writing with young children.

February 15 - 9:30-10:30 a.m. **Let's Share Breakfast** - We'll celebrate Valentine's Day. Bring a food from your culture or something you just love to eat to share with other parents. Heart-shaped foods NOT required!

February 22 - 9:30-10:30 a.m. **Keeping Kids Safe On-Line** - McNair technology specialist Mrs. Jones will share information about Internet safety for families.

March 8 - 9:30-10:30 a.m. **Ask a Primary Grade Teacher** - Second grade teacher, Mrs. Wines, will share information and answer questions about curriculum in grades 1-3.

March 15 - 9:30-10:30 a.m. **"Writing with Your Child"** - Our reading teacher will share ideas about writing with your child. We'll experiment with writing a family memory story.

March 22 - 9:30-10:30 a.m. **Family Field Trips for Spring** - We'll share ideas for local family outings that take advantage of the outdoors. We have some ideas, bring your suggestions to share too!

March 29 - 9:30-10:30 a.m. **Writing a Resume** - Local businesswoman, Laura McCarthy of Qualified Search, Inc., will meet with us to share tips for writing resumes. Laura's tips will be of benefit to a job search in any field.

Points to Ponder
Professional Learning Communities

Rick DuFour and his colleagues have identified ten attributes of professional learning communities. He is adamant that professional learning communities are not a series of meetings or events, but rather organizations that operate with the following mindset:

- Clarity of the knowledge and skills all students should acquire
- Agreement on and consistently applied assessment practices
- Development of common formative assessments
- Use of formative assessments to identify and provide students with timely intervention
- Use of data to assess effectiveness of instruction
- Establishment of SMART goals
- Commitment to and focus on improved instructional practices
- Sharing of researched-based best practices
- Determination to help all students achieve at high levels
- Use of team time to focus on student learning

For in-depth information from Rick and Rebecca DuFour and their colleagues on their professional learning communities work, see ***Learning by Doing: A Handbook for Professional Learning Communities at Work***. Also visit the website: **All Things Professional Learning Communities** at www.allthingsplc.info/about/aboutPLC.php

Why Professional Learning Communities?

A review of the literature reveals that schools with fully functioning professional learning communities see the following results:

- Continuous professional growth and student learning
- Reduction in isolation of teachers
- Increased commitment to the school's vision
- Shared responsibility for the success of students
- Increased use of best practices
- Increased satisfaction, higher morale, and lower rates of absenteeism
- Advances in adapting instruction to meet students' needs
- Commitment to making lasting change
- More learning for more students more of the time

## III

Characteristics of
Professional Learning Communities (PLCs)

In schools that truly function as PLCs, one finds:

Shared Values and Vision about Student Learning

- All staff members are involved in creating a shared vision and using the vision in making decisions about teaching and learning.
- A core value in the vision is the complete focus on student learning.
- The norms of behavior of the school consistently focus on every student's potential achievement.
- Relationships among individuals are valued. All involved learn to trust and care about one another.

Collective Focus

- All staff members continually focus on creating the results they want.
- New and creative ways of thinking are nurtured.
- People learn and grow together.

Shared Leadership

- All stakeholders develop leadership skills.
- The school leaders provide and active nurturing of the entire staff's development as a community.
- The traditional pattern that "teachers teach, students learn, and administrators manage" is completely altered.
- There is no longer a hierarchy of who knows more than someone else, but rather the need for everyone to contribute.

Data-Driven Discussions and Decisions

- All participants build knowledge and skillfulness at analyzing, interpreting, and acting on multiple sources of data about effectiveness of instructional practices and on student learning. Discussions include:
  - Knowledge of what data to collect
  - Knowledge and skillfulness in identifying gaps in data and creating data sources to gather needed information
  - Skillfulness in identifying individual problems as well as patterns and trends
  - Skillfulness in taking action based on the data analysis and interpretation
- All opinions and generalizations are based on evidence or data.

Characteristics of
Professional Learning Communities

Public Accountability

- Accountability reports/minutes for collaborative team meetings can be electronic or paper and will be maintained as a collective record of efforts and accomplishments of the team.
- Data is published and shared publically in support of collaborative team work.

Shared Personal Practice

- Teaching is made public through peer observations, planning together, and looking at student work together.
- Teachers develop productive relationships with one another.
- All become more comfortable and skillful with debate, discussion, and disagreement.
- All celebrate each other's triumphs and offer support when practices do not work.

Lessons from the Field
Successful Cultures for Learning
Bruce Oliver

Across the nation educators are working hard to create cultures for learning not only for the students but for adults as well. Many districts and schools are embracing Rick DuFour's approach to professional learning communities (PLCs). Others are developing learning communities via Critical Friends Groups (CFGs), an approach originally designed by the Annenberg Institute for School Reform at Brown University and now supported by the National School Reform Faculty (NSRF) in Bloomington, Indiana. Stevi Quate and her colleagues at the University of Colorado, Denver have been particularly proactive in their work with this initiative. Shirley Hord, Michael Fullan, Andy Hargreaves, and Mike Schmoker have added mightily to the dialogue. All agree that creating a culture for learning requires leadership commitment, support, and understanding that it is neither an announcement nor an event, but instead a complex journey to increased student learning.

From firsthand experience, I can attest to the power of professional learning communities. Prior to my retirement I introduced DuFour's PLC concept at **Thoreau Middle School, Fairfax County Public Schools (FCPS), Virginia**. Following several days of training with a team of teachers, I led small group discussions with staff members introducing them to the ideas and building a case for why the professional learning community concept had the potential to make a difference in student achievement. We began slowly at the mid-year point and I had the chance to watch the levels of conversations flourish. For the next school year, the teachers indicated that they wanted to continue meeting in curriculum teams but they needed time during the work day to meet and collaborate. As we began our second year, we developed a master schedule that allowed the teams to meet throughout the day. I felt that the level of commitment by the teachers had reached new heights when I realized I could drop in on a meeting and the high-powered conversations would continue. I was not someone who interrupted the meeting; the teachers came to understand that I was there to learn from them and to witness firsthand the excitement they brought to their collaborative efforts.

Brenda Kaylor, ASK Group Senior Consultant, and Stevi Quate worked with the leadership and teaching staff in **Mesa County Valley School District #51 in Grand Junction, Colorado**. The K-8 schools in that district focused for two years on creating cultures for learning in a standards-based environment. Well-versed in both DuFour's work and the Critical Friends work, Brenda and Stevi provided professional development support that was ongoing, job embedded, and multifaceted through site-based coaching and structured training sessions. Vernann Raney, principal, and the staff of Dos Rios Elementary School in Grand Junction reported that in their first year of this work they began by establishing

Lessons from the Field
Successful Cultures for Learning

norms of behavior for their grade level collaborative teams, examining current student data, and identifying one SMART goal for student learning based on the data analysis. When establishing their goal, the teachers participated in extended conversations to make sure the goal was SMART: specific, measurable, attainable, results-oriented, and time bound. The real excitement started happening when teachers developed common assessments and started discussions about how to ensure that there was inter-rater reliability as they assessed student learning. Using the protocols they learned through the Critical Friends work enabled them to become much more consistent in their conclusions as they examined student work. When Vernann visited team meetings, she described the work teachers were doing as unstoppable.

Darren Reed, former principal at **Cora Kelly Elementary School, Alexandria City Public Schools, Virginia**, introduced the PLC concept with the Cora Kelly staff, set up training for the entire staff, and devised a master schedule that allowed grade level teachers common planning time during their work day. Each grade level team decided on a team leader and established norms of communication. As Darren visited team meetings, he found that the conversations were much more focused on student learning. The teachers shared responsibility for the tasks they undertook. For example, the third grade teachers worked collaboratively to create review materials for the annual state assessments. One kindergarten teacher who is a technology enthusiast took it upon herself to search the web for new ideas that she and her teammates could use to match the needs of their young students. When Darren found a common area on which his teachers needed additional information, he quickly arranged for the appropriate professional development to occur. For example, at a faculty meeting the staff focused on higher level questions and took time during the meeting to develop questions for an upcoming unit. Overall, the teams thrived as they focused their conversations on best teaching practices, common assessments, and ways to support struggling students. The workload was shared equally among team members and, according to Darren, "their level of professionalism reached new heights."

At the middle school level, Mark Greenfelder, the current principal of **Thoreau Middle School in FCPS**, has put in place a system of electronic assessments that allows teachers to create and administer common assessments on a quarterly basis. After students complete the online assessments in math, science, social studies, and English, the teachers have instantaneous results. They are able to respond immediately and work with students who are not successful; additionally, students have additional chances to demonstrate mastery level learning. In addition to continuing and refining the previously mentioned master schedule, Mark applied for and received a teacher leader grant which provides financial compensation for their time used to examine the work they are doing and to develop plans to improve the learning for all students. An outgrowth of their work was the institution of the **Time to Soar** program in the middle of the school day. Any student who is not achieving at a passing level must work with an assigned teacher for a short period in the middle of the school day. In addition, all special education teachers have additional time to work with their students to reinforce learning that occurred during the regular class setting.

At **George C. Marshall High School** another Fairfax County Public School, Principal Jay Pearson and the Marshall staff have in place **Lunch and Learn**, an hour-long period in the middle of the school day during which students participate in enrichment or intervention activities. This important inclusion in the school day has proven to be hugely successful in meeting the needs of a very diverse student population. In addition, all teachers at Marshall have uninterrupted time every Friday to work with fellow teachers who teach the same subjects; they use the time to create common assessments and determine how best to respond to the needs of individual students. These practices have become an essential part of the culture of the school and have resulted in notable achievement gains for its students.

In order to create a strong culture for learning and have learning communities become a lasting part of the school's culture, the principal must make commitments which will allow the collaborative teams to flourish. Commitments from principals which have proven to be efficacious include:
- Providing time for teachers to meet as collaborative teams on a regular basis during the school day
- Implementing appropriate professional development and providing resources as identified by teams
- Protecting the school from competing initiatives
- Creating systems to give students additional time and support when they experience difficulty.

These remarks, written by Bruce Oliver, were originally published in the May 2007 issue of *Just for the ASKing!* Over eighty issues of *Just for the ASKing!* are available at no charge at www.justaskpublications.com.

IV

Professional Learning

Best Practice in Professional Learning

The professional learning program of the St. Vrain Valley School District, Colorado:
- Reflects the district's purpose
- Is both district and school-based
- Is integrated with a comprehensive change process
- Is more effective and meaningful when there is ownership and responsibility for collaborative planning, shared decision making, and timely implementation
- Recognizes that professional learning takes many forms
- Is driven by analyses of data that show the gap between the goals set for student learning and actual student performance
- Recognizes that the value of professional development ultimately should be measured by its impact on staff and the students they serve

Brenda Kaylor
Former Director of Professional Development

Every educator engages in effective professional learning every day so that every student achieves.

Learning Forward (NSDC)

Planning Professional Learning Opportunities

Because our colleagues

- need to be validated for what they already know and do; we need to recognize and build on their experience
- experience a dip in their sense of self-efficacy when new initiatives with new skills and language are introduced; we need to provide encouragement and recognition of effort
- spend much of their time with children; they need opportunities to be congenial and socialize at the beginning of conferences and work sessions
- value choice, they should be offered choice in how they learn, as long as what they are learning is based on the mission and vision of the organization, all available data, and is in the interest of student learning; we need to provide multiple learning formats and environments
- internalize and use strategies that they experience far better than they internalize strategies that they only hear or read about; we need to structure our interactions to include opportunities for staff to experience proven teaching/learning strategies
- engage when they are asked what they would like to know about the topic; we need a repertoire of ways to gather, analyze, and use the data about their concerns, goals, and needs
- need to see and hear examples from situations similar to the ones in which they work; we need to locate and save examples from all content areas and grade levels
- want to know why and how the supervisor, mentor, or coach is qualified to lead their learning and whether or not the leader has "walked the talk;" we need to be storytellers...but not braggarts
- respond to humor; we need to be able to enjoy the moment and, as appropriate, build in humorous stories
- expect feedback on work they do; we need to not only give them appropriate feedback, we need to teach them strategies and protocols for asking for and giving each other feedback

This chapter explores the RPLIM model for designing professional development, an array of approaches to professional learning including peer observations, learning walks, looking at teacher work, professional conversations online, and attending professional conferences as a team, setting professional learning goals, needs assessments, and tips for assessing the impact of professional learning.

IV

RPLIM
Readiness, Planning, Learning, Implementation, and Maintenance

Considerations for Planning
Results-Based Professional Development

The RPLIM Model is a synthesis of ideas emerging from the literature in organizational development, adult learning, school change, leadership behavior, and professional development. Its five stages of planned change form a structure for thinking about improvement systematically. School leaders use these stages to design for and facilitate change for successful, long-term school improvement.

Sara DeJarnette Caldwell
Professional Development in Learning-Centered Schools

Readiness

☐ Is a shared sense of purpose/vision being created?
☐ Is there a climate/environment conducive to learning in our school/district?
  • Is there frequent, concrete talk about teaching?
  • Do we observe one another in our practice?
  • Do we collaborate together?
  • Do we teach each other what we know about teaching, learning, and leading?
  • Do we ask for and provide one another assistance?
  • Is there a focus on continuous improvement?
☐ Have we examined our student data carefully?
☐ Have we examined our current classroom and school-wide practices?
☐ What are the connections (or lack of) between our current practices and student results?
☐ Have staff examined their core beliefs about student learning?
☐ Have we examined and researched best practices?
  • Are there sites making gains in student achievement that have challenges similar to our own that we can visit?
☐ Do we have visible support from leadership?
  • Principal
  • Central administration
  • School Board

RPLIM
Readiness, Planning, Learning, Implementation, and Maintenance

Planning

☐ Is there a compelling vision that embodies high expectations for student learning, teaching, and professional development?

☐ Do we have specific and measurable goals?
  - Are the goals based first on student and staff need?
  - Is there evidence that these are goals that will make a difference in student achievement?

☐ How will we evaluate this professional development work?
  - Have we considered:
    - Budget for evaluation?
    - Timeline?
    - Need for an external evaluator?

☐ Who needs to be involved in the planning?
  - Content expert(s)
  - Meeting facilitator(s)
  - Logistics coordinator
  - Communicator(s)
  - Evaluator(s)
  - Stakeholders

☐ Organized Abandonment
  - Before we begin this new work, what are we going to stop doing?

☐ Are our logistics well-planned?
  - Timelines
  - Current financial resources
  - Long-term financial commitment

☐ Do we have a commitment from the:
  - Board of Education?
  - Teachers' Association?
  - School community?
  - Community?

☐ How do we plan to maintain the momentum over time?

RPLIM
Readiness, Planning, Learning, Implementation, and Maintenance

Learning

☐ Does our learning design include:
  - Variety and choice?
  - Accommodation for diverse learning styles?
  - Support for learners at the various levels on the CBAM continuum?

  ↑ collaboration
     impact
     management
     personal
     information
     awareness

  - Formal and informal learning structures?
  - A strong plan for ongoing follow-up?

☐ Which combination of the learning models and strategies would best help staff acquire the new knowledge, skills, and attitudes?
  - Training
  - Process Model
  - Professional Study Teams
  - Action Research
  - Coaching/Mentoring
  - Independent Study

☐ Selecting a Program
  - How does the training program align with our specific professional development goals?
  - Can the training be customized to fit our specific needs?
  - Are there references to call where the program is in place?
  - What results (student and staff) have been reported with respect to this program?

Implementation

☐ Are we collecting formative data throughout the implementation?

  ↑ Student learning
     Staff usage of the innovation
     Staff learning
     Staff reaction

☐ Do we have time and resources structured for staff to:
  - Observe one another?
  - Coach and provide feedback to each other?

RPLIM
Readiness, Planning, Learning, Implementation, and Maintenance

- Participate in dialogue or implementation problem-solving groups?
- Ask emerging questions of the consultant?
- Receive the materials/resources necessary for successful implementation?

☐ Do we celebrate/recognize progress?

Maintenance

☐ Are the responsibilities for maintaining momentum shared by teachers and administrators?

☐ Does the data we are collecting tell us to:
- Modify our efforts?
- Budget more/less resources?
- Abandon this work?
- Increase/decrease individual accountability for implementation?

☐ Do we systematically introduce this professional development work to new staff members?

☐ Do we systematically support new staff members as they acquire the new skills, knowledge, and attitudes?

☐ Are there system structures that need to be modified for congruency with this work?
- School schedules
- Calendars
- Incentives for learning
- Time for collaboration
- Association agreements
- Other

©Just ASK Publications

Professional Learning
An Array of Approaches

Over 30 approaches to professional learning are listed below. Many of them are discussed in other chapters because professional learning is at the heart of a culture for learning. To that end, the page numbers where approaches may be found are listed after the approach. The approaches discussed in this chapter are looking at teacher work, peer observations, learning walks, and attending professional conferences as a team.

- Action Research: See pages 235-244.
- Analysis of Videotaped Teaching and Learning Episodes: See page 154.
- Book Clubs: See page 150.
- Case Studies
- Collaborative Teams: See Chapter III.
- Collegial Conversations (Coaching, Collaborating, Consulting): See pages 57-68.
- College Classes
- Co-Teaching: See pages 78-80.
- Common Assessments: Development, Use, and Analysis: See pages 245-249.
- Critical Friends Groups
- Critical Incident Discussion - "What Do You Do When... ?"
- Demonstration Teaching
- Data Dialogues and Analysis: See pages 254-259 and 262-272.
- Focus Groups/Study Groups
- Journals: Planning, Reflective, or Dialogue: See page 149.
- Learning Clubs: See pages 150 and 151.
- Learning Walks/Walk-throughs: See pages 154-170.
- Lesson Study
- Looking at Student Work: See pages 250-253.
- Looking at Teacher Work: See pages 144-146.
- Meetings Focused on Teaching and Learning: See pages 115-120.
- Mentoring Relationships: See pages 76-77 and 81-83.
- Observations for Peer Coaching and Peer Poaching: See pages 152-154.
- Online Conversations and Collaboration: See pages 147-148.
- Parallel Planning
- Podcasts and Webinars
- Professional Conferences: See pages 186-190.
- Role Playing
- School Improvement Teams: See pages 282-283.
- Teacher-Leader Cadres (Building In-House Capacity)
- Workshops/seminars: See pages 151, 174-176, and 192-194.

Formats for Professional Learning

	In place and functioning smoothly	We are working on this one	Good idea we need to try	Would like to know more
Action Research				
Book Studies				
Case Studies				
Classroom Observations				
Co-Teaching				
Collaborative Teams				
Common Assessment Work				
Critical Incident Discussions "What Do You Do When... ?"				
Data Dialogues				
Demonstration Lessons				
Journals				
Learning Walks				
Lesson Study				
Looking at Student Work				
Looking at Teacher Work				
Meetings Focused on Teaching and Learning				
Mentoring Relationships				
Online Conversations: blogs, discussion forums, wiki, and email				
Parallel Planning				
Planning Conferences				
Podcasts				
Post/Reflective Conferences				
Professional Conferences				
Video Conferencing				
Videotaped Classroom Episodes, Analysis of				
Webinars				
Workshops/Seminars				

Self Assessment: Formats for Professional Learning template is available online.

Looking at Teacher Work

The Planning Process

A review of lesson plans often reveals that, in many cases, teachers write topics, page numbers, or standard, benchmark, and indicators as "lesson plans." While these words and numbers may well be code for much more complex thinking and planning, we need to be able to communicate that thinking in either written or oral form. Collaborative team members as well as supervisors, mentors, and coaches need to ensure that we are knowledgeable about planning in a standards-based environment and hold each other accountable for such planning. That is, we need to be clear not only about what we are teaching, but why we are teaching it, how we are teaching it, and when we are teaching it.

One of the biggest challenges facing teachers in a standards-based environment is the planning process. It can be an even bigger challenge for supervisors because many do not have experience with this process. While many districts have had curriculum guides for years, for some teachers how closely those guides were followed was a matter of personal choice. In fact, in many districts staff proudly pointed out the autonomy with which teachers have engaged in their practice. In a standards-based environment there is still a great deal of autonomy around how to instruct, but much more external direction and accountability about what to teach and how the learning will be measured. This external direction and accountability demands that the planning process function like a well-oiled machine and that means that collaborative teams, supervisors, mentors, and coaches must engage in frequent discussions about the planning process.

Planning and pacing for the year needs to precede unit design to ensure that time is appropriately allocated throughout the year for the essential knowledge and skills. In past practice we often started at the beginning of the book and worked our way through the chapters and, of course, ran out of time before we reached the end of the book. One often hears the phrase "I have so much to cover" in reference to this march through the pages. If the school district has not mapped the curriculum or developed pacing guides, discussions need to be held with teachers around their thinking about how they map out the year. It is only after that thinking is done that units of study can be designed with some assurance that there is sufficient time in the instructional calendar to devote to each unit. The **Standards-Based Classroom Operator's Manual**, listed in **Resources and References**, provides printable forms for the planning process from planning for the year to examining the cause and effect of teacher decision making on student achievement.

Points to Note in the Review of a
Standards-Based Lesson or Unit

Analyze the lesson or unit plan using the following criteria. Note strengths and consider what changes, if made, might make the most difference in student learning.

Addresses district **standards, benchmarks,** and **indicators** at the appropriate grade level

Data:

Focuses on **essential understandings, key concepts,** and **big ideas**

Data:

Incorporates **formative** and **summative assessment** components with a feedback loop clearly articulated

Data:

Uses **assessment strategies** that allow students to demonstrate what they know in **different ways**

Data:

Provides public and precise **assessment criteria** communicated to the learners prior to beginning the work (If possible, exemplars are provided.)

Data:

©Just ASK Publications

Includes a thorough and detailed **task analysis** of the standards and the assessment task

Data:

Includes instructional strategies which address **required knowledge and skills** identified in the task analysis as necessary for mastery

Data

Includes strategies that **Frame the Learning** by accessing prior knowledge, providing opportunities for meaning making and real-world connections, and having students summarize their learning to promote retention and transfer

Data:

Requires **rigor** and **complex thinking skills**

Data

Provides **scaffolding** and **extensions** to meet the needs of a wide range of learners

Data:

Includes an emphasis on **literacy** across the curriculum

Data:

Standards-Based Lesson or Unit Design: Points to Note template is available online.

Planning Meaningful and Reflective
Professional Conversations Online

There are a multitude of ways to have meaningful and reflective professional conversations online. In fact, it's so easy to find a place and start a group or a conversation that it might seem like all one needs do to build a successful collaborative online community is to simply start a blog or a virtual classroom and get going. But it's not that simple. When considering the use of blogs, discussion forums, wikis, or other online conversation tools including email, it is important to have a plan.

The plan should include:
● Purpose of the conversation
● Online tools to be used
● Structure and management of the conversation
● Evaluation of conversation

Purpose of the Conversation
● What are the topic or topics to be discussed?
● Why is there a need to converse online?
● To what end will the conversation focus on those topics?
    ● Document learning?
    ● Share ideas?
    ● Support reflective talk?
● Who is the audience? Why?
● What are the anticipated outcomes of the conversation?

Whatever the purpose, make sure that the conversation is structured in a way that makes it clear what participants are to talk about and why that is the focus of the conversation.

Online Tools for the Conversation
The purpose(s) will, to some degree, dictate a tool or tools that support those purposes.
● A private conversation might not best be conducted online, but if the decision is made to have a private conversation, consider a discussion forum.
● If a wider, more public audience is desired, a blog might be a good way to go.
● Wikis make sense when building a text or set of documents collaboratively.
● Joining one of the larger professional communities online rather than creating your own space is also an option.

Bud Hunt, Instructional Technologist, St. Vrain Valley School District, Colorado

Planning Meaningful and Reflective
Professional Conversations Online

Whatever tool is chosen, do a trial run before using it with others. In addition, consider these practical considerations when choosing a tool:

- Is the website to be used blocked by district filters?
- Is it an easy tool for the group that you are working with?

Structure and Management of the Conversation

- How will the conversation be structured and managed to support the stated purposes?
- Who will dictate the topics? Will everyone? One person?
- How will the conversation be guided so that participants are on track? Is going "off track" acceptable, considering the purposes and audiences?
- What is the plan for supporting participants in learning about the tool or tools to be used?
- What guidelines will the group follow in their professional conversations?
- Will the guidelines be established collaboratively?
- Is there a schedule for posting?
- Will a certain number of posts, comments to others' posts, or a combination of both be required?
- How will participation be tracked?

Evaluation of the Conversation

- What is the compelling need for the conversation?
- What will a successful conversation look like?
- How might the learning of individual participants be monitored and measured?
- What indicators will provide data that the instructional objectives have been met?
- How might the impact of the conversation on classroom practice and student learning be measured?

Bud Hunt, Instructional Technologist, St. Vrain Valley School District, Colorado

Journals

Planning and Reflective Journals

Journals are both a data collection tool and a professional growth tool. This makes them an excellent means of communication for many professionals. Journals can be organized chronologically or thematically and can be kept electronically or in a traditional log. Possible entries or sections include:

- goals and action plans
- success or problems with a lesson, unit, program, training session, work session, etc.
- parent-teacher conferences
- interactions with peers
  - collaborating
  - coaching and mentoring
  - problem identifying and solving
  - dealing with different perspectives
- interactions with individual students or the entire class
- daily thinking...aha's and questions, general musings
- responses to discussions, professional development opportunities or professional readings
- set priorities and schedules
- identify and solve problems
- record and evaluate practices and effectiveness of efforts

Dialogue Journals

A dialogue journal can be kept in a traditional journal format, as a printout of computer entries or kept electronically. When geography or time constraints limit the frequency of face-to-face interactions these journals can be a productive way to fill the gaps. They can only be effective if response turnaround time is quick, if the two parties trust one another, and this form of communication matches the information processing styles of both parties. Brenda Kaylor used dialogue journals with induction coaches and clinical professors when she was Director of Professional Development in St. Vrain Valley School District, Longmont, Colorado. The coaches wrote in their journals on an ongoing basis. Since they were expected to be out in schools working with teachers as much as possible, these dialogue journals proved to be a great communication tool. Brenda could read them and write responses in individual journals and, as the person in charge of the induction program, could identify patterns and trends in the experiences not only of the coaches, but also of the new teachers with whom they were working across the district. This helped her identify future professional development needs.

Learning Clubs and Book Clubs

Learning Clubs

Learning Clubs are small groups of teachers who meet regularly to discuss their lives as teachers. During a learning club meeting, each teacher takes a turn discussing some aspect of her teaching life. In running her part of the meeting, the teacher selects one of five types of discussion:

- **Review**: The teacher asks the group to focus on an instructional strategy they have studied together and explain how it is working in each of their classes. The discussion would focus on how it worked and what they learned from their initial attempts to use the strategy.

- **Problem Solving**: The teacher presents a problem he is currently facing and asks the group for help in clarifying the problem and brainstorming possible actions to take. A structured problem-solving model will yield the best results.

- **Now Hear This!** The teacher announces that she wants to use her time to either share a success story about a recent or current instructional encounter, or to complain about a dilemma she is facing. In a **Now Hear This!** session, the group members' responsibility is to appear interested and use active listening. They do not offer solutions or suggestions.

- **Lesson Design**: The teacher asks the group to help plan a lesson or unit, or to review a plan he has designed.

After a teacher has announced what kind of help he wants, and the group has focused on his issues for approximately 15 minutes, his turn ends and another teacher begins her turn by declaring what kind of session she wants. Once each group member has had a turn, the group spends five to ten minutes discussing the ideas shared during the meeting and the implications of each for their professional practice.

Book Clubs

Prior to meetings, group members all read an article or a chapter in a jointly selected book. The meeting revolves around a discussion of the book and the implications for classroom practice. An alternative is to have each member of the group bring a different article related to a group-identified issue or to have each member read a different book on a topic. Each participant then shares a review of that article/book over a series of meetings. The discussion focus is on the implications for decision making and classroom practice. There are now many study guides for books on instructional practice available online.

Collegial Discussions

Use these questions to structure your discussions about what you did differently in your classroom as a result of your previous focus group, learning club, or workshop.

1. What You Tried

> Give a brief description of the strategy(ies) you tried. Identify the standard on which the learning was focused and explain why you chose to use this strategy.

2. How It Went

Successes Experienced
- What worked well?
- What pleased you?
- How were you able to know that the use of this process helped achieve the desired learning?

Problems Encountered
- What frustrated you?
- Was the process a good one for the content to be learned?
- Were there any logistical problems?

3. What You Learned

Possible Revisions
- What changes might you make when you use this strategy again?
- What revisions would deal specifically with the problems you encountered?

Critical or Interesting Incidents
- How did your behavior, or that of your students, match what you expected?
- What intrigued you?
- What questions were raised in your mind?

4. Next Steps
- Where do you go from here? Where might you use this strategy next?
- What do you need to do to remember to use this strategy again?
- With whom should you share your success/the usefulness of this strategy?
- With whom could you problem solve?

Adapted from Geoff Fong and Ray Szczepaniak, Department of Defense Dependent Schools

Collegial Discussions template is available online.

The Principals' Perspective
Peer Observations

A good starting point for embedding peer observation into the life of the school is learning walks and school-wide initiatives like **Peer Poaching** and **Treasure Hunt**.

Peer Poaching

Dianna Lindsay, Assistant Superintendent for Instruction in the Williamsburg-James City County, Virginia school district and former Principal of Worthington-Kilbourne High School, Columbus, Ohio, provided each staff member with three peer poaching passes. They were to visit three different classrooms to gather teaching ideas they might use. Upon leaving the classroom, they were to leave their passes on the teacher's desk. The teacher who was visited signed the pass and placed it in a fish bowl in the front office. Once a month, Dianna drew a pass out of the fish bowl to identify winners who were applauded for their collaborative practice and public teaching with time to talk and plan or materials they could use in their instructional programs.

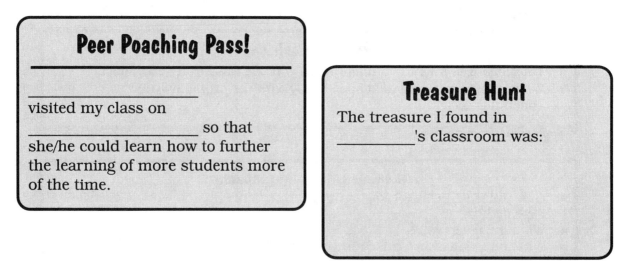

Peer Poaching Pass!

_____
_____
visited my class on
_____ so that
she/he could learn how to further
the learning of more students more
of the time.

Treasure Hunt

The treasure I found in
_____'s classroom was:

Treasure Hunt

Bruce Oliver, former Principal of Thoreau Middle School, Vienna, Virginia, had all faculty members draw the name of another faculty member out of a hat at a staff meeting. They were instructed to visit the classroom of the teacher whose name they had drawn and to complete an enlarged version of the form shown above. See page 98 for more information.

Peer Poaching Pass template is available online.

Peer Observations

At last, the practice of peer observations is becoming part of the fabric of school cultures. It is about time!

It was in the 1980s that peer observations first became a topic of conversation among the staff developers with whom I worked. We quickly embraced the idea because we believed that **Judith Warren Little** was right on the mark with her research findings. She found that student achievement could be directly linked to collegial collaboration when it included frequent concrete talk about teaching, use of a common vocabulary and concept system, asking for and providing one another assistance, and frequent observation of one another in our practice. Embracing the idea was one thing; implementation was another story. Despite the best counsel of **Sue Wells Welsh** and **Beverly Showers** and words of wisdom from **Art Costa** and **Bob Garmston**, teachers with whom we worked in the '80's and '90's completed the rounds of peer observations required as a part of course work. They then retreated back into the privacy of their classrooms. This occurred even though almost all who completed those required peer observations wrote glowingly about how much they learned from the experience. The reason for not continuing was almost always the same. Time! That is, there was no time to do the observation, participate in planning or reflective conferences, prepare the lesson plans to leave for the substitute, or to deal with the fallout from having a substitute in the classroom. Perhaps we managed to make the process too complex.

Thirty years later, peer observation is coming into its own. One of the primary reasons is the increase in the number of induction and mentoring programs that require, or at least recommend, peer observations as a format for mentoring interactions. Another reason for the widespread use of this professional development approach is that many colleges and universities include classroom visitations in their teacher preparation programs and require pre-service teachers to both observe and be observed with more focus and frequency. A third reason is that we are redefining peer observation to better match the realities of the work life of teachers. Finally, the Gen-Xers and Millenials, who have grown up receiving information and instant feedback through technology, want and expect instant feedback at work. Two or three observations a year culminating in a formal appraisal in the spring is not their idea of instant feedback. In fact, most young teachers are more than eager to not only be observed but to be given the opportunity to observe other teachers.

Peer Observations

Videotape Analysis

If your school district does not provide release time for teachers to get into one another's classrooms, the use of technology can fill the void. Watching videotaped episodes of teaching and learning together can provide a powerful alternative to actual classroom visitations. If staff members are not quite ready to videotape themselves for self or peer analysis, there are many commercially prepared videotapes that provide exemplars of teaching and learning suitable for viewing and analysis by educators.

Watching and analyzing videotaped teaching and learning episodes can lead to a strong desire for teachers to observe together in actual classrooms in their own school or at other school sites. These peer observations can be extended to include focused observations of expert teachers or a series of short visits in multiple classrooms across the school. A twenty to twenty-five minute walk through multiple classrooms observing how different teachers handle that situation provides rich data for dialogue about repertoire and decision making.

Learning Walks

Shared experiences around teaching practice are important for professional growth. Meetings and conferences where classroom practice is discussed are the usual forum; the reality is that we have been missing important learning labs all around us. When small groups of teachers identify a focus and then walk through their own buildings looking for evidence of that focus, the learning curve is steep, the dialogue is rich, and professional relationships are strengthened.

If those participating in a learning walk are participating in a learning club, book club, or focus group, they can make the focus of their learning walk the same as the focus of their study group. Other focuses might include areas identified in school, department, or grade level improvement plans. Mentors and novice teachers walking together can gather important data about classroom practice that can frame their discussions for months.

In large schools with multiple administrators, learning walks by administrative teams can refine and expand their repertoires and knowledge about instructional practice. When an administrator is given the assignment of supervising a grade level or department for which he does not have direct experience, a series of learning walks with a knowledgeable team leader, department chair, curriculum specialist, or other administrators with background in that arena can provide a rich learning experience.

Learning Walks and Walk-Throughs

Walk-throughs and learning walks are informal brief classroom visitations that may be used for generic data gathering or focused on particular teaching and learning behaviors.

Several education researchers and consultants have written about and advocated the use of these brief and more frequent classroom visits. Madeline Hunter talked about conducting classroom observations using a 5 x 5 schedule. She suggested that supervisors could spend thirty minutes visiting five classrooms for five minutes each and thereby greatly increase the frequency of their classroom observations. Dr. Carolyn Downey of San Diego State University and Dr. Lauren Resnick, Director of the Learning Research and Development Center at the University of Pittsburgh, have focused their work around the power of increasing the frequency of classroom observations. Dr. Resnick's efforts have been focused on various stakeholders participating in learning walks to look for conditions that would promote student achievement of high standards while Dr. Downey has focused on walk-throughs as a component of data gathering in the supervision and evaluation process. The New Teacher Center at the University of California, Santa Cruz calls the short but frequent observations Quick Visits in its training program for mentors.

What to Notice During Walk-Throughs: The Experts Say...

Ellen Muir, Executive Director, and the staff at the New Teacher Center suggest that the focus of the **Quick Visit** should be as follows:
- Content: What are the students learning?
- Strategies: How are they learning/practicing/applying skills, knowledge, and concepts?
- Alignment: How does this learning correlate to district standards and to the needs of the students?
  - How does this work help students meet performance standards?
  - How have student needs been assessed?
  - Does the pacing match student needs?
  - How is instruction differentiated?

Dr. Resnick recommends that observers:
- Look at the work in which students are engaged
- Examine student work that is displayed in the classroom
- Talk to students
- Talk with the teacher

Learning Walks and Walk-Throughs

What to Notice: Conversations with Students

Given our focus is on student learning, it is important to include looking at student work, watching students at work, observing student/teacher interactions, and asking students questions about their work. Questions to pose to students include:

- What are you supposed to be learning?
- How is what you are doing helping you learn that?
- How will you and your teacher measure your success?
- How are you doing in the learning journey?
- What are the next steps for you?
- How do you know what excellent work looks like?
- In what ways do you do self-assessments of your efforts and your work?

Bruce Oliver wrote about the power of learner-focused observations in "Just Ask the Kids," the December 2007 issue of *Just for the ASKing!* He shared comments from administrators who participated in multiple rounds of walk-throughs focused on student learning:

- "So much insight is gained by listening to students talk about what is happening. They reveal their understandings but also their own struggles, concerns and questions. One leaves feeling invigorated by the connections and excited by the learning."
- "By doing frequent walk-throughs and asking students questions about their learning, I can come away with valuable and insightful data to share with the teacher."
- "To me, it was extremely informative to look at what students were doing, how they were completing their tasks, what they understood the relevance of the tasks to be, and what they could tell me about what their learning was leading to next."

Learning Walks and Walk-Throughs

What to Notice: Looking at Student Work

Another area of focus could be the kind of work students are doing .Variables to note include:
- Type of task (note taking, reading, collaborating, listening, etc.)
- Knowledge students were expected to master or demonstrate in the task
- Skills students were expected to be using or demonstrate
- Level of thinking required of the students in completing the task

See **Tools Section** for a form on which to note observations about student work.

What to Notice: Using the Common Core Standards, District Performance Criteria, Data-Analysis, etc. as the Focus

Short classroom visits might focus on:
- A complete set of criteria as identified by the district, the induction program, or a professional development program.
- Areas of focus from the Common Core Standards
- One or two areas of focus as selected by the district, the observer, the teacher, or a combination thereof
- One or two variables across all the classrooms in the school/district
- An action research project
- Strategies the staff is studying in book clubs or study groups
- Alignment and consistency across teachers and/or buildings

See the **Literacy Walk-Through** form on page 167-168. The form is attributed to Greece Central School District, New York.

What to Notice: A Collaborative Approach

Use the **Graffiti** technique described on page 119 to have staff generate lists of look-fors or to further personalize and quantify Common Core Standards or district performance criteria. See lists of look-for's generated by the staff of Patrick Henry Elementary School, Alexandria City Public Schools, Alexandria, Virginia, on the next pages. In the weeks following the creation of these lists, Marcia Baldanza, Principal, and the Teacher Leader Cadre did learning walks on a regular basis and left "I Noticed That..." notes as they exited the room. Teachers were comfortable with the process because they became active members of the process when they created the lists of look for's and listen for's.

Patrick Henry Elementary School Learning Walk Look-For's and Listen-For's

Framed Learning

Looks Like:

- Standards of learning posted
- Internalized standards
- Lots of students' work depicting standards learned
- Confidence and a sense of direction
- Standards guide all classroom decisions
- Objectives stated in terms students can understand
- Close activities
- Structured curriculum with coherence between grade levels
- Pruned textbooks
- Purposeful and focused curriculum and instruction

Sounds Like:

- Yesterday we... today we are going to...
- Students can state what they are learning and why
- Students are engaging by working in small groups (telling/sharing interests)
- At the end of the unit, you will be able to...
- Students relate current learning to past learning
- Productive activity
- Students, teachers, and parents all speaking the same language

High Expectations

Looks Like:

- Syllabus/course study laid out
- Objectives posted
- Rubrics with "going beyond expectations" posted
- Positive work samples available
- Communication of expectations to parents
- Students understand what is expected
- Students think and perform "out of the box"
- Students actively engaged
- Learning styles are respected and addressed
- Students take risks and use knowledge in new ways
- Achievement charts
- Work is connected to real-life applications
- Purposeful and focused curriculum and instruction

Sounds Like:

- Clear statements of learning outcomes
- "Do your best work!"
- Productive student chatter
- Wait time for students
- "Now, how can you make it better?"
- "Just do it!"
- Children sharing their ideas
- "Look at the great idea ____ had!"
- "I did extra to earn a 5."

The staff of Patrick Henry Elementary School, Alexandria City Public Schools (ACPS), Virginia, brainstormed these indicators using **Graffiti** during a staff meeting.

Safe and Organized Environment

Looks Like:
- Flexible arrangement of desks allowing for different activities
- Area is free of obstacles to ensure ease of movement and lack of injury
- Students are taking risks
- Students are sharing thoughts with one another
- Materials are clearly labeled
- Teacher can move easily from student to student
- Students understand procedures...know where to be and what to do
- Inappropriate student behavior is redirected privately
- Interactions are positive
- Students move comfortably around the room and are respectful of others

Sounds Like:
- Enthusiastic, but moderate voices
- Students sharing in small groups and with whole class
- Guided group discussion
- Respective tone
- System for students to be responsible for organizing materials
- "I can do this."
- "I have an idea to try."
- Excitement about learning
- All students participating in class activities and discussions
- Learning noise

Checking for Understanding

Looks Like:
- Portfolios with exhibits
- Varied assessments
- Children using visual cues to show understanding
- Rubrics on walls
- Conversation among peers
- KWL charts
- Demonstrations
- Exit Slip. "Today I learned..."
- Graphic organizers and Venn diagrams
- Students re-teaching what they have learned

Sounds Like:
- Tell me what you think when you solve problems
- Peer tutoring
- What did you just do and why?
- How we apply information we just learned to everyday situations?
- Students repeating or modeling what the teacher taught/said
- Can you, in turn, teach this to another?
- Reviewing
- Thumbs up, thumbs down
- "I could use the information or skill to..."
- Orally answering
- Students talking about how they are doing with the standards
- Processing and summarizing throughout the lesson

Whole School Observation Form

Use this form to capture data about the implementation of the best practices you see across the school or throughout a department or grade level. Use the district's performance criteria or strategies the staff is studying together as the focus of the data gathering. You can provide feedback electronically or in a newsletter.

Teacher Name	A	B	C	D	Data

In the areas designated A, B, C, and D insert the specific behaviors for which you are observing on a given day. You may choose to observe for only one or two at a time. In the Data column include teacher actions, student actions, and artifacts.

Whole School Observation Form template is available online.

Data Log for
Peer Observations and Learning Walks

Teacher's Name _____

Date _____

Subject/Grade _____

Focus of Observation/Learning Walk (Optional) _____

Standards/Indicators being addressed:

Students were:

Teacher was:

Evidence of rigor:

Evidence of positive and productive environment:

Points to ponder:

Data Log for Peer Observation and Learning Walks template is available online.

Standards-Based Education Learning Walk

School _____ Date _____

Observers _____ Grade Level/Teams _____

Focus Question: To what extent is the SBE Planning Process being implemented?

+ = Appropriate implementation observed
X = Evidence seen
# = Did not observe

1st Oval: What should students know and be able to do?

____ Standards drive curriculum planning and classroom decisions.
____ Learning outcomes and agenda for the lesson are communicated to the students before the lesson begins.
____ Lessons are linked to essential understandings, key concepts, or big ideas.
____ Students can articulate what they are expected to know and be able to do as a result of the lesson or unit.

2nd Oval: How will the students and I know when they are successful?

____ Public and precise criteria are communicated to students prior to the beginning of the lesson or unit.
____ Exemplars, where appropriate, are provided for processes and products.
____ Students can explain how they are going to be evaluated.

3rd Oval: What learning experiences will facilitate student success?

____ The teacher has planned the lesson/unit with the end in mind.
____ A task analysis is used to determine the required skills and knowledge and the level of understanding demanded, (writing, small group instruction, individual student-teacher conferences, group sharing.)
____ Students are provided an opportunity to access prior knowledge and/or experiences about the topic to be studied.
____ Misconceptions and naive understandings are identified and addressed.
____ The learning experiences are aligned with lesson and outcomes and information revealed by the task analysis.
____ Accommodations are made for different readiness levels and learning styles of students.

Standards-Based Education Learning Walk

____ Scaffolding is provided so that students have appropriate levels of support and structure to be successful as learners.
____ Scaffolding is withdrawn as the students become more independent in their learning.
____ Extensions are provided for accelerated learners.
____ Pauses for processing and summarizing new information are built into the lesson.
____ Clear explanations of assignments are provided so students know exactly what they are supposed to do.

4th Oval: Based on data, how are learning experiences refined?

____ On-the-spot adjustments are made based on how well the lesson is meeting the needs of students.
____ Teacher decisions are guided by formative and summative assessments.
____ The results of formative and summative assessments are used to inform students of their learning and next steps in their own learning.

Comments:

Standards-Based Education Learning Walks template is available online.

FCPS Cluster I Priority Schools Initiative
Learning Together, Achieving Together

In Fairfax County Schools (FCPS), Virginia, all schools are expected to build professional learning communities that employ FCPS's **Best Practices for Teaching and Learning** to raise the bar and close the achievement gap. In Cluster I, Educational Specialist Barbara Walker developed several data gathering and analysis tools for use in dialogues with the principal, collaborative team visits, and classroom visits. These tools focused on the Priority School Initiative Indicators listed below. An example of one of those tools is found on the following pages.

Priority Schools Initiative (PSI) Indicators:

Learning as Our Fundamental Purpose
- Team knowledge of state standards and Program of Study
- Implementation of best instructional and assessment practices
- Best practice focus on checking for understanding, relationship-building, and student engagement
- Use of team-developed common formative assessments
- Use of eCART/Horizon to assess learning
- Additional time to provide intervention and support for student learning on a daily basis
- Intervention efforts monitored and adjusted as needed

Building a Collaborative Culture Through High Performing Teams
- Time structured during the school day for team meetings
- Interdependent collaboration by teams to clarify student learning, analyze the data
- Identification of most powerful teaching strategies for all team members
- Implementation of unified policies and procedures for all teams
- Use of SMART Goals for team strategic planning

A Focus on Results
- System of gathering data - use of Horizon reports
- Analysis of data from common assessments to inform instructional decisions
- Identification of students - by name, by need - for intervention and support

Barbara Walker, Educational Specialist, Fairfax County Public Schools, Virginia

Professional Dialogue Tool
Learning Together, Achieving Together

School_____ Cluster_____

Indicator	Next Steps
Data- Evidence of proactive analysis of student data (i.e., formative and summative) in effort to predict areas of instructional strengths and weaknesses. Comments:	
PLC- Evidence of a professional, instructional culture that is focused on learning as the fundamental purpose, building a collaborative culture through high performing teams, and analyzing results. Master schedule provides embedded collaborative team time. Comments:	
Intervention- System of monitoring students for instructional intervention. Master schedule provides time for embedded review, remediation, and enrichment for students. Comments:	
Communication- Evidence of ongoing internal and external communication of School Improvement Plan for all staff and community members. Comments:	

Professional Dialogue Tool
Learning Together, Achieving Together

Indicator	Next Steps
Classroom Visits- Evidence of student learning through implementation of Best Practices that include a focus on the following: checking for understanding, relationships, and engagement. Comments:	
Goals- Evidence of implementing goals specific to School Improvement Plan Comments:	

_____   _____
Visitor   Date

Barbara Walker, Educational Specialist, Fairfax County Public Schools, Virginia

Professional Dialogue Tool - Learning Together,
Achieving Together template is available online.

Literacy Walk-Through Guide

School _____   Date _____
Observers _____   Grade Level/Teams _____

Focus Question: To what degree is the District's Balanced Literacy Framework being implemented?

□ = **Appropriate implementation observed**   □ = **Evidence seen**

Assessment

____ Evidence that assessment is used to guide instruction
____ Use of running reading records
____ Use of anecdotal records
____ Teacher-student individual conferences held

Reading

____ An organized, well-stocked classroom library and reading area
____ Evidence of a Reading Workshop structure (i.e., mini-lesson, independent reading, small group instruction, individual student-teacher conferences, group sharing)
____ Daily read-aloud of quality literature
____ Evidence of scaffolded instruction (modeling, guided practice, independent practice, authentic application)
____ Shared reading (i.e., teacher reading while students follow along using multiple copies or enlarged text)
____ Small group reading instruction (i.e., guided reading, strategy groups, or literature circles)
____ Independent reading with self-selected, appropriate books at students' instructional or independent levels
____ Reading opportunities across a wide variety of genres
____ Student responses to reading are meaningful and varied
____ Teacher explicitly targeting specific reading outcomes
____ Skills instruction is connected to real reading and writing (whole-part-whole)

Writing

____ Evidence of a Writing Workshop structure (i.e., mini-lesson, independent writing, small group instruction, individual student-teacher conferences, group sharing)
____ Teacher modeling writing (both processes and products)

Literacy Walk-Through Guide

____ Interactive writing at the emergent writer levels (teacher and students share the pen)
____ Shared writing (i.e., teacher writes while composing with students)
____ Writing/publishing is for real audiences and authentic purposes
____ Conventions of writing are taught in the process of writing (not through separate exercises)
____ Many opportunities are provided for student-selected writing topics
____ Skills instruction is connected to real reading and writing (whole-part-whole)

Language and Word Study

____ Evidence of students actively involved in the exploration of language and about the structure and meaning of words
____ Evidence of attention to words that provide powerful examples of how to take words apart while reading for meaning
____ Evidence of attention to words in writing that help students to develop effective spelling strategies
____ Direct teaching about how words look, sound, and mean
____ Word Walls display commonly used words and word patterns
____ Students are held accountable for spelling Word Wall words correctly

Application of Literacy Instruction

____ Evidence of literacy instruction across the curriculum, in all content areas
____ Evidence of opportunities being made for students to share their reading and writing
____ Evidence of student use resources (i.e., teaching wall charts, District Language Resource Guide, Word Walls)

Comments:

Literacy Walk-Through Guide template is available online.

Learning Walks

To: **Parkland-Brookside Teachers**
From: Ray, Heather, and Connie
Re: **Learning Walk Observations**

It is evident as we walked around our buildings this week that folks are working hard to enhance the quality of the teaching and learning process. As we continued data gathering on constructivist teaching and learning, we gathered data that teachers are working to differentiate instruction on the basis of students' needs and interests, help students attach relevance to the curriculum, and structure lessons around big ideas, not small bits of information.

Here are some of the exemplary practices we observed:
- In second grade, we saw a differentiated lesson integrating language arts and science where students were working on specific performance indicators and using graphic organizers differentiated by readiness.

- In fifth grade, we observed the use of literature and technology to support the mathematical concept of polygons. Students had an opportunity to plot the coordinates of their polygons on the computer and use the data to make comparisons.

- In pre-kindergarten, students were working with a "hula hoop Venn Diagram" to compare two science concepts; transparent and translucent.

- In third grade, students were working with partners to create various arrays on chart paper and sharing their understandings of multiplication.

- Special area teachers were integrating math and science concepts into daily instruction.

- In grades pre-K, 1, and 2, teachers were collaborating on student management, organization, and engagement in guided reading centers.

- In grades 3, 4, and 5, teachers were collaborating on strategies for processing text with understanding in small, guided reading groups.

As we continue our hard work of helping children to construct their own meaning, let us be ever purposeful in our assessment of student learning in the context of daily classroom investigations, and continue to help students demonstrate their knowledge every day in a variety of ways.

From the Doorway...
Peeks into Pedagogy

Standards-based or Standards-referenced?

The stages of being standards-based are as follows:

- Knowing that the standards exist
- Knowing where to find a copy
- Reading the standards
- Posting the standards
- Occasionally referring to the standards during planning and with students
- Checking to see if what is being taught can be found in the standards
- Beginning to understand the power and focus the standards provide and working to identify the essential understandings that are embedded in and that transcend the standards as they are written in the documents.
- Being able to truly say "I am standards-based because I used standards to design assessments and instruction and I used student work to judge whether or not instruction was well designed for this content with these learners."

Do you just reference the standards or are you truly a standards-based educator?

Reprinted from *Why Didn't I Learn This in College?*

In the middle school...

- Mr. Rugg visited Jessie Bliss' classroom and noted the active, hands-on learning taking place. Also apparent was the fact that classroom expectations had been established. Students were aware of the expectations and followed them.
- Laurie Rayhill, special education teacher, brought one of her students to Mr. Rugg's office at the beginning of this week. The student was not in trouble, but practiced giving an oral report in front of Mr. Rugg in preparation for giving her report to a classroom audience.
- Students in Mrs. Prodanovich's class watched a "Charlie Brown" video last week. The students were then asked to compare and contrast Linus and Charlie Brown. I was reminded of Mrs. Prodanovich's activity when reading the article "Invitations to Learn" by Carol Ann Tomlinson, in which she wrote, "The impetus to learn gradually does not come first from content itself, but rather because a teacher has learned to make the content inviting."

In the high school...

- A week of "mockery" in the high school! Students in the middle school and high school participated in the mock election conducted on Tuesday, November 5. This was the end activity of a unit that covered polling and the creation of brochures to educate the "public." Voter turnout was impressive (see results). Thanks to Kent Willmann and student teacher Anna Gardiner for organizing the mock election. What an excellent way for students to gain a deeper understanding of the political process.
- Hillary Jackson, student teacher in Mr. Lathrop's class, held a mock trial in English 11. The class read *Frankenstein* and the assignment was to try Dr. Frankenstein in a civil case that was brought forth by the "creation." Before "going to trial," the students had to learn about the court system and define terms such as malpractice, negligence, and emotional and physical distress. In preparation for the trial, students had to find quotes and passages from the book that supported their views. This activity incorporated reading comprehension skills and argumentative speaking.

Jessica Overboe, Silver Creek High School, St. Vrain Valley Public Schools, Colorado

Multiple Pathways to Professional Learning
A McNair Elementary Case Study Artifact

Whole Faculty Professional Development
Instruction for All Students
All staff members are provided a copy of *Instruction for All Students*. This text is used in a variety of ways:
- Faculty Meetings
  - Active learning strategies
  - Lesson design
  - The Assessment Continuum
  - Differentiation of instruction
- With individual teachers
  - During goal setting conferences
  - With Instructional Coaches
  - After classroom observations
  - In general discussions

Meeting the Needs of Diverse Learners
All staff members are provided with a copy of *Meeting the Needs of Diverse Learners*. This is used at staff meetings as we seek to address meeting the needs of all students.

Virginia Grade Level Alternative assessment (VGLA) Workshops and Work Sessions
Our assistant principals shared the VGLA overview at a general faculty meeting. They have subsequently provided work sessions for general education, special education, and ESOL teachers to review strategies.

Professional Learning Communities: Bruce Oliver spent a day with us revisiting the basic tenants of Professional Learning Communities.

New Teachers

New Colleague Learning Group: Teachers who are in their first and second year at McNair meet with our instructional coach once or twice monthly to review best practices, prepare for upcoming events, and receive additional help and support based on their identified learning needs.

Why Didn't I Learn This in College?
This book is provided to all first and second year teachers and has been used in the New Colleague Learning Group. It provides teachers with strategies for both instruction, classroom management, parent conferences, etc.

Multiple Pathways to Professional Learning
A McNair Elementary Case Study Artifact

Mentor Resource Teacher (MRT): Our part-time MRT works with our first year teachers. She meets with them on a regular basis and provides individual support when she and the teachers meet together. This includes modeling teaching, co-teaching, and planning for instruction.

Individuals and Groups of Teachers

Mathematical Reasoning Assessment (K-2)

(K-2) Assessment on eCART (multiple-choice, free response, performance-based tasks) used to measure students progress in mathematics. Teachers are able to use the results of the assessment to adjust their instructional practices to meet student needs.

Balanced Literacy Class (3-6)

Most 3-6 teachers participated in the balanced literacy class to review the basic components of best practices in literacy.

Guided Reading Class (3-6)

All 3-6 teachers have been required to take the guided reading class to support their efforts to improve student learning.

Technology Carousel

McNair teachers have shared their strengths with each other through our technology carousel. We will have one more prior to the end of the school year. Areas of focus included using the SMART board, creating SMART Board lessons, Learn Start, Math Programs, and Using Maps.

SMART School Teams Handbook

This handbook is provided for all teacher leaders who are on the leadership team. This is a resource for team leaders as they work to develop professional learning communities.

Differentiation of Instruction (K)

The kindergarten team is reading ***Making the Most of Small Groups: Differentiation for All*** with the support of our reading specialist. They are using this to study and better understand small group literacy instruction.

Every Day Counts Calendar Math (K-6)

This has been provided on an individual basis for teachers new to the school or who need a review to teach this program effectively. Interactive program of elements are used to teach mathematical concepts every day. Concepts are spiraled throughout the year and are linked to what students are learning during math class.

Multiple Pathways to Professional Learning
A McNair Elementary Case Study Artifact

Math Workshop
Title I Math teachers have taught teachers how to implement this so that they can differentiate instruction and teach concepts in small groups. Groups are formed by student need/enrichment. Teacher facilitator groups are also leading a small group to reinforce concepts. This is based on readers'/writers' workshop.

Individual Grade Level Math Support
Math specialists introduce Partner Games which are interactive math games to actively engage students in learning mathematical concepts. Teachers learn to use these games to differentiate instruction. SUM teachers introduce games throughout the school year linked to the pacing guide during CLT meetings.

Individualized Reading Support
Our reading specialists work with individual teams on each grade level to support guided reading instruction and writers workshop. They model whole group activity and small group work, and co-plan for instruction.

Classroom Observations
Our math specialist invites teachers to observe other classrooms with her. They hold a pre and post observations conference and discuss learning strategies.

Learning Forward (NSDC) Conference
Nine teacher leaders were invited to attend the Learning Forward conference when it took place locally. They have been able to apply their learning to work with teachers and share best practices discussed at the conference.

National Council of Teachers of Math
Six teachers represented our school at the NCTM conference. They learned new ideas and brought them back to share with our faculty.

Reading Conference
Our literacy team attended the greater Washington area reading conference. They also worked on learning best practices to improve instruction.

Planning Professional Development

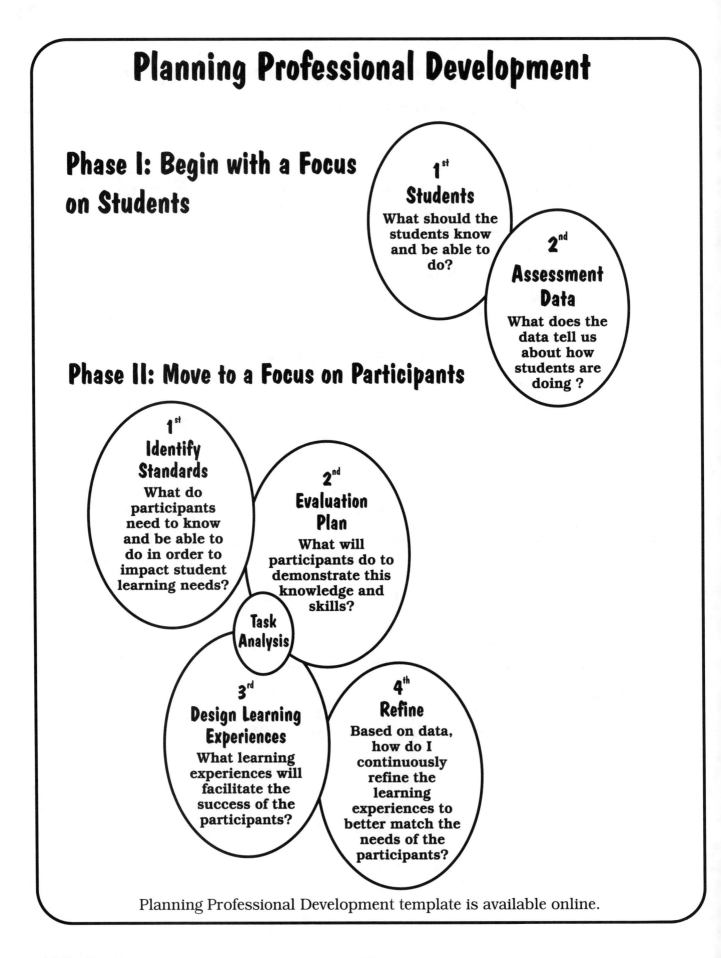

Phase I: Begin with a Focus on Students

1st
Students
What should the students know and be able to do?

2nd
Assessment Data
What does the data tell us about how students are doing ?

Phase II: Move to a Focus on Participants

1st
Identify Standards
What do participants need to know and be able to do in order to impact student learning needs?

2nd
Evaluation Plan
What will participants do to demonstrate this knowledge and skills?

Task Analysis

3rd
Design Learning Experiences
What learning experiences will facilitate the success of the participants?

4th
Refine
Based on data, how do I continuously refine the learning experiences to better match the needs of the participants?

Planning Professional Development template is available online.

Session Planning

Getting Started Segment
Welcome: Use Visual: Welcome
Introductions
Essential and/or Focus Question(s)
- Develop and communicate essential and/or focus questions/understandings for the workshop series and for each session.
- Communicate the program goals/understandings and the session goals/understandings in each session.

Agenda
- Develop the agenda based on the essential and focus questions and on the time available.
- Agendas can be presented in multiple ways. You can choose to include the agenda in the handout packet, post it on a chart, display it on a PowerPoint slide, or overhead transparency.
- Keep the number of agenda items listed to around five.
- Do not post times. Your own copy of the agenda should have times but do not box yourself in by publicly announcing times.

Community Builder
Variables to consider in selecting a community builder for each session
- Are participants sitting in seats of their own choice, in seats selected by you, or by random methods?
- Do the participants know each other in their table groups and in the large group?
- How recently did the group meet?
- How long is the session?

Collegial Discussions
- When there are multiple workshops or support sessions, always include an opportunity for participants to share what they have learned, accomplished, or encountered since last they met.
- If the participants were asked to complete a specific task, have them engage in collegial discussions about that work.

Session Planning

- If the participants are asked to submit work, be sure to not only read it but to give them feedback about patterns and trends the next time you meet. If they offered new ideas or approaches, compile and distribute the list to group members the next time they meet. If they are not meeting again, email the information to them.

Learning Focus Segments
General Guidelines
- In a three-hour session there may be two or three learning focus segments. In a full-day session there would be several focus segments.
- Always use the following sequence:
  - Access prior knowledge
  - Input of new information
  - Process new Information
  - Summarize
- Build in choice whenever possible.
- Use 10:2 Theory.
- Model best practice in instruction.
- Be explicit about the strategies you are using. Keep a chart: **Strategies We Have Used or Studied**.
- Process not only the content but the process as well.
- Address the four questions from McCarthy's 4Mat model:
  - Why?
  - What?
  - How?
  - What If?

Reflection and Next Steps Segment
General Guidelines
- Be purposeful about asking/expecting participants to take action.
- Advise participants to do informal action research in their classrooms and come to follow-up sessions with reflections and artifacts to support their discussion of their practice.

Session Planning template is available online.

Questions to Drive the Development of
Professional Growth Plans

Data Collection and Goal Development
- How could I grow professionally to meet the needs of my students?
- How could I engage in learning within my school setting?
- How will I identify goals that are critical to my professional growth and to student learning?
- How can I further building and district goals?
- In what areas do I feel most or least competent?
- In what areas do my students excel?
- In what areas do my students struggle?
- What can I do differently that will affect those areas in which my students struggle?

Developing and Implementing the Plan
- How does this student impact plan link to what I already know?
- Why am I considering this particular plan?
- What resources do I need for this plan and how can they be obtained?
- How does this plan relate to other learning activities I intend to pursue?
- How comfortable will I be engaging in this plan?
- What will be the easiest and most difficult parts of this plan?
- How will I change as a result of this plan?
- Will this plan foster collegiality?
- How can I link this plan to the work of my colleagues?
- How can my plan benefit my colleagues?
- Whom can I call upon for feedback?
- What evidence of my learning will I produce?
- What will I observe, count, or measure to determine whether the changes in practice as a result of this plan have improved student learning?

Analysis and Reflection
- What did I do for this plan?
- What did others do for this plan?
- How did the anticipated plan compare to how it actually went? What went as I planned and what did not?
- What have I learned from this plan?
- What new questions do I have as a result of this plan?
- What am I doing differently in my teaching and learning practice as a result of this plan?
- What are my students doing differently as a result of this plan?
- What do I want to do now?
- With whom do I want to share the results of this plan? How and when do I do that?

Professional Learning Goals Worksheet
Theresa West

Teacher_____   Grade/Subject Area_____

Personal Learning Goal(s)

Reflect on your instructional strengths and potential areas of growth. Identify one or more skills or practices you plan to improve or acquire that relate specifically to the act of improving your teaching (e.g., differentiation of instruction, student performance assessments, lesson pacing) and, by extension, the performance of your students. Consider ways that you can participate in workshops, tap into the expertise of colleagues, and/or locate relevant readings or reference materials. Identify each personal learning goal and respond to the listed questions to complete your plan.

1. How does this goal support our school's student achievement objectives in math and reading?

2. Identify activities you will participate in and/or methods you will use to acquire/improve the skill.

3. How will you build opportunities for repeated practice of the skill into your plan?

4. What methods will you use to get feedback on your performance (from other professionals and from students)?

5. What data will you collect to demonstrate your progress?

6. What indicators will demonstrate that you have achieved (or made progress toward) your goal?

Professional Learning Goals Worksheet template is available online.

Individual Professional Development Plans

Florida requires that each teacher have an **Individual Professional Development Plan**. In Orange County (Orlando), Florida, the form used for designing and recording that plan provides the following categories and questions:

- **Baseline Data**: What specific student achievement data indicates the need for improvement?
- **Needs-Based Question for Professional Inquiry**: In reflecting on this achievement data, what instructional questions(s) come to mind?
- **Expected Student Achievement Goal(s)**: What is your expectation of student achievement as a result of your professional development?
- **Related Professional Development Objectives**: What practices will you need to enhance/develop in order to answer your questions and meet your stated student achievement goals?
- **Related Professional Training and Learning Experiences**: How will you use research-based knowledge and strategies that will help you achieve your stated professional development objectives?
- **Classroom implementation**: What practices have you implemented as a result of your professional development?
- **Documented Results**
- **Collaboration**: How do you plan to share what you learned?

Professional Development Needs Assessment

Sherri Stephens-Carter designed the survey displayed on the following pages in her work with Westminster Elementary School in Colorado. In collaboration with Julie McVicker, Sherri used the results of three administrations of the survey to determine next steps in professional learning opportunities. Sherri and Julie led multiple data-driven professional development sessions with staff and completed several walk-throughs identifying best practice in action with the administrative staff and teacher leaders. Julie also conducted phone-based coaching sessions with the principal.

Staff Survey of Use of Best Practice in Teaching and Learning
Sherri Stephens-Carter

Level (circle one)   Primary   Intermediate   No grade/All Grades

Role in the school (circle one)   Teacher   Specialist   Support Staff   Other (please list)

Please respond to the statements by circling the number in the column that best describes your practice.
The choices include:

I am confident in my use of this and can provide artifacts: **Confident with artifacts**

I am using or doing this but am not yet confident: **Doing this but not confident**

I know about this but am not doing or using it: **Know about but don't do**

I don't know about this: **Don't know about it**

	Creating a Positive Learning Environment	Confident with artifacts	Doing this but not confident	Know about but don't do	Don't know about it
1	I make a strong effort to interact positively with each student each day.	4	3	2	1
2	I develop and use a system for monitoring the nature and frequency of interactions with individual students.	4	3	2	1
3	I display student work both in the classroom and in public areas and identify the standard of learning the work represents.	4	3	2	1
4	I set up conditions where students can assess the effectiveness of their learning habits and learn to make the necessary adjustments.	4	3	2	1
5	I teach students to self-assess the appropriateness and effectiveness of their social skills.	4	3	2	1
6	I practice equity and explain to students the difference between equity (get what you need when you need it) and equality (all get the same thing at the same time).	4	3	2	1
7	I provide student choice of learning process, teach them to make good choices, and analyze why the choices were or were not the best choice.	4	3	2	1

IV

#		Confident with artifacts	Doing this but not confident	Know about but don't do	Don't know about it
8	I explain the reason why I am doing what I am doing or making the decision I am making.	4	3	2	1
9	I change strategies to meet students' needs rather than expecting students to change to meet teacher needs.	4	3	2	1
10	I reinforce students' attempts to solve problems and exert effort.	4	3	2	1
11	I include students in developing classroom expectations and consequences for meeting and not meeting those expectations.	4	3	2	1
12	I use a clearly articulated range of consequences for both met and unmet expectations based on the quality, intensity and frequency of the action.	4	3	2	1
13	I promote intrinsic motivation (I did it!) rather than extrinsic motivation (I got a sticker!)	4	3	2	1
	Communicating High Expectations for Student Learning	Confident with artifacts	Doing this but not confident	Know about but don't do	Don't know about it
14	I communicate clear expectations including what students are expected to learn and criteria for success such as rubrics, task performance lists and exemplars of good performance.	4	3	2	1
15	I provide feedback from multiple sources so that learners are able to use the feedback and make adjustments in their future work.	4	3	2	1
16	I design units around authentic assignments and assessments.	4	3	2	1
17	I make sure that students know how every classroom activity fits into their learning targets.	4	3	2	1

IV

#	Statement	Confident with artifacts	Doing this but not confident	Know about but don't do	Don't know about it
18	I coach students in setting challenging yet attainable goals and in designing and implementing action plans for attaining those goals.	4	3	2	1
19	I help students build skills in recognizing how the current lesson is related to and builds on previous lessons.	4	3	2	1
20	I encourage students to think about how the information they are learning relates to other subjects and their lives beyond the school day.	4	3	2	1
21	I explicitly teach students the connection between effort and achievement and reinforce both.	4	3	2	1
22	When planning instruction, I do a thorough task analysis of the components, knowledge, and skills in a lesson plus an analysis of student readiness, background knowledge, interests and processing styles.	4	3	2	1
23	My instructional plans include what I will do if some students already know the content and what I will do for those students who are not successful in learning the content.	4	3	2	1
	High Quality Learning Activities	Confident with artifacts	Doing this but not confident	Know about but don't do	Don't know about it
24	I create a text-rich environment by collecting, displaying and using a wide variety of subject-related books, magazines and posters in the classroom.	4	3	2	1
25	I provide opportunities for students to locate, organize and use information from various sources to answer questions, solve problems and communicate ideas.	4	3	2	1
26	I teach reading as a process of constructing meaning through the interaction of the reader's prior knowledge and experiences, the information presented in the text and the context or purpose of the reading.	4	3	2	1

		1	2	3	4
27	I provide a balanced literacy program that includes reading to students, reading with students, independent reading by students, writing for and with students and writing by students.	1	2	3	4
28	I use small, flexible groups to provide appropriate instruction in reading and other content areas.	1	2	3	4
29	I help students build a repertoire of reading strategies and help them learn when to use which one.	1	2	3	4
30	I model my thinking aloud so that students hear what to do when they are tackling complex problems.	1	2	3	4
31	I present students with explicit, ongoing guidance in identifying similarities and differences within a unit or content.	1	2	3	4
32	I provide students with strategies and opportunities for summarizing in a wide variety of situations.	1	2	3	4
33	I teach students strategies for taking effective notes as a regular part of instruction.	1	2	3	4
34	When I assign homework, the purpose is clearly identified and articulated, the duration is appropriate for the grade level, and students receive feedback on their work.	1	2	3	4
35	I explicitly teach a variety of non-linguistic representations including graphic organizers, models, and drawings.	1	2	3	4
36	I provide my students with training and opportunities to work in cooperative groups.	1	2	3	4
37	I provide opportunities for students to respond to and ask thought-provoking questions.	1	2	3	4

#	Statement	Confident with artifacts	Doing this but Not confident	Know about but don't do	Don't know about it
38	I design learning experiences in which thinking processes are named, modeled, and practiced in a variety of situations.	4	3	2	1
39	I build decision-making and problem-solving situations into learning experiences.	4	3	2	1

Assessment

#	Statement	Confident with artifacts	Doing this but Not confident	Know about but don't do	Don't know about it
40	I communicate to students at the beginning of a unit or learning block how their learning will be assessed.	4	3	2	1
41	I go beyond grading student work to critiquing and analyzing student work to see which components of the learning targets are mastered and which are in need of re-teaching.	4	3	2	1
42	I select assessment tools from a wide range of options including, but not limited to, projects, performances, and paper and pencil assessments.	4	3	2	1
43	I do a pre-assessment as part of the planning for units and lessons.	4	3	2	1
44	I check for understanding across all students by using a variety of strategies such as signal cards, slates and think pads.	4	3	2	1
45	I design and give assessments that provide opportunities for practice and rehearsal before the final assessment.	4	3	2	1
46	I include student self-assessment as a regular part of the assessment process.	4	3	2	1
47	I teach students to give each other feedback through explicitly taught protocols for peer review.	4	3	2	1

Staff Survey of Use of Best Practice in Teaching and Learning template is available online.

	4	3	2	1
48	I engage students in the creation and use of rubrics.			
	4	3	2	1
49	I have students score work to help them understand how the scoring criteria are used to evaluate student work.			
	4	3	2	1
50	When I have students work in groups, I structure the assignments to assure individual accountability for the work.			
	4	3	2	1
51	I regularly look at the progress my students are making in their attainment of the learning targets and adjust my teaching to their needs.			

Conference Planning, Learning, and Sharing
Brenda Kaylor

Attempts to improve education are doomed to failure unless educators have an opportunity to learn from each other, use the best research available, carry out their own research, work together to solve problems and make decisions on the best way they can improve education.

Pre-conference

This form will help your team focus on the need for attending this conference.

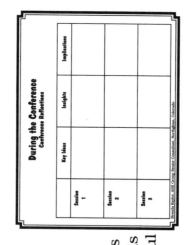

During Conference

Use these sheets to summarize the key message(s) presented during the sessions attended. Include insights and the implications. This information will be helpful when your team gets together to debrief each evening

Post-Conference

Use the key questions to guide your discussion as you debrief the conference experience. Team members should be prepared to present what the group has learned to a variety of staff members.

This page will help your group prepare for what you expect to learn and how you will share your learning during the conference. Use it as a tool to focus questions and your evening dialogue.

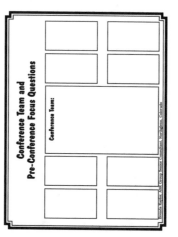

Attending a Professional Conference

A sound investment of both time and resources is a team commitment to attend a professional conference together. It is a place where individuals representing the district will significantly increase their capacity for understanding and implementing solid professional learning that focuses on increasing achievement for all students in our schools. Preparation for the conference has been outlined as follows:

I. Pre-Conference

Based on district and school needs, focus groups at the school or district level will form to generate questions and learning goals with conference participant(s).

Conference registration will be completed, focusing on the specific needs and goals identified by the school(s) and district.

Conference participants will refine guiding questions that the team will use in seeking and integrating information.

II. During Conference

Team debriefs/reflections will be scheduled throughout the conference for application and discussion purposes. Initial pre-conference questions will drive discussions.

Throughout the conference, participants will also network and explore ideas with presenters and conference participants from around the nation.

III. Post-Conference

Multiple study sessions with school/district staff members will be scheduled to share the key learnings from the conference.

Integration of key learnings with current school culture and district/school improvement goals will be a focus.

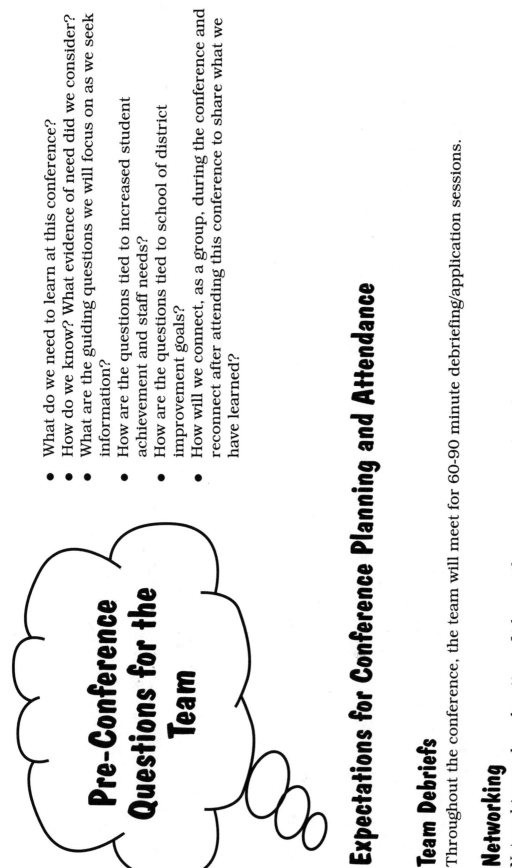

Pre-Conference Questions for the Team

- What do we need to learn at this conference?
- How do we know? What evidence of need did we consider?
- What are the guiding questions we will focus on as we seek information?
- How are the questions tied to increased student achievement and staff needs?
- How are the questions tied to school of district improvement goals?
- How will we connect, as a group, during the conference and reconnect after attending this conference to share what we have learned?

Expectations for Conference Planning and Attendance

Team Debriefs

Throughout the conference, the team will meet for 60-90 minute debriefing/application sessions.

Networking

Networking and exploration of ideas with presenters and conference participants from around the nation will occur throughout the conference.

During the Conference
Conference Reflections
(Add pages as needed)

	Key Ideas	Insights	Implications
Session 1			
Session 2			
Session 3			

Post-Conference Questions for the Team

- What did we learn in terms of our key questions?
- What did we learn in addition to information matching our key questions?
- How can we apply what we have learned in our schools? In our work across the district?
- What specifically will we share with others? How and when will we do this?
- What research and data did we gather and how can we use it to guide our efforts?

Expectations After Conference Attendance

- Thoughtful presentations will be prepared and offered to the appropriate school communities and district staff.
- Study sessions with school and district staff will be scheduled utilizing the key learnings from the conference.

Assessing the Impact of Professional Development

Level 1: Reaction Data
- a participant satisfaction index which is often referred to as a "happiness index" or "smile sheet"
- uses questionnaires which are distributed and completed at the conclusion of a session or program
- questions often deal with reactions to the design and delivery of the program around content, learning activities, level of instruction, and learning environment
- an important component of the evaluation process which should not be used in isolation
- patterns of reactions rather than isolated comments should be addressed

Level 2: Learning Data
- measures whether participants are building skills and knowledge around the intended goals
- reveals whether participants can demonstrate progress toward mastery of the stated objectives with job-site practice
- data sources include reflective or planning journals, portfolios or performance assessments such as simulations or skill demonstrations, teacher and student work resulting from classroom application of learning

Level 3: Application Data
- is measured three to six months after new information is introduced
- measures whether participants have integrated their learning from the professional development into their ongoing practice
- data sources include interviews, walk-throughs, unit development, team journals over time, and comparisons to baseline data

Level 4: Impact or Results Data
- provides evidence that a professional development initiative has resulted in teacher growth and, in some cases, student learning
- student work can provide valuable data at this level
- research reveals that professional development must include job-site practice and collegial collaboration to obtain significant results (Warren-Little)

Adapted from ***A Practical Guide for Supervisory Training and Development*** by Donald Kirkpatrick, Addison-Wesley, 1983

Professional Development Evaluation

Please evaluate the professional development opportunity with the following scale:
5= always, 4= usually, 3= sometimes, 2= rarely, 1= never

Should you rank an item 3, 2, or 1 please indicate in the comments section how this variable could have been, from your perspective, more positive.

____ 1. The content and processes learned are relevant and will be of practical use to me.

____ 2. There were opportunities for me to be involved in hands-on learning.

____ 3. There were opportunities for me to apply what I already knew.

____ 4. I was able to integrate new knowledge and skills in my own bank of knowledge and skills.

____ 5 I understood why the particular knowledge and skills were emphasized.

____ 6. The learning environment offered multiple opportunities to work with a partner or group.

____ 7. There were options and/or flexibility in the assignments.

____ 8. The amount of work was reasonable for the amount of time.

____ 9. Active participation was allowed and encouraged.

____ 10. Effective two-way communication was established and maintained.

____ 11. The furniture, equipment, etc., was sufficient for my needs.

____ 12. The facilitators offered expertise, both in knowledge and preparation.

____ 13. The facilitators conducted the sessions with understanding and consideration towards the participants.

____ 14. The facilitators showed enthusiasm for the course, the content, the participants, and the profession of teaching.

____ 15. The facilitators showed clarity in their teaching, their explanations of assignments, and the workshop discussions.

Comments (List item number and suggestions.)

I would have liked more _____

_____

I would have liked less _____

_____

There was just the right amount of _____

_____

Tina Grayson, CLT, Prince William County Public Schools, Virginia
Professional Development Evaluation template is available online.

Countdown Evaluation
for Ongoing Professional Development

List **5** new ideas/practices you have tried (or plan to implement) since taking this class. Explain how they affected your practice or why you plan on trying them.

5.

4.

3.

2.

1.

Name **4** resources you are now aware of that you did not know about before.

4.

3.

2.

1.

Identify **3** issues or concerns you continue to work on in your practice.

3.

2.

1.

Describe **2** critical observations you have made about the content or organization of this ongoing professional development opportunity.

2.

1.

Tell about **1** overarching concept, theme, or idea discussed that has impacted your professional practice and will continue to do so over time.

1.

CLT, Prince William County Public Schools, Virginia
Countdown Evaluation for Ongoing Professional Development template is available online.

Professional Learning Reflections
Sarah Wolfe Hartman

Please take a few moments and reflect on the outcomes for today's session. Your feedback is important to us.

List three concepts/processes we discussed today that were meaningful to you. Please explain why.
-
-
-

Describe one way the key concepts we learned today connect to what you do in your current position.

Name one process strategy introduced today that you will use in your classroom.

What questions do you have about topics discussed today?

Turn to a table partner and discuss ways we might adjust our strategies for providing you with feedback on your work/performance. List 2-3 ideas you come up with together.
-
-
-

Look ahead three months. What processes or content ideas do you think you will be continuing to implement and why?

Professional Learning Reflections template is available online.

We cannot accomplish all we might until we see ourselves as part of a greater whole and expand our efforts for working collaboratively. We must agree on, and become much more clearly focused on, what students should know and be able to do; then we must focus our time and energy on moving all students toward those goals. It is no longer good enough for the lesson to be a "good lesson," it must also be the "right lesson."

There is a strong likelihood that we will all accomplish far more if we engage in our practice with:

- A sense of self-efficacy
- A focus on clearly articulated standards
- An ever-growing repertoire of skills for teaching and assessing diverse learners
- A passion for engaging all students in the learning process
- The use of data to make and assess instructional decisions
- A mission to promote high standards and expectations for both students and educators
- A commitment to collaborate with colleagues and parents

V

Best Practice in Teaching and Learning

Teaching, Learning, and Leading in the
21ˢᵗ Century Standards-Based School

Standards guide all classroom decisions.

This statement represents where we want and need to be. Across the United States educators have access to the newly developed Common Core Standards, standards developed at the state level, and outcomes identified at the local level, that should guide instructional decision making. The reality is that not all educators can say that they are standards-based. What we can say so far is that they are standards-referenced. That is, many refer to the standards to see if they can justify what they had planned to teach based on teachers' manuals, on programs purchased by the district, or by what they have always done. Teachers who are new to the profession seem to more readily engage in practices that are standards-based because they have no "old habits," units, lessons, or activities to give up.

The journey from standards-referenced to standards-based goes as follows:
- Knowing that the standards exist.
- Knowing where to find a copy.
- Reading the standards: It is, however, possible to read the standards without really understanding the depth and breadth of the standards for a course of study. There is a danger that we will march through indicators in much the same way that we have, in the past, marched through pages in texts or workbooks.
- Posting the standards: Posting standards in "educationaleze" in a primary classroom or posting the standard, benchmark, or indicator numbers in any classroom does not meet this criteria. Announcing the number as in, "Today we are working on Standard/Benchmark/Indicator II-Vb" is a waste of time.
- Occasionally referring to the standards during planning.
- Checking to see if what is being taught can be found in the standards: It is at this point in the journey that many get stuck.
- Beginning to understand the power and focus the standards provide and working to identify the essential understandings that are embedded in and that transcend the standards as they are written in the documents.
- Finally being able to say, "I am standards-based because I used the standards to design assessments and instruction, and I used student work to judge whether or not the instruction was well-designed for this content with these learners."

Teaching, Learning, and Leading in the
21st Century Standards-Based School

The first six bullets are more representative of **standards-referenced** than they are of **standards-based**. Teachers have to include the last two before they can say that they are **standards-based**. The following five sections further clarify variables that must be in place before teachers can accurately say, "**I am standards-based.**"

The focus is always on student learning.

"I have so much to cover" continues to be the cry of many teachers. It is true that the amount of information and the number of skills we are asked to ensure learners master is mind-boggling. Given that, we have to be thoughtful and focused about how we spend the currency of education: time. We need to make sure that every single learning experience students engage in is not only an interesting activity, but also the right exercise for moving their learning forward. Just because an exercise is next in the textbook, or because teammates have been using it for years, is not sufficient reason for having students do it. As professionals, we must hold each other accountable by asking the following questions:

- Is this the right lesson for these students right now?
- Given the school-year time frame, is this learning experience worthy of the time it will cost?
- Is there another way to approach this learning that might work better for these learners or be more efficient in moving them along?

Expectations for learning are the same for all students, even those who have traditionally performed at low levels.

At the same time the standards movement was sweeping across the land, IDEA made legally imperative what was already our moral responsibility. It required that all students have access to the same rich curriculum and be held to the same level of understanding as all other students. The implications are huge. The percentage of students who have been labeled as "special needs" and the percentage of English Language Learners (ELLs) is staggering.

This mandate and these students are the reason we hear so much about differentiation of instruction. Differentiation must start with a strongly focused curriculum based on the standards. We need strong knowledge and skillfulness with the content, a thorough understanding of how students learn, and a deep and wide repertoire of instructional strategies for connecting the students and the content.

Teaching, Learning, and Leading in the
21st Century Standards-Based School

Only then can we ensure that students are being provided the scaffolding, extensions, and multiple pathways to learning they need to succeed. The current move away from a deficit model in identifying students who need special education services increases the need for not only all teachers but instructional leaders as well to constantly refine and expand knowledge and skills around key concepts to be taught, the use of data to inform instructional and leadership decisions, and best practice in instruction. Response to Intervention (RtI) provides us with an opportunity to be more collaborative in our work, more purposeful in the selection of strategies, and more data-driven in analyzing the effectiveness of those decisions.

The final determination of the effectiveness of instructional practices is whether or not they result in higher levels of achievement for students.

We need to first gather and analyze pre-assessment or baseline data about what our students know and can do as they enter the learning experience. Unfortunately, many teachers do not make this a regular part of their practice. The analysis of that data leads to an instructional plan which includes the ongoing gathering and use of formative assessment data in the classroom setting. This data informs us and the learners about whether or not they are moving toward mastery of the identified standards. The question is not did students complete all the assignments and do their homework, but rather, did they learn what they were supposed to learn, did they retain it over time, and can they use it in ways that demonstrate that transfer has occurred.

Assessment results are used to inform the teacher about the effectiveness of curricular and instructional decisions.

This fifth category is different from the previous one in that it forces the issue of using not only classroom data but external data to inform our practice. The data we glean or that we are given may reveal that the pacing of instruction needs to be adjusted, that the curriculum needs to be re-examined, or that instructional practices need to be revamped to promote retention and transfer. As we look at assessment results across schools, departments, and classes, we can examine and redesign instruction to more closely align with what is working most effectively in similar settings. When we look at the data longitudinally across the year and over several years, we will be able to identify patterns and trends. When we reach the point where all stakeholders engage in this work collaboratively and automatically, we should see astonishing results in student achievement.

A Teacher's Perspective: My Professional Journey
Becoming a Standards-Based Teacher

I recall my first experiences more than a decade ago with mapping the K-5th grade science curriculum with a group of teachers within the school division. As we mapped the objectives and created a pacing guide, there were many discussions regarding the essential understandings for each objective. I had to think in-depth about what key concepts and big ideas and connections were most essential. These were not clear and we had to work through many ideas to clearly identify these understandings.

As a result of this four weeks of intense work during the summer, I found that when I returned to my classroom in the fall, I was very aware of the objectives, pacing and where I would need to focus the students' attention as I shared with them these essential understandings. I found that my lessons became more effective for the students because they were very aware of the nature of the big ideas. The students actually began to enjoy science.

I went through my file of science lessons that I had saved from prior years and sorted them according to the level of alignment with the key concepts of the objectives. I found that I threw out more lessons than I kept. Some were very minimal in challenging students to think critically; others were "cutesy" replications that I had gathered over the years that I thought the students liked. However, the lessons that I did keep all had a few things in common:
- The lessons could be differentiated easily for the needs of my students.
- The lessons could be used as formative assessments.
- The lessons could be integrated in such a way that key concepts could be connected to their prior knowledge and experiences.
- The lessons focused upon higher order thinking rather than on learning simple basic skills.

As the new school year began, I started to plan my lessons from the ones that I had saved. The organization and format of the lesson plan was no longer the criteria for a great lesson. Instead, I judged the lesson on whether or not it accomplished the intended outcome. Since I knew the end results I wanted for my students, I felt like I had a clear road map of where the students were heading. I also began to share with the students the purpose of the lesson. They became more motivated to perform as a result.

As I became more proficient in the process, I added on another piece of the Standards-Based Planning Process. I became more comfortable in conducting simple task analyses of the skills and knowledge that students would need to learn as we moved through the objectives. I also set up a simple recording system to track where the students were in mastering these skills. I had never used analysis in this manner so it was a bit confusing at first. I had trouble trying to

A Teacher's Perspective: My Professional Journey
Becoming a Standards-Based Teacher

define and sequence all of the skills and knowledge for each objective. I had to go back and read all of the essential understandings in the curriculum map to guide me in the analysis. Eventually, I began to get better with practice. I realized that the amount of time up front in planning this way was worthwhile to save time at the end of the teaching cycle.

Now as a reflective practitioner, I can't imagine teaching without using the Standards-Based Planning Process. I feel that I would be limiting the effectiveness of the lessons and just returning to my old ways to simply teach to the activities, not teaching to ensure student learning. I view the planning as a cycle now. My assessment informs what I teach next, how it will be taught, and to whom.

Planning Instruction
How Am I Doing?

Mark each item: (W) Working Well   (S) Sometimes   (N) Not Yet

_____ I use the Common Core Standards, state standards, and district outcomes to plan for the year, the unit, and the lesson.

_____ I use the standards-based planning process to plan and pace for the year.

_____ I use the standards-based planning process for units and lessons by aligning assessments and learning experiences with the standards.

_____ I identify the focus of the content areas being taught.

_____ I design summative assessments prior to deciding on learning experiences for units or lessons.

_____ I design learning experiences that give students practices and rehearsals at the same level of understanding as the level at which the standards are written.

_____ I communicate how any given lesson/learning experience is directly related to the standards.

_____ I state standards in lesson plans.

_____ I analyze instructional materials for match to district outcomes.

_____ I identify supplemental materials and design learning experiences to fill any gaps in standard materials.

_____ I use the task analysis process to identify the knowledge, skills, and level of understanding required by the standard and the assignment or assessment task, consider where individuals and the group of students are with the required knowledge, skills, and level of understanding, and plan learning experiences accordingly.

_____ I include knowledge of student readiness levels, interests, and learning styles in designing learning experiences.

_____ I build pauses for processing into the lesson design and use 10:2 Theory and Wait Time as guidelines.

_____ I plan and write out the key questions to ask during a lesson.

_____ I analyze text structure, point out the structure, and teach students to use graphic organizers to represent the thinking processes used by the author and to capture the key information in the text.

_____ I align assignments including homework with standards and assessments and am purposeful about examining homework results for evidence of learning.

_____ I eliminate lessons and learning exercises that do not move students toward meeting the standards.

_____ I collaborate/consult with support staff about special needs students.

Self Assessment: Planning Instruction template is available online.

The Planning Process in a Standards-Based Environment

Planning in a standards-based environment is often called "backwards" because we "begin with the end" in mind. In fact, we almost always begin with the end in mind when we plan vacations or weddings or purchase new automobiles. It is the way our colleagues in business and industry do project management and action planning. In school, teachers have always planned with "the end in mind." Often though, the end we had in mind was to work our way through the book, chapter by chapter, or through the year, project by project.

In a standards-based environment, we must be clear about "the end" we have in mind and be certain that we are working together from pre-kindergarten through twelfth grade to lead students to the achievement of commencement level standards. It is within this context that we focus on the standards, benchmarks, and indicators that have been identified as the ones students are to master during the grade or courses we teach. The end in mind cannot be a particular activity or project, chapters in a book, or completion of a packaged program. We have to be clear about how what students are doing in the classroom is tied to the outcomes we seek this year and throughout their K-12 educational experience.

Just like we have a clear picture of that perfect vacation, car, wedding, or ad campaign, we need to have a clear picture of what it looks like when our students are competent with what we want them to know and be able to do. Just as that vacation, wedding, or ad campaign will not happen without an action plan, we need an action plan for guiding our students to be able to demonstrate the learning we have in mind for them.

The first step in this planning process, both inside and outside the classroom, is identifying the outcome we want. The second step is creating our vision of what it looks like when we get there. Next we analyze the outcome and vision to figure out what we have to do in the third step in order to accomplish the first and second steps. It makes no sense to start the third step without **THE END** in mind.

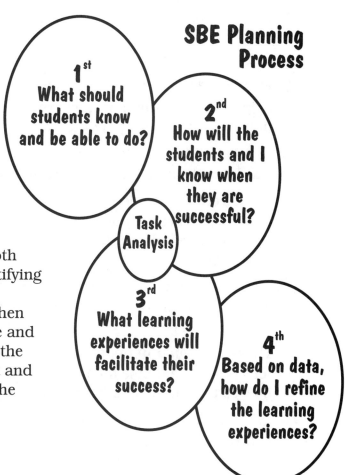

SBE Planning Process

1st What should students know and be able to do?

2nd How will the students and I know when they are successful?

Task Analysis

3rd What learning experiences will facilitate their success?

4th Based on data, how do I refine the learning experiences?

Building on the SBE Planning Ovals
Top Ten Questions
to ask myself as I design lessons and units

Oval One

1. What should students know and be able to do as a result of this lesson? How are these objectives related to national, state, and/or district standards?

Oval Two

2. How will students demonstrate what they know and what they can do? What will be the assessment criteria and what form will it take?

Oval Three (Questions 3-10 address Oval Three)

3. How will I find out what students already know (pre-assessment), and how will I help them access what they know and have experienced both inside and outside the classroom? How will I help them build on prior experiences, deal with misconceptions, and reframe their thinking when appropriate?

4. How will new knowledge, concepts, and skills be introduced? Given the diversity of my students and the task analysis, what are my best options for sources and presentation modes?

5. How will I facilitate student processing (meaning making) of new information or processes? What key questions, activities, and assignments (in class or homework) will promote understanding, retention, and transfer?

6. What shall I use as formative assessments or checks for understanding? How can I use the data from those assessments to inform my teaching decisions?

7. What do I need to do to scaffold and extend instruction so that the learning experiences are productive for all students? What are the multiple ways students can access information and then process and demonstrate their learning?

8. How will I Frame the Learning so that students know the objectives, the rationale for the objectives and activities, the directions and procedures, as well as the assessment criteria at the beginning of the learning process?

9. How will I build in opportunities for students to make real-world connections and to learn and use the rigorous and complex thinking skills they need to succeed in the classroom and the world beyond?

10. What adjustments need to be made in the learning environment so that we can work and learn efficiently during this study?

Facts Are Important...But They Aren't Enough!
Concept-Based Instruction

The brain can hold only so many isolated facts. It continually seeks a connection or patterns on which to hook new information. The more we know, the more we learn.

We have obtained an increase in student achievement by aligning the curriculum to learning standards. Much remains to be done. To see further increases, it is essential that we adjust instructional practices so that students have a greater chance of retaining and transferring knowledge and skills to new situations.

High school teachers in Greece Central School District, New York, were not able to create interdisciplinary units until they moved beyond the standards and indicators in each of their courses. Through the use of Lynn Erickson's book, **Concept-Based Curriculum and Instruction**, they moved beyond thinking that they had little common ground in their courses to seeing that they could indeed design meaningful integrated units while preserving the integrity of each course. The key points that moved the work forward are explained below.

Essential Understandings
- are generalizations that show the relationship between two or more concepts
- may be written as statements or questions

Concepts
- are big ideas that are timeless, universal, broad, and abstract
- have a set of examples that share common attributes

Facts
- are pieces of information to know
- are embedded in concepts

Therefore
- Essential knowledge is fact-based.
- Essential understandings cannot be fact-based. They must be concept-based!

In addition to the fact that students learn at a higher level when we use concept-based instruction, it is important to note that this instruction also leads to higher standardized test scores as well. Even though many standardized test questions are written at the factual or recall level, when students learn at a conceptual level they are better able to sort through the possible answers in a multiple-choice item and eliminate the alternatives that do not fit the big idea of the question.

Concept-Based Instruction
Concepts, Key Ideas, and Generalizations

Framing lessons and units around concepts, key ideas, and generalizations leads to improved teaching and learning. Generalizations, also known as essential understandings, can be presented as statements or questions. The question format promotes learner curiosity and facilitates inquiry. The following statements and questions were developed by participants in the workshop series **Instruction for All Students**™.

- All living things need to adapt to their habitat to survive and thrive. (Grade 4 Science)

- All living things need each other to survive. (Grade 4 Science)

- How does the study of language help us understand and experience the world around us? (Languages Other Than English)

- What makes a book worth reading? (Middle School English)

- How do geographical, economic, technological, religious, and social variables affect the course of history? (Grade 5 History and Social Science)

- There are positive and negative consequences of revolutions. (Grade 5 History and Social Science)

- Math is a language. Effectively communicating mathematical ideas is a critical component in solving real-life problems. (Geometry)

- Numbers tell the story of a business. (Accounting)

- Is the world a fair and just place? (High School English)

- How does literature affect your life, and how does your life affect your interpretation of literature? (High School English)

- The three big ideas of Chemistry are structure and properties of matter, atomic structure, and chemical reactions. Everything we study will fit into those categories. (Chemistry)

- Observations lead to model building that helps explain past observations and predict future events. (Grade 2 Science)

- The study of mathematics is the study of how to organize information to solve problems. (Mathematics K-12)

- Why war? (Middle School Social Studies)

- All life on earth is interdependent. (Grade 4 Science)

- Data that occurs in real-world situations can be examined for patterns and trends. These patterns may exhibit linear or non-linear relationships. (High School Math)

Task Analysis

Task analysis is the systematic breakdown of the tasks we ask students to complete. It allows us to identify the skills, both academic and process, that the students need in order to successfully complete the task, assignment, or project.

How To Analyze a Task

- Make sure the task is worth doing and that it is aligned with the standards of learning.
- Note and list all the components that go into accomplishing the task.
- Note and list all the skills (procedural knowledge) and bits of declarative knowledge students need to have in order to be successful with the task.
- Identify the levels of understanding they will need to complete the task.
- Use cognitive empathy to check through the task one more time. Better yet, if it is a high-stakes assignment, have someone not in your class (student, teacher, or friend) read through the task and the directions to check for possible problem areas.
- Identify which students have mastered which skills. If unknown, decide how to find out or how to circumvent the need for the skill.
- Design your instruction by deciding what to do about the skills or knowledge the entire group needs, what to do about those students who lack the prerequisite skills to be successful even with the beginning components of the task, and what to do about those students who have already mastered the knowledge and skills required by the task.

- While there may be many skill sets and chunks of knowledge you include as learning experiences for the entire class, you may choose to organize mini-lessons for small groups. These mini-lessons may focus on skill remediation, extension of learning, or provide the information students will need to complete a particular part of the task. Prevention of problems, frustration, or failure, rather than intervention later, will make you and your students more successful. In the end, it will save time and energy for all involved.

The ultimate goal is for our students to task analyze independently. We should be explicit about teaching gifted and accelerated learners how to task analyze and then expect them to become skillful at task analyzing the independent studies they organize for themselves.

Task Analysis Exemplar

English 11 Standard: Students will write a multi-paragraph persuasive essay.

Assessment Task: In this RAFT students assume the role of teenager from a specific country or the position of a teenager in the United States. After studying a selected country in detail, they write letters to the President of the United States, suggesting the role the U.S. should play in the political/economic future of that country through its foreign policy practices.

Knowledge	Skills
What must students know?	What must students be able to do?
Know (nouns):	**Be able to do (verbs):**
• characteristics of argumentation/persuasion	• form arguments
• role of fact/opinion	• create a rationale for position
• paraphrasing	• locate facts to support position
• direct quotations	• support points with specific facts
• summarization	• express thought in complete sentences
• background (political/historical) information about a specific area of the world	• use transitions to combine sentences into paragraphs and to connect paragraphs
Understand (nouns):	• arrange paragraphs in a logical order
• U.S. foreign policy goals	• frame an introduction and conclusion to serve the focus of the writing and ideas in the paragraphs
• U.S. foreign policy tools	
• elements of persuasion	• appeal to a specific audience
• thesis	• create a call to action in a multi-paragraph essay
• the call to action	

Task Analysis

Knowledge	Skills

- Is there background knowledge or a level of understanding the entire group is lacking? How about individual students?
- Are there academic or social skills the entire group is lacking? How about the skill level of individuals?
- What shall I do in a proactive way to prevent frustrations and problems with learning?
- What shall I do with students who already know and can apply this information?

Students	Potential Problem	Possible Intervention

Task Analysis template is available online.

Formative Assessment

If It Hasn't Been Caught, It Hasn't Been Taught!

Leaders cannot be called leaders if no one is following. The same is true for teachers. Presenting or telling information is not teaching. In order to call ourselves teachers, our students have to be learning from the learning experiences we orchestrate. A significant component of our teaching repertoire has to be checking to see if our students are with us on the learning journey, or if we are going on the trip alone.

Strategies to find out where to "pick them up" for the learning journey are essential. Many of the active learning strategies we use to help students make meaning of the work can provide us with important assessment data. When we do a task analysis, access prior knowledge, or surface misconceptions and naive understandings, we gather a great deal of information about what students know and at what levels they can use that knowledge and those skills. In fact, we may find that we do not need additional pre-assessment data, but simply need to use the data we collect through those exercises.

In order to facilitate learning, we have to adjust the design of the learning experiences based on the data we collect not only at the beginning of the learning experience but throughout the work. In many instances the data is right in front of us but we are not seeing it as "data" that can inform our decisions.

Formative or Summative?

Formative assessment results inform teachers about how well students are learning and inform students about where they are in the learning process. Summative assessment results reveal how students can apply the key concepts and essential understandings they are studying.

Any assessment can be formative or summative. While many forms of formative assessment are informal, it is not the format that determines its status; it is, instead, the way the results are used.

When we use assessment for formative purposes, students should receive growth-producing feedback and have the opportunity to make adjustments to their work based on that feedback. Of course, that means averaging grades is not an option.

Formative Assessment

We are not checking for understanding when we ask:
- "Are there any questions?"
- "Are you all with me?"
- "Am I going too fast?"
- "This is an adverb, isn't it?"

Given that the above are negative examples, what is checking for understanding? It is asking questions that can only be answered if students understand. Using Howard Gardner's definition of understanding, this would mean that students are able to use knowledge and skills in new situations in appropriate ways. While recall of significant information is an important part of learning, checking for understanding is not the same as checking for recall or memorization.

Another classroom dilemma is one that we all experienced as students. We sat in classrooms where the teacher asked many questions to the entire class and called on one student to answer. Given the number of students and the limited amount of time, the chances were pretty good that any one student was called on only once during the period. There are two big problems with that approach. One problem is that the teacher only knows if the one student who answered the question knows or does not know the answer to, or, has or does not have an informed opinion on the point being discussed. The other problem is that the rest of the students can tune out if only volunteers are called on, or if the teacher makes it a practice to call on all students one by one. After students have answered they are off the hook. Why do we, as teachers, even consider continuing this practice year after year? If we want to scaffold or extend learning it is essential that all students are actively engaged in demonstrating their current level of understanding so that we can match our interventions to their learning needs.

There are ways to check across many students on the same concept or skill in a relatively short time. As we incorporate **10:2 Theory** into our practice, a strategy that is easy to implement is **Think-Pair-Share**. This strategy meets the needs of the introverted learners who want time to think before talking because there is a short think time before any answers are accepted. Other possibilities include signal cards, slates, sort cards, journal entries, and homework. It also meets the needs of extraverted learners who need to talk to create meaning.

Providing Growth-Producing Feedback

Feedback is an incredibly powerful teaching tool; Grant Wiggins writes that when growth-producing feedback is provided, most students can achieve at the same level as the top 20% of students. He also asserts that feedback has a positive impact on student engagement. Put quite simply, students who are given specific information about the accuracy and quality of their work will spend more time working on their academic assignments.

Grades Are Not Growth-Producing Feedback

It is important to have a clear definition of growth-producing feedback. Wiggins says that feedback is not about praise or blame, approval or disapproval. Good feedback describes what a student did or did not do for the purpose of changing or maintaining a behavior or performance. Robert Marzano and associates concur that effective feedback should provide students with an explanation of what they are doing correctly and what steps they must take to continue to make progress. Typical feedback includes such comments as "Nice work," "Unclear," "You need to improve your study habits," "C+," or "75%." These types of statements or grades show either an approval or disapproval of what a student has done, and are evaluative in nature. This type of feedback has very little effect on student learning and can have a negative impact on student motivation to learn. Students tend to ignore comments when they are accompanied by grades or numerical scores. Students pay much closer attention to written comments when they are not accompanied by a grade. Stephen Chappuis and Richard Stiggins found that "replacing judgmental feedback with specific, descriptive, and immediate feedback benefits students." Productive feedback tells students where they are on the continuum of mastery of given standards or benchmarks, what they are doing right, and next steps to take toward mastery.

Following Growth-Producing Feedback

Providing students growth-producing feedback is not enough. Students must have the opportunity to respond to the feedback, make adjustments in their work, and resubmit their assignments for further comments. When students are given these opportunities, they begin to develop skills of self-assessment and self-adjustment. We do not want students to be completely dependent on teachers to let them know if they are learning. We want them to develop skills that result in their having greater aspirations to succeed in the future, enjoying greater satisfaction from their learning, and setting future performance goals.

Adapted from the October 2006 issue *Just for the ASKing!* by Bruce Oliver.

Providing Growth-Producing Feedback

Feedback is not about praise or blame, approval or disappointment.
Feedback is value-neutral. It describes what you did and did not do.
Praise is necessary but praise only keeps you in the game. It doesn't get
you better.

Grant Wiggins

Positive Examples

- Take a look at the example on the board. Look at my second step and compare it to what you have done.
- Remember that the objective is to make all your letters touch the line. Go back to your seat and fix the letters that don't follow that pattern.
- You must follow the steps in the recipe precisely. Go over the steps in the recipe and identify the step you missed.
- It's clear from your explanation that you have grasped the main ideas. I would recommend one change. Think about your third statement and see if you can make a better argument for your thesis statement.
- In number four, you are dividing fractions. Remember to invert the fraction and then multiply.
- Review the footnote format I gave you at the beginning of the assignment. Check to verify that all your footnotes match the guidelines and fix the ones that do not.
- I want you to listen to the tape again. Listen to how the narrator pronounces his words. Then come back and try your recitation with me again.
- Remember... *i* before *e* except after *c*. Using this rule go back and correct your spelling words.

Negative Examples

- I'm not sure you studied hard on this test. I expected better results from you.
- There are just too many careless errors here. Take your paper back and correct your mistakes.
- I feel that I have presented this information in a clear cut manner. I've done my part. You just are not paying attention.
- Your work is showing great improvement. You're doing much better.
- C+ (without a rubric)
- Your writing lacks clarity and focus.
- Great work! You are becoming an excellent student.
- Your book report was just superb this time. I enjoyed reading it so much.
- You did not sound good today. I hope you improve before next week's concert.

SBE and Multiple Pathways to Learning

Differentiation of instruction does not mean that you individualize instruction or provide something "different" from the normal lesson for struggling or advanced students. It means that you think proactively and, from the beginning, the "normal" lesson includes more than one avenue for success. It means that you think about the diversity of your learners when you are planning and don't fall into the trap of thinking that "one size fits all." Use what you know about the **SBE Planning Process** and the needs of your diverse learners to answer the following questions:

1. Identify a standard/benchmark/indicator you will be addressing in the near future.

2. What assessment opportunities might you give students to demonstrate what they have learned about the above concept?

3. Given the task analysis, what information and skills should all students experience? List a few instructional strategies and practice and/or processing activities which would facilitate that learning.

4. What might you do to extend and expand the thinking of students ready to and/or interested in going beyond what you've planned? Include both inside and outside of class possibilities.

5. What do you know about your struggling learners that you need to address up front? What about your ESL students? Your special education students? List specific examples of instruction strategies, adaptations, support systems that would be helpful to small groups?

6. What might you do to reteach or help students having difficulties in understanding this concept? Include both inside and outside of class possibilities.

SBE and Multiple Pathways to Learning template is available online.

Differentiation Non-Negotiables

We Must

- Be knowledgeable about and skillful with the **content** to be taught.
- Acknowledge, understand, respect, and respond to the **differences** in, and **needs** of, the learners to be taught.
- Hold and select purposefully from a deep and broad **repertoire of instructional strategies**.
- Use **multiple sources of data** to inform decisions about instruction.
- Realize that differentiation is not a set of strategies but is instead a **way of thinking** about the teaching and learning process.
- **Not differentiate who will learn what** but rather, **how we will teach** so that all students have access to, and support and guidance in, meeting or exceeding the Common Core Standards, state standards, and district outcomes.

How am I Doing in Taking Action around the Non-Negotiables?
(A) Always   (S) Sometimes   (N) Not Yet

_____ We base the lessons and units we design on the Common Core Standards, state standards, and district outcomes.

_____ We design learning experiences based on a task analysis that includes an analysis of the skills and knowledge embedded in the standards and the task plus an analysis of student readiness, background knowledge levels, interests, and information processing styles.

_____ We provide sources of information at various reading levels, in different languages, and in varying formats to match the needs of learners.

_____ We provide appropriate scaffolding and extensions.

_____ We provide students precise and public criteria and for assessment prior to the beginning of the learning experience or assessment; We include models and exemplars with the guidelines.

_____ We ensure that grouping is flexible so that students are working and learning with a variety of classmates.

_____ We orchestrate the learning environment so that the student is given both choice in and responsibility for learning.

_____ We regularly collaborate with colleagues around the design, implementation, and effectiveness of instruction.

_____ We consider parents equal partners in the education of their children and our interactions with them are representative of that belief system.

_____ We ask ourselves:
- What will we do if some students do not learn?
- What will we do if some students already know what I want them to learn?

Differentiation Non-Negotiables template is available online.

Self-Assessment
Ways to Scaffold and Extend Instruction

We base our planning on the key concepts/essential understandings of our curriculum. To provide additional challenges, or additional support, we move from those understandings to deciding what support systems students need to master those essential understandings as well as what we will need to do to provide rigorous and challenging learning experiences for those who can easily demonstrate mastery of those understandings.

Read through the statements below, mark with an X those that you already consider in your planning, and reflect on those that you need to use to guide your thinking as you plan future instruction.

☐ I design lessons and units based on the essential understandings, key concepts, big ideas, and level of understanding required by the Common Core Standards, state standards, and district curriculum.

☐ I make abstract concepts more accessible through semi-abstract (pictures or graphs) or concrete (realia/props/exemplars) representations.

☐ I promote learning by linking new concepts and ideas to familiar concepts or experiences.

☐ I purposefully learn about my students readiness levels, interests, and learning strengths and design standards-based learning experiences that build on their current status.

☐ I increase/decrease accessibility by providing alternative resources, by giving more/less guidance, or by supplying resources.

☐ I ensure that students' working at all skill levels constantly build expertise at accessing resources for increasingly independent learning.

☐ I break the task or goal into simpler parts...such as chunking the task, providing check-in points and time guidelines, or having advanced students do more independent investigations.

☐ I provide more/less structure as needed.

☐ I adjust the level of independence to ensure success without enabling.

☐ I adjust the frequency of feedback so that students can adjust their learning efforts.

☐ I adjust the time for input of new information, the meaning making, and the demonstrations of understanding as needed.

☐ I extend and enrich the learning experiences for those who are able to do complex quality work and demonstrate understanding in a short time.

Self-Assessment: Ways to Scaffold and Extend Instruction template is available online.

Just ASK Resource Center
Teaching and Learning Resources

Access the Resource Center at www.justaskpublications.com

Just ASK has an extensive online Resource Center where you can access many tools to support you as you design and implement, coach, or supervise teaching and learning in a standards-based school. There are brief descriptions below of some of those resources.

Standards-Based Planning Templates

The following templates are available as Word documents. They can be edited and expanded to accommodate your own content while designing units.

A Guide to Unit Design in the Standards-Based Classroom: Download this template and use the guiding questions in the design of your own units. Also, see the exemplar units below that use this template.

One-page **SBE Unit Plan** and Two-page **SBE Unit Plan**
Explore alternative formats for designing and recording unit and lesson plans. Download these templates and see if they have potential for use in your practice.

Concept-Based Unit Design and **Concept-Based Integrated Unit Design**
These two templates are adaptations from Greece Central School District, New York that use the idea of concept-based instruction: framing lessons and units around concepts, key ideas, and generalizations. They have designed meaningful integrated units that preserve the integrity of each course.

Standards-Based Planning Process: A Guided Approach
This template is an adaptation from Prince William County Public Schools (PWCS), Virginia which they use as a guide in the planning of standards-based units. See an exemplar unit using this format designed by Beth McKinney below.

Top Ten Questions to Ask Myself as I Design Lessons
Use this worksheet to add detail to the standards-based planning process ovals and help identify the variables you need to consider when designing lessons or units.

Standards-Based Unit Exemplars

First Grade Unit: Persuasive Writing
This unit, developed by Cheryl Ebertz, Carolyn Hammerschmidt, and Ann Lenzi, Greece Central School District, New York, asks first graders the essential question: How can I persuade others?

Just ASK Resource Center
Teaching and Learning Resources

Second Grade Unit: Ghana

This unit, developed by Laura Cork, Newton Public Schools, Massachusetts, asks students to explore the construct that events are shaped by the ideas and actions of both individuals and groups in response to meeting fundamental needs. Big ideas they investigate are the similarities and differences between and among cultures of people and that people express their culture in many ways: writing, literature, architecture, celebrations, everyday tools, and objects, etc. High school teachers will be amazed by the work these second graders are doing and the level of planning by the teacher.

Middle School Science Unit: Force and Motion – The Science Behind Sports

In this unit, developed by Karen Finter, West Irondequoit Central School District, New York, students are asked to analyze the underlying physics concepts behind a sport or leisure activity. First, students gather technical information on a sport of their choice, using both printed and electronic resources. After they complete their initial research, students develop, conduct, and analyze an original experiment based on a scientifically sound problem. Finally, students present their research and experiment results throughout the grade level in a student-led symposium.

High School Science Unit: Comparing and Contrasting Plant and Animal Cells

This unit, developed by Beth McKinney of Prince William County Public Schools, Virginia, asks students to investigate and understand relationships between cell structure and cell function while answering the question: What are the similarities and differences between plant and animal cells?

High School Science Unit: Interdependence of Organisms

In this ecology unit, developed by Janice Creneti, instructional coach at Pinellas County Public Schools, Florida and former teacher at Fairfax County Public Schools, Virginia, students are asked to explore how their individual actions and those of society impact the ecosystem and how we can be responsible stewards of the earth. Through extensive, well-planned, creative lessons and projects, students explore possible answers to these essential questions.

Additional Resources for Teaching and Learning in the 21st Century

Points to Note in the Review of a Standards-Based Lesson or Unit

Use this worksheet as a checklist when critiquing or submitting your standards-based lesson or unit for peer review.

Just ASK Resource Center
Teaching and Learning Resources

Staff Survey of Best Practice in Teaching and Learning
This survey, developed by Sherri Stephens-Carter, is a tool that can be used multiple times throughout the year to identify staff perceptions of their own knowledge and skills around key components of best practice. It serves as an excellent needs-assessment for the design of professional learning opportunities.

Standards-Based Classroom Self-Inventory
You can't get to where you want to go unless you know where you've been and where you are right now. A mutual understanding of the content standards and standards-based teaching and learning is a critical foundation for increasing student learning. This self-inventory helps you analyze where you are in terms of curriculum, instruction, assessment, and student learning using points on a continuum that describe classrooms in transition to ideal classrooms based on standards. Complete the self-inventory to find out where your practice and your students are on the continuum.

Essential Roles and Responsibilities
Standards-Based Education (SBE) only works well when everyone in the system is focused on doing everything necessary to ensure that all students are learning at high levels. This tool describes how all members of the SBE system might do their work. As an individual, use this tool for self-assessment and goal setting. Groups may use it to start conversations, discussions, and dialogues about how different roles support SBE.

Results-Based Professional Development Models
This text, edited by Brenda Kaylor, provides all the tools professional developers need to introduce and implement five results-based models: coaching/mentoring, independent study, inquiry, process, and training.

Access these resources at www.justaskpublications.com.

Just ASK Resource Center
Just for the ASKing!

Access the following issues of *Just for the ASKing!* that focus on best practice in instruction, assessment and meeting the needs of diverse learners at www.justaskpublications.com. You are authorized and encouraged to duplicate each of these for your own use or for use in professional learning initiatives.

Are We Having Fun Yet?
Chaotic Situations
Closing the Achievement Gap
Common Assessments: Uncommon Results
Differentiation of Instruction
Don't Jump to Conclusions
Dropouts: Our Ultimate Left Behind Children
Engaging Experiences
Fostering Student Resilience
Framing the Learning
Growth-Producing Feedback
It Seemed Like a Good Idea at the Time
It's a Feedback World
Ladies and Gentlemen, Start Your Engines
Making the Case for Standards-Based Grading
Moving Out of the Assessment Dark Ages
Peeks into Powerful Pedagogy
Resistant and Reluctant Learners
Response to Intervention (RtI): An IDEA Whose Time Has Come
Rethinking Assessment Practices
Setting Students Up for Success: Filling in the Blanks
Social Security
Stop! ... In the Name of Learning!
Success Factors in Diverse Schools
The Homework Dilemma
Time: We Have to Spend It Wisely
Unlocking Potential
When Students Already Know the Content
When Students Don't Learn

Making Connections
With Your Classroom Practice

Top Ten Questions I Ask Myself When I Design Lessons
Questions 3-10 address Oval 3 of the SBE Planning Process and the question: What learning experiences will facilitate student success? See page 204 for the ten questions. Access the Top Ten Questions Template online.

Other lesson design approaches that address Oval 3 are:

The 5 Es of Constructivism
- Engage: Students access prior knowledge, establish relevance, and make real-world connections.
- Explore: Students interact with concepts and processes being studied and used.
- Explain: Learners engage communicate what they have learned in a variety of formats and with a variety of audiences.
- Elaborate: Students apply what they have learned to new situations and connect new learning to their own lives, to other content areas, and to what they have learned before.
- Evaluate: Students engage in formative and summative assessments that include self-assessment and opportunities for responding to growth-producing feedback.

LEARN Model, Fairfax Public Schools, Virginia
The components are:
- Link
- Engage and educate
- Active learning
- Reflect
- Now and then

Gradual Release Model
- Demonstration
- Shared demonstration
- Guided practice
- Independent practice

Marzano's Nine Strategies also address Oval 3 of the SBE Planning Process.
1. Identify similarities and differences
2. Summarizing and note taking
3. Reinforcing effort and providing recognition
4. Homework and practice
5. Nonlinguistic representation
6. Cooperative learning
7. Setting objectives and providing feedback
8. Generating and testing hypotheses
9. Questions, cues, and advance organizers

Curriculum Map
Julie McVicker

Subject _____

Grade _____

	Month of _____	Month of _____
Essential Questions		
Content		
Standards/Skills/Benchmarks		
Assessments		
Learning Experiences		
Differentiation Strategies		
Technology		

Curriculum Map template is available online.

Language Arts Classroom Guidelines
A McNair Elementary Case Study Artifact

The First Twenty Days of Reading mini-lessons are to be completed no later than October 9.
Reading Workshop Format: 60 minutes each day

10 - 15 minutes	**Focus Lesson** **Shared reading/modeled reading/thinking aloud**
40 - 45 minutes	• Guided reading groups • Teacher/student conferences about reading • Literature discussion groups • Literacy centers • Independent reading • Students working independently on a variety of tasks such as reading notebooks • Ongoing assessments (running records, anecdotal notes, checklists, etc.
5 - 10 minutes	**Share and wrap-up**

Writing will begin on the first day of school.
Writing Workshop Format: 60 minutes each day

10 - 15 minutes	**Focus/Mini Lesson about writing process, craft or procedures**
40 - 45 minutes	**Independent writing time** • The majority of writing should be authentic and student generated. • When appropriate, prompt writing can be taught as a unit of study. • Ongoing assessments, editing checklists, writing rubrics)
5 - 10 minutes	**Share and wrap-up**

What needs to be in place?

• Physical arrangement of room should provide for whole group instruction, small group instruction, table/chairs for use by instructional support staff (SPED, ESOL), cooperative student learning, one-on-one instruction/conferencing.
• Word walls should be alphabetized, color coded (red-language arts, green-science, orange-math, blue-social studies) for each subject area, and updated on a regular basis; there is evidence of ongoing use.
• Classroom library should be organized by genre, topics, authors, and leveled books, in clearly labeled baskets.
• Routines are established for reading and writing assignments, moving through the writing process, etc.
• Writing supplies are organized and available for student use.

©Just ASK Publications

Grades 4-6 Writing Rubric
A McNair Elementary Case Study Artifact

Student: _____ Date: _____ Grade: _____

	4 Proficient Control	3 Basic Control	2 Partial Control	1 Minimal Control	
Composing	• strong central idea • many important details • good organization • strong beginning/middle/end • strong lead and closing • purposeful/stayed on topic • evidence of prewriting/planning	• has central idea • some important details • limited organization • has beginning/middle/end • lead and closing • some off topic ideas • attempt at prewriting/planning	• weak central idea • few details • poor organization • weak beginning/middle/end • lead or closing • off topic • few signs of prewriting/planning	• no central focus • no details/elaboration • no organization • off topic • doesn't make sense • jumps from point to point • no signs of prewriting/planning	
Written Expression	• powerful message • precise information • vivid and descriptive vocabulary • varied sentences/structure • strong voice/mood • rhythmic flow • strong imagery	• good word choice • some important details • some descriptive vocabulary • some varied sentences/structure • attempt at voice/unsteady mood • good imagery	• awkward construction • few important details • bland words • little sentence variety • little/no voice/mood • choppy • some imagery	• void of detail • repetitive ideas/words • no sentence variety • vague • no voice/mood • general/boring • no imagery	
Usage (Grammar) and Mechanics Punctuation, Spelling and Capitalization	• proper sentence formation • complete sentences • proper capitalization • proper punctuation • use of correct spelling • paragraph indented • minimal to no errors	• mostly proper sentence formation • many complete sentences • good control of capitalization • good control of punctuation • use of spelling patterns • most paragraphs indented	• poor sentence formation • some complete sentences • poor tense agreement • capitalization/punctuation errors • many spelling errors • some paragraphs indented • many errors/readable		

Tier 1 Reading Instruction (Grades K-2)
Teacher Self-Assessment

The following is a list of the essential components of a **Primary Reading Workshop**. Identify your level of use of the activities and structures that need to occur if your students are ultimately to achieve reading success. This reflection tool is a starting point for ongoing collaboration, practice, and continual learning school wide and in your grade level.

Essential Component	Frequency	Always: 95%+ Usually: 75%-95% Sometimes: 40%-75% Rarely: 0%-40%	If unable to mark Always, my plan for reaching the goal of this Reading Workshop component is:
1. **I read aloud** to the class each day allowing time for discussion among the students.			
2. During **interactive read-aloud** I ask questions to elicit higher level thinking and stimulate rich discussion.			
3. I use **shared reading** to teach students reading strategies. Children can all see the text and can read along.			
4. I plan for and provide **guided reading** groups for each student reading below grade level using appropriate leveled text; small group explicit instruction based on students' needs.			
5. I plan for and provide **guided reading** groups for each student reading on/above grade level using appropriate leveled text; small group explicit instruction based on students' needs.			
6. I provide each student with an individual book box with texts at each student's appropriate level (e.g., guided reading books) for **independent reading**. I provide time for independent reading.			

Jay McClain, Principal, Bailey's Elementary School, FCPS, Falls Church, Virginia - Access template online.

225

Tier 1 Reading Instruction (Grades 3-5)
Teacher Self-Assessment

The following is a list of the essential components of a **Intermediate Reading Workshop**. Identify your level of use of the activities and structures that need to occur if your students are ultimately to achieve reading success. **This reflection tool is a starting point for ongoing collaboration, practice, and continual learning school wide and in your grade level.**

Essential Component	Frequency	Always: 95%+ Usually: 75%-95% Sometimes: 40%-75% Rarely: 0%-40%	If unable to mark Always, my plan for reaching the goal of this Reading Workshop component is:
1. I **read aloud** to the class each day allowing time for discussion among the students.			
2. I plan for and provide **guided reading** groups for each student below grade level using appropriate leveled text; small group explicit instruction based on students' needs and reading level.			
3. I plan for and provide guided reading groups for each student on/above grade level using appropriate leveled text; small group explicit instruction based on students' needs and reading level.			
4. I provide each student with an individual book box with texts at each student's appropriate level (e.g., guided reading books) for independent reading, I provide time for independent reading.			
5. I provide students with the opportunity to participate in in-depth analysis of one or more aspects of literature study-author study, genre study, picture book study.			
6. I provide small groups of students the opportunity to participate in literature discussion groups around a text-picture books, nonfiction texts, poetry.			
7. Each student in my class keeps a Reader's Notebook where he/she articulates thoughts, questions, comments and predictions about texts and I respond on a regular basis. Each of my students also keeps a reading log.			

226

Jay McClain, Principal, Bailey's Elementary School, FCPS, Falls Church, Virginia - Access template online.

Tier 1 Math (Grades K-5)
Teacher Self-Assessment

The following is a list of the essential components of a **Math Workshop**. Identify your level of use of the activities and structures that need to occur if your students are ultimately to achieve math success. **This reflection tool is a starting point for ongoing collaboration, practice, and continual learning school wide and in your grade level.**

Essential Component	Frequency	Always: 95%+ Usually: 75%-90% Sometimes: 40%-75% Rarely: 0%-40%	If unable to mark Always, my plan for reaching the goal of this Math Workshop component is:
1. I have a **daily** math workshop of at least 60 minutes (Monday-Friday).			
2. I start my math block with an engaging **opening** that focuses on a specific strategy, (i.e. counting, vocabulary development, test-taking strategy, etc.)			
3. I launch students into a discovery of certain standards/concepts through a focus lesson.			
4. I plan for and provide guided math groups with explicit instruction based on students' needs.			
5. I prepare meaningful math tasks for small groups and/or individual students (i.e. centers, targeted games, math journals, other investigations).			
6. I dedicate time at the end of the math block for students to reflect on the math concept through whole group discussion, exit tickets, journal writing or think-pair-share.			

Jay McClain, Principal, Bailey's Elementary School, FCPS, Falls Church, Virginia - Access template online

227

4th Grade Remediation Plan
A McNair Elementary Case Study Artifact

Math	Reading	Social Studies	Duration of the Program	People Responsible for Implementation	SOL Data
• "Club" Fridays will be for 30 minutes every week. Based on our exit tickets and assessments we will create groups to go to a certain "club" that will be run by one of the fourth grade teachers. Each teacher will be guiding a certain concept in math. • Morning time (2 teachers) or quiet time (2 teachers) will be used for 15 minutes of remediation for students. • Our math resource specialist is pulling students every Monday for thirty minutes. • We will offer math tutoring for students once a week in the afternoon from 3:35-4:35 pm	• Students below reading level are being seen twice a week by the reading specialist. After lunch, students are reading independently for 10-15 minutes while the teacher focuses on at-risk readers. • During the student's morning routine, the teacher is pulling at-risk readers for running records.	We will begin a Social Studies remediation group (Junior Virginians) in the mornings once a week for 1 hour.		**David** 4th Grade Advanced Academics Teacher **Nicole** 4th Grade Advanced Academics Teacher **Deb** 4th Grade Teacher **Alex** 4th Grade Teacher **Georgina** ESOL Teacher	<table><tr><th>Content</th><th>Scores</th></tr><tr><td>Reading</td><td>71.4%</td></tr><tr><td>Math</td><td>83.3%</td></tr><tr><td>Social Studies</td><td>76.0%</td></tr></table>

6th Grade Intervention/Enrichment Plan
A McNair Elementary Case Study Artifact

Grade/Subject _____   Dates _____   Action Plan _____

SIP Goal: We will implement a schoolwide intervention and enrichment block to meet AYP proficiency goals of 89% in reading and 87% in math and to increase the percentage of pass advanced students by 10% over the next school year in each grade level.

Student Names	Student Data	Instructional Goals	Strategies, Actions, Resources, and Evidence
Suzanna, Robert, Arnav, John, Juan, Pete, Rohan, Bruce, Amir, Tom, Amy, Anya, Jose, Raina, Bob, Jack, Chaya, Nicole	Test score 70% and below	6.4 Compare and order whole numbers, fractions, and decimals	• Reviewed test • Practiced skills and computations with teacher-made compare and sort games using decimals and fractions and teacher-made ordering fractions by place value matching game. • Decimal Spokes Game with partners • Reassessed with 10 multiple-choice questions
Jaspreet, Shilpa, Keja, Daniel, Suraj, Jenna, Antonio, Ryan, Louis, Ross Patricia, Joseph, Alex, Christine, Anika	Test score between 70% and 85%	6.4 Compare and order whole numbers, fractions, and decimals	• Teacher-made matching and ordering numbers, fractions and decimals game.
Omar, Beza, Karen Marian, Tim, Rishi, Jabeen, Julia, Brandon, Luzia, Dwight, Beth, Laura, Riya, Isabella	Test score above 85%	6.4 Compare and order whole numbers, fractions, and decimals	• Groundworks: Reasoning with Numbers pages 80-86/Grand Sums • Geometer's Sketchpad with Accelerated Learning Specialist using proportions/fractions

Intervention/Enrichment template is available online.

Top Ten Tips
Teaching and Learning in the 21ˢᵗ Century

1. Begin with the end in mind...the end of the year, the end of the unit of study, the end of the lesson. Always ask myself what students are supposed to know as a result of the lessons I plan.

2. Make the use of 10:2 Theory and Wait Time as much a part of my professional practice as brushing my teeth is of my personal life!

3. Help students access and use prior knowledge at the beginning of each new unit of study! Don't ever skip this step!

4. Have students process and summarize their learning inside and outside of class. Use homework as formative assessment data rather than as a management tool.

5. Use a wide range of assessment strategies including pre-assessment. Help students develop strong self-assessment habits.

6. Use the research on differences in learners (learning styles, multiple intelligences, modality preferences, second language learners, etc.) as a check and balance system on my instructional decisions.

7. Make learning active and relevant! Be sure that my students are the workers not spectators watching me work! Help them make real-world connections.

8. Analyze the levels/kinds of thinking required in the learning standards and make sure the questions, learning experiences, assignments, and assessments I design are rigorous and aligned with the thinking required by the standards. Remember to go beyond fact-based teaching.

9. Use student work and classroom assessment data in combination with standardized achievement results to inform my instructional decisions.

10. Always remember: Kids are people and deserve to be treated accordingly. When setting up routines and procedures, focus on learning rather than compliance and control.

Words of Wisdom from Albert Einstein

Not everything that can be measured matters, and not everything that matters can be measured.

Insanity: Doing the same thing over and over again and expecting different results.

We can't solve problems by using the same kind of thinking we used when we created them.

Einstein's words combined with Mike Schmoker's advice to "keep it simple" provide the framework for this chapter.

Data gathering, analysis, and areas of focus include:
- Self-assessment
- Selected formats
  - Action research
  - Common assessments
  - Looking at assignments and student work
  - Assessment walls
- Tools for data-driven discussions and decisions
- Practitioner examples
- Data beyond the text

The use of data to inform practice is discussed in all the previous chapters as well because its use impacts our communication, our collaborative practices, our professional learning, and our classroom practices.

Student Learning is the Goal!

Control and compliance is not the goal! Seat time is not the goal! All students on task is not the goal! It is student learning for which we have to hold ourselves accountable. We must build and use a body of evidence around student learning, including classroom data, data from department, grade level, or district common assessments, as well as state and national assessments.

Analyzing data is not optional and it is not enough. It is the data-driven adjustments we make in our professional practice that make a difference. We must, therefore, get over being defensive about data and use it to inform our practice. It is the decisions we make and the actions we take as a result of the data analysis for which we need to be held accountable.

We need to build expertise at identifying what data is important, the situations in which it is important, and in making sense of it in such a way that it can inform instructional decision making and classroom practice. Whatever data is identified for analysis must be analyzed carefully following the guidelines from best practice in data analysis. Mike Schmoker and Victoria Bernhardt provide us with clear guidelines on how to proceed. Readers should consult their work for in-depth guidance on the process.

The stages we go through to get over being defensive about data to owning the data and the responsibility for responding to that data are varied and depend greatly on the interactions we have had with colleagues in looking at student work, the relationship we have with our supervisors, and our very real anxieties about statistics and numbers in general.

More and more educators are analyzing data, but the stumbling block comes when determining action as a result of the data analysis. In this chapter, readers will find self-assessments, exemplars from practitioners, multiple tools and templates, and points to ponder that are intended to move us to action. Out of the huge body of research on data gathering, analysis, and use, a selected few approaches are explored here. Those are action research, common assessments, looking at assignments and student work, and assessment walls.

How Are We Doing?
Data Analysis and Integration

We use data to:	Skillful Use	Learning to Use	Need to Learn
• build a body of evidence to include classroom, district, state, and national data			
• improve the instructional program			
• provide teachers feedback on the effects of their efforts			
• provide students feedback on their performance			
• develop a common understanding of quality student performance and how close we are to achieving it			
• measure program results, efficiency, and cost effectiveness			
• understand if what we are doing is making a difference over time by tracking students			
• understand if what we are doing is making a difference over time by examining programs, curricula, and departments			
• ensure that students/groups of students "do not fall through the cracks" by disaggregating the data in multiple ways			
• identify cause and effect relationships			
• guide curriculum development, integration, and revision			
• develop School Improvement Plans			
• design professional development plans			
• meet district, state, and federal requirements			

Self Assessment: Data Analysis and Integration template is available online.

Getting Started with
Action Research

In ***Results-Based Professional Development Models***, edited by Brenda Kaylor and available online at www.justaskpublications.com, we learn that action research is:

- A methodical evaluation of topics or issues about teaching and leadership practice and student performance
- Research-based, data-driven, and centered on student learning
- A structure for determining areas of focus for research, for gathering data, and for writing summary reports that describe observations and findings
- Generating information that is talked about, shared with students and colleagues, and acted upon

While action research may be conducted by individuals, the results should be shared with colleagues and impact their practice as well. A team approach to action research could provide valuable school improvement information and probably develop on-site expertise on the selected area of study. ***Results-Based Professional Development Models*** cited above, as well as several ***Tools for Schools*** from Learning Forward (NSDC) and a variety of books from ASCD, provide in-depth information on the action research process.

Possible Purposes of an Action Research Project

- To develop reflective, inquiry-based skills as a professional
- To enhance instructional or leadership decision making
- To pursue, in depth, a topic or research question that is important to you or your students
- To enhance student learning opportunities
- To transfer your discoveries to classroom or leadership practices

Questions to Ask When Selecting a Research Question or Topic

- What questions do I have about instruction, assessment, or leadership either in a general sense or in the context of my own work? (Examples: How should phonics be incorporated in instruction? How should I teach spelling? When/How should I group for math instruction? How do I best support collaborative teams?)
- What issues have I been wrestling with as a teacher or administrator?
- What teaching or leadership methods would I like to investigate more fully in an action research study?
- What topics interest me most?
- Based on student data, what do I/we need to know or learn?

Getting Started with Action Research
Important Questions to Consider

Issue
- What is the focus of your action research?
- Why is this an important challenge or issue?
- What needs to be understood or developed?
- How will learning more about this issue contribute to improved learning for students?

Guiding Questions or Hypotheses
- What do you know already?
- What does research or a review of the literature tell you?
- What question or hypothesis will guide your research?

Methods and Procedures
- What will you do to answer the question?
- How will you do the research and what resources will be used?

Data Gathering and Reporting
- What data will you gather?
- How might that data answer your question?
- How can you ensure that data gathering methods are replicable?
- How can you use multiple sources of data?
- How will you include multiple perspectives?

Data Analysis
- What does the analysis of the data reveal?
- What patterns or trends did you discover?
- What relationships did you see between data?

Action Planning Implications and Significance
- What have you learned and what will you do as a result?

Reporting Results
- What new questions emerged as a result of your study?
- What documentation will you include with your report?
- How will the results be shared with colleagues?

Getting Started with Action Research
Data Collection Possibilities

We are surrounded by data. We need to get over being defensive about it and use it to inform our practice. This list provides a starting point for thinking about the data that is, or could easily be, available to us.

- Pre/post test scores
- Attendance reports
  - Grade distribution sheets
  - Across departments
  - Across teachers
  - Across schools
  - Longitudinal
- Standardized test results
- Student portfolios
  - Across students
  - Same students across time
- Student work
  - Across the same assignments
  - Across grade levels
  - Across schools
  - Across teachers
  - Using rubrics
- Field notes
- Recordings
- Chart patterns over time
- Videos
- Student journals
- Interviews
- Questionnaires
- Surveys
- Review of the literature
- Document analysis
  - Provides perspective
  - Provides context and background
- Case studies
- Chart patterns over time

This information on action research is adapted from *Results-Based Professional Development Models* edited by Brenda Kaylor and published by Just ASK. That text includes information on coaching/mentoring, independent study, inquiry, process, and training models. It is available online at www.justaskpublications.com.

Action Research: A Principal's Perspective
Highly Mobile Students
Julie McVicker

The complexities of Indian Peaks Elementary School, a bi-lingual school in Longmont, Colorado, were immense. Not only was instruction in English and Spanish, 45-60% of students were on free and reduced lunch. Of our total Hispanic population (currently 58%) only about 40% were in bilingual instruction which meant that the remainder was taught in English. In addition, there was a high student turnover rate, mostly during the summer months, but there were also peaks during December and January. The school had between 360-390 students per year, and each year we enrolled and dropped between 110-115 students.

The remarkable aspect of this school was the staff. They were a committed group of individuals who enjoyed working with the students and their families. When I was appointed principal, the teacher turnover rate, however, was 50%. The first summer, I hired 17 teachers out of a staff of 35. As we looked at the data, we confirmed the concern the District and parents had for the school. Neither our English or Spanish-speaking students were doing well academically, but the data for our Spanish learners was particularly bad. Their dismal performance on assessment measures did not help the overall achievement picture of the school.

To address our turnover rate and low levels of student achievement we applied for and received a grant through the Colorado Department of Education, Special Education Unit, and our local BOCES. The goals of this grant were to increase literacy achievement for all students, increase the use of data to affect achievement, and increase collaboration among teachers. We formed a Building Leadership Team that received training and in turn came back to the building to train the staff. During this time, we reconfigured the entire school and began to collaborate on a regular basis. As we learned, we began changing our practice. One of the outcomes of this process was the creation of a pyramid of interventions based on the work of Rick DuFour. We knew that we needed to do a better job of placing students with teachers, based on learning styles, teaching styles, and student needs. We also realized that the students who came to us during the year were placed in classes strictly based on numbers of students already in a teacher's classroom. This led us to create a student placement interview. (See the **Placement Interview** following this report.)

When we began in the mobility action research project, the logistics of how we would accomplish this task were still unknown, but we had talked about rotating the interviews with parents through the staff. The more we thought about this the less we thought it would work. Parents would arrive at the school at any time during the day and we did not want to use a teacher's plan time. The other complicating factor was the language of the parents. Many of our mobile students

Action Research: A Principal's Perspective
Highly Mobile Students

speak Spanish. This meant fewer people were able to help with the interviews.

During the first cycle of our research we clarified the questions we would be asking parents and students. I met with our homeless liaison and added some of the critical information she needed as we determined the status of families. Our hope was to create a document that could be used district-wide to help schools better know their families and children and serve their needs. When we initiated a conversation with our Department of Learning Services, they were overwhelming supportive.

Again, the question of logistics arose. Who would interview the family and when? After many conversations with our bilingual counselor, we came up with a tentative plan. We did our first interviews together so we were consistent in our approach to the questions. If we were available, we would do the interview when the parents arrived at the school to enroll their child. Of course, this would not always be the case, so we agreed that during this first cycle, if we weren't available our records clerk would set up an appointment for the family to meet with us. Our goal was to get the interview done as soon as possible so we could thoughtfully place the child with a teacher and get them started right away.

Our first new student arrived when we were both in the office. She was a third grader, named Sabrina, whose father worked construction. During the interview with Sabrina and her mother, we learned that this was Sabrina's 7th school as her family would move as the father was sent to different states or parts of states to work on jobs. We decided that she needed a stable teacher and a classroom that had a community environment. Our counselor trains all our classes in conflict resolution and knows the students well. We chose a classroom that had empathetic students who were good at welcoming new students. While we felt good about Sabrina's placement, we were still struggling about what to do with the rest of the information gathered. Our musings included how to get information to the teacher in a timely manner and determining which other service agencies might provide appropriate support for the family.

Our next new student was a cousin of a student currently enrolled in our school. Josie was attending a school across town and her mother wanted her to come to Indian Peaks because her sister liked our school for her sons. Josie had attendance problems in her previous schools. Indian Peaks was to be her third school as a second grader. During the interview we were able to address the attendance issue and the impact of constantly changing schools. Josie's mother had made arrangements for her sister to bring Josie to school and Josie's mother would pick her up. We felt that this would assure Josie's daily attendance based on the attendance of the sister's children. All in all we felt our first two

Action Research: A Principal's Perspective
Highly Mobile Students

conversations with parents were successful.

The third new student was part of a Spanish-speaking family. Lisa conducted the interview alone and shared the information with me. It took us three days to schedule an interview. When we realized how long it would be before they could meet, we started the student. We placed him based on the information provided by the record's clerk. Obviously, this was not what we had planned but the student needed to get started in school.

Lisa and I were also discovering that some of the questions we were asking were difficult for parents to answer. After some revision, we were ready to try again. We also felt that we each knew how we wanted the interviews to go and the type of information we wanted to receive. At this point we decided that we could do the interviews individually. We were still struggling about what to do with the information besides using it to place students. We knew we needed to get to the teacher before the student started school but again, logistics questions started. How, when, and what specifics would we share?

As we started our second cycle we revised the questions, had a plan to get information to the teachers, and felt better about conducting the interviews. The teachers were anxious to get the information on their new students so were willing to meet at lunch, plan time, recess, or after school. Most of our new students during this cycle were from Spanish-speaking families so Lisa conducted the interviews. We were able to place students with teachers who matched their learning styles. Our students who stay with us are used to having students come in and out during the year and the teachers have prepared them to be helpful. They use a buddy system within the classroom and then a group of students to help on the playground and lunchroom. As I was in the lunchroom daily, I made sure to check up on the new students to see if they had questions and to ensure that the other students were being helpful.

It is clear that the interviews started students and families off on a positive note with the school. We developed relationships with the families and we knew much more about the circumstances of their lives. While we may not have prevented children from moving, we did make their time at our school productive, worthwhile, and caring. We helped them access services in the community, and they knew we were here to help. The student was placed in a class that we felt best met his/her needs and the transitions went much smoother. The students appeared to be happy with their class and teacher and exhibited well adjusted behaviors. They knew the expectations of our school up front and were not surprised about the quality of work or homework required. We were able to help them with school supplies, as needed, or clothing because

Action Research: A Principal's Perspective
Highly Mobile Students

of our community connections. They felt that we cared about them personally.

A logical next step would be the development of an exit interview to get the perspective of parents and students leaving Indian Peaks. Once again, logistics would be key to making this an effective practice. How would we get them to the families and get them returned? Should it be a personal interview? Would families that are moving give us the time to talk with them regarding their experiences here? Helping teachers make transitions smooth for children is always an area for growth. Another possible next step would be providing after- or before-school interventions for those students who are significantly behind because of mobility.

This process has made me realize how important it is to establish good communication with families and students as they come into a new school setting. The relationships we established were invaluable and worked to improve the education of the children.

A summary of this action research project was included in the Colorado Department of Education's report: **Colorado Educators Study Homeless and Highly Mobile Students**. Access it at: www.cde.state.co.us/cdeprevention/download/pdf/COPAR%20Book%20Fin al%204-25-05.pdf.

The introduction to the report reads: In 2003-04, the Daniels Fund, in partnership with the Colorado Department of Education and the Center for Research Strategies, sponsored a year-long professional development opportunity for school teams to focus on homelessness and high mobility issues using participatory action research. A total of 17 teachers, principals, a school social worker and an education director at a youth shelter comprised this cohort for the school year. The expectations of the "Colorado Participatory Action Research," or COPAR, project were demanding, as it required six full days of class work supplemented with individual research, planning, and implementation in between class sessions. Self-reflection and dialogue among the group members and with the facilitator were integral to the flow of the project.

At year's end, each of the nine sites reported their processes, insights and conclusions. Their heartfelt stories of action and research comprise the following chapters. They detail their year-long engagement, questions, struggles, ahas! and action steps.

Highly Mobile School
Placement Interview
Julie McVicker

Child's name _____ **Date** _____

Parent's Name _____ **Grade** _____

Educational Background

What is the child called at home?

Who are the members of the child's family? Who among these lives with the child?

Who should receive communications from the school that concerns the child?

How should these communications be made?

Who will respond to communications from the school? How will those communications be made?

How many schools has your child attended?

Has your child had any disciplinary referrals? If so, for what?

Has your child been in any special programs?
- ☐ Special Education (IEP or 405 Plan)
- ☐ Title I
- ☐ Literacy Plan
- ☐ Gifted/Talented
- ☐ Preschool: ____ Head Start ____ Child Find
- ☐ Other _____

Is your child currently on a literacy plan?

Placement Interview

Language

What language did your child first speak?

What language was your child instructed in at their last school?

How much English does your child speak?

Learning Style

What would you like me to know about your child?

What do you see as areas of strength for your child?

What do you see as areas in need of improvement for your child?

Describe the teacher with whom your child has been the most successful.

How does your child learn best?

Health

Does your child have her immunizations?

Is your child on any medications? Will he be taking them at school?

Does your child have any severe allergies?

Has your child been hospitalized in the last 2 years? If so, for what?

Are there medical issues/concerns we should be aware of?

Does your child have insurance?
- ☐ Medicaid
- ☐ Child Health Plan Plus (CHP+)
- ☐ Private Insurance
- ☐ None

Placement Interview

Behavioral Concerns

What type of discipline is used at home?

What works?

Legal

Are there any legal issues/custody issues (arrangements)?

Is there a current restraining order?

Parent Involvement

What do you hope your child will get out of school this year?

In what ways do you think you can help at home to support your child's education?

What roles do you see parents having at the school site to support the education of their children?

What can a school do to make you feel welcome?

Interview conducted by _____

Language in which interview was conducted _____

Attendees _____

Highly Mobile School Placement Interview template is available online.

Points to Ponder
Common Assessments FAQs
Bruce Oliver

An emphasis on assessment practices is all around us. All the ideas sound promising, but there are so many that one wonders how we can keep all the ideas straight. New terminology is flooding the articles, books, and workshops giving fresh, and potentially overwhelming, ways to look at how students are assessed. Assessments are described as transformative, in-the-moment, formative, summative, and balanced. There are power assessments, system-level assessments, and benchmark assessments. Even the most dedicated and open-minded individual may find it impossible to keep all of the ideas straight or to know where and how to start using the information.

There is, however, one practice that seems to be sensible, reliable, and most promising to positively impact student learning. This practice is the consistent development and use of common assessments by teams of teachers. When teachers take the time to clearly investigate and understand how common assessments can augment student achievement, they become excited and motivated to continue their collaborative work. Educators often have questions about how to get started with common assessment. Below are FAQ's along with some suggestions as to how to bring the concept alive and sustain its use.

What is a common assessment?
A common assessment is a uniform tool developed and administered in a given time frame by all teachers in a grade level or course. The assessment includes various types of questions to measure students' understanding of essential knowledge. After administering the assessment, the teachers score the students' work and compile the results. Data from the assessments are shared at a team or department meeting in order to determine how teachers should respond to the assessment data. Ultimately, the goal is to use assessment data to provide immediate feedback and support to students in order to ensure student learning and academic progress.

What is the purpose of using common assessments?
The goal of using common assessments is to ensure that the continual focus is on higher levels of achievement for all students. When teachers develop and use common assessments, they must provide all students with access to the same essential knowledge and skills regardless of who their teacher is. When teachers openly talk about the content they teach, there is a greater likelihood that all students will have a common educational experience. After there is concurrence on the content that must be taught, teachers create assessments that accurately measure student learning. The professional dialogue which occurs while the results of the assessments are analyzed is an important payoff from this collaborative process.

Points to Ponder
Common Assessments FAQs

How are common assessments developed?

Common assessments may be developed in a variety of ways. Some teachers create assessments by having each team member bring possible assessment questions to a planning meeting. Others provide questions from previous assessments they have used to determine if previous questions accurately and adequately measure student learning. Still others review possible assessment items from released questions from former statewide assessments. Finally, some districts create common assessments centrally and schools are required to use district-wide common assessments. Regardless of how the assessment is developed, what is most important is that all teachers teach the same knowledge and skills, and that all teachers teaching the same content work together to create assessments which are clearly matched to standards.

What forms can common assessments take?

Common assessments may take a variety of forms depending on the standards, the curriculum being taught, the make-up of the student population, and the desired outcomes. Assessments may include multiple choice questions, require students to respond to essay questions or writing prompts, or be performance-based in nature. However, common assessments should not be excessively long, unnecessarily complicated, or hard to analyze. Regardless of what form the assessment may take, the main purpose of the assessment is to determine if the students are mastering the required standards.

What are some misconceptions about common assessments?

Some teachers who are just learning about common assessments have misunderstandings about what they are and how they should be used. Misconceptions include the following:

- **Common assessments are used to "grade" the teacher**. Some teachers feel that they become vulnerable when the results from the common assessment are publicly presented and discussed with fellow teachers. They feel that the data from the assessments may be used to evaluate their effectiveness as a teacher. This practice by leaders would be a step backward. The purpose of common assessments is to encourage honest, open dialogue among practitioners and the sharing of best practices. The misuse of data from those discussions as part of a teacher's evaluation will only lead to distrust among the teaching staff and cause teachers to be more isolated.

- **Every assessment must be a common assessment**. Teachers who develop and utilize common assessments still maintain individual autonomy to develop and use additional assessments that will help them measure

Points to Ponder
Common Assessments FAQs

student learning.

- **Common assessments require lockstep pacing and uniform instruction on the parts of teachers**. When teachers agree to devise and administer common assessments, it is important for the assessment to be given to students within a certain window of time. However, teaching is not a mechanical process and students are not all the same. Thus, a teacher must pace instruction to meet the needs of his or her students. While it is true that the teachers must teach the same standards, teachers do not have to deliver their lessons in the same exact manner as their peers. Just as students learn differently, individual teachers have different skills, different stories and examples, and different methods of teaching their content.

- **Common assessments will require an inordinate amount of extra work**. Some teachers believe that common assessments are extra assessments above and beyond the assessments they already use. Teachers should not be required or feel the necessity to develop more or different assessments. Teachers who have worked with their peers over time in the development of common assessments actually have found that the practice is a time saver. When teachers jointly develop an assessment, the questions are often clearer, they accurately measure student learning, and they may be used when the content or unit is taught again.

How should teachers analyze the data from common assessments?

Collaborative teams can analyze the results from common assessments in several ways:

- Some teams compile data question-by-question and look at student responses to each question. The ensuing conversations can help teachers identify the instructional methods that were most effective in leading to student understanding.

- Some teams bring samples of student work to team meetings and sort the work into different categories based on whether student work was above standard, met the standard, or was below standard. Once again, the close examination of the work and agreement on levels of achievement can result in a more consistent evaluation of student learning.

The truly important part of the analysis of assessment data is the accompanying discussions to determine which specific teaching methods elicited the greatest results.

What should teachers do with the results from common assessments?

Thomas Guskey, who writes extensively about assessment practices, has noted that assessments by themselves do little to improve student learning. He

Points to Ponder
Common Assessments FAQs

stresses that "what really counts happens after the assessments." Some grade level or curriculum teams develop what Rick DuFour calls a "pyramid of interventions" of student support strategies. These responses provide timely assistance so every student can move toward higher achievement. Possible interventions include:

- Small group or one-on-one instruction by an individual teacher
- Small group or one-on-one instruction by a student or students
- Use of all time during the school day – before school tutoring, instruction during a designated support period in the school day, or after school support sessions
- Feedback to students and the opportunity to be reassessed to determine if a higher level of achievement has been reached

What are some unique practices related to common assessments that schools are using?

Some creative and potentially effective strategies are being carried out in schools across the country. Here are some options schools may wish to explore:

- One practice that has shown some positive results is **advanced planning**. As teachers teach their current unit, they meet to collaborate on a future unit. They discuss the standards all teachers must address and create common assessments prior to the beginning of the next unit. When teachers know well in advance how students' learning will be assessed, they can plan instruction that is more likely to lead to improved student learning and success on assessments.
- While some teachers develop common assessments that are more in line with state-required multiple choice tests, other teachers have developed rubrics to measure success rates on common assessments.
- Some schools have found success in having short, weekly common assessments (five questions) so that teachers are able to respond to student misunderstandings more quickly.
- Successful collaborative teams have made an adjustment in their way of thinking in that they focus on **results** and not **intentions**.
- When teachers "begin with the end in mind," they complete a task analysis during the planning process and create their assessment(s) at the beginning of the planning process. As they instruct, they frame their learning so that students can be successful when they complete their assessment(s). The result is that remediation, intervention, and follow-up are minimized or non-existent because students are successful the first time around.

When teachers meet together to develop common assessments, it is essential that there be explicit trust among the participating members. Confidentiality is

Points to Ponder
Common Assessments FAQs

paramount if teachers are willing to share their thoughts, and perhaps doubts, with their peers. The work to develop these assessments may be rocky or frustrating. But with persistence, the collaborative efforts can lead to powerful and exciting learning on the parts of determined professionals. Rick DuFour has stated, "Hosts of researchers have concluded that substantive change inevitably creates discomfort and dissonance as people are asked to act in new ways." No important change can occur without some frustration and hard work. The subsequent learning that can occur from the development and use of common assessments can transform the way teachers teach and assess, and lead to unforeseen results previously unattained.

These remarks, written by Bruce Oliver, were originally published in the November 2008 issue of *Just for the ASKing!* All eighty issues of *Just for the ASKing!* are available at no charge at www.justaskpublications.com.

Looking at Assignments and Student Work

Much has been written about ways to productively look at student work in collaborative settings. When teachers engage in these processes, it makes a great deal of sense for the principal to sit in on the meetings. Several of the protocols or processes currently in use are described below.

Education Trust's Standards in Practice

Education Trust created this process to help teachers align classroom work with standards. The scoring tool is used to focus participants on the quality of classroom assignments and their direct connection with standards. Use of this approach can help teachers design rigorous assignments. Analysis of student products helps identify adjustments needed in the assignment directions and levels of teacher support needed to ensure student success. The process is:

- The teacher presenting the assignment explains how and when the assignment was given and what the students were expected to learn as a result of completing the assignment. The presenting teacher also spends a few minutes working through the problem or explaining what the response should look like.

- The collaborative group asks questions about the assignment. They in essence do a task analysis of what students would have to know and be able to do to successfully complete the assignment.

- Next the group identifies the standards, benchmarks, and level of thinking required by the task using Bloom's Taxonomy.

- The team then generates a rubric or other scoring tool to describe successful completion of the assignment.

- The teacher presents student work from the assignment and the team scores the work using the scoring tool they have generated.

- After the scoring, the group discusses possible revisions to the assignment and what to do about students who did not demonstrate competency with the standards the assignment addressed.

The last step in the Education Trust process is quite different from traditional practice around the data obtained from student work. In the past the norm was to simply record the number correct or the grade in the grade book and move on. While planning standards-based instruction is a challenge in and of itself, revision of instruction and assignments as a result of the analysis of student work requires a completely new way of thinking and working. Discussions about the significance of this shift provide learning opportunities for both teachers and administrators.

Looking at Assignments and Student Work

Project Zero
Steve Seidel and his colleagues at Harvard's Project Zero created a process that provides opportunities for teachers to examine and discuss pieces of student work in structured conversation with their peers, coaches, and supervisors.

Project Zero's Collaborative Assessment Conference
- **Getting Started**: The presenting teacher or team shares copies of the selected student work without making comments about the work or the assignment.
- **Describing the work**: The other participants examine the work and describe what they notice without making any judgments about the quality of the work or their personal preferences.
- **Raising questions**: They then pose questions about the student, the assignment, the curriculum, etc. The teacher/team members take notes but do not respond. The participants "guess" what the child was working on when he/she created the piece. This could include the standards, benchmarks, and indicators on which the student was focused or the skills the child was trying to master, questions the child was trying to answer, or ideas he/she was trying to express.
- **Teacher response**: The teacher or team responds to the comments made in the review process. She/they provide information to clarify intent and contextual background, engage in reflective discussion with the reviewers and ask their own questions.
- **Closing the Conference**: The group reflects on their learning and the process. The presenting teacher's efforts and presentation are acknowledged. The implications of this process for teaching, learning, and leading are tremendous. Attention and energy is appropriately focused on the work of students and of the school. It requires that there be a high level of trust in the competence and benevolence of all participants and that the presenting teacher or team of teachers not be defensive about data, data analysis and questioning.

Resources for Looking at Student Work
- www.lasw.org (lasw = looking at student work) This website features the collaborative assessment conference and provides multiple links to related web sites.
- www.annenberginstitute.org/Products/list.php

Looking at Assignments and Student Work

Writing Rubrics Using Student Work

This process is a productive way to engage staff in collegial discussions about student work and to establish consistency across teachers about what work does and does not meet the standards of performance established by the school community. As the educational leader, you can either facilitate or participate in these discussions and at the same time gather data about the thinking of teachers about what excellent work looks like. These discussions help staff meet school goals of consistently clear and high expectations, provide the opportunity for informal professional development for staff, and the teaching staff leaves the meeting with rubrics ready for classroom use.

The Process

- Sort the work into broad categories: excellent, okay, and needs work.
- Identify two or three strong examples of each category.
- Start with the excellent examples and list the attributes that make them excellent.
- Continue the process with the okay and needs work examples.
- Write these attributes into a holistic rubric.
- Be sure that an attribute listed in any one category is also listed in the other two. If you want to turn your holistic rubric into an analytical rubric, sort by attributes and assign a rating to each of the attributes.

Getting Started

The ninth grade English team at West Springfield High School, Springfield, Virginia, developed a rubric to assess student writing. On Thursdays they had a brown bag lunch and scored the work of each other's students using the rubric they designed.

Teachers in Churchville-Chili School District, Churchville, New York, examined second grade student work using a district-wide writing rubric. A collection of student writing samples from September, November, January, and March were scored and the ratings recorded in a different color for each month. This enabled them to see growth over time and to pose questions as to what the data told them and to design next steps in working with those students.

Looking at Assignments and Student Work 3-D Teams

These Data-Driven Decision (3-D) Teams are groups of teachers who meet once or twice a month to review and analyze student work in an effort to use data to make solid instructional decisions. These teams may be grade level teams, departmental teams, vertical teams, or collaborative teams from multiple schools. The analysis, reflection, and collegial collaboration provides a framework for decision making about future instruction. This practice is a particularly useful tool for teachers who are striving for consistency across classrooms in a standards-based learning and assessment environment.

The group members bring samples of student work to the meeting. Hanson, Silver and Strong, in descriptions of their **Authentic Achievement Teams**, suggest that each teacher bring six pieces of students' work to the meeting; they further recommend that the samples represent different achievement levels or different levels of success on this particular assignment. For example, two might be from the top third of a class, two from the middle, and two from the bottom. An alternative approach would be to analyze the work of "regular" students and that of ESL, advanced, or inclusion students. It is also helpful to bring copies of any directions given to the students.

If the group members have not planned together, ten to fifteen minutes are spent looking through the student work samples and any teacher artifacts so that all participants get a good idea of what kind of work they will be discussing and analyzing.

The participants can agree to analyze all the work of their students around the same set of criteria, or each teacher can indicate the questions, concerns, or criteria to be considered for that set of student work. In either case, the outcomes of the discussion might be directed toward:

- checking for **validation** about the appropriateness of the work for the developmental stage of the students
- checking to ensure that the task is **congruent** with the stated mastery objective and/or state or district standards
- checking for **consistency** of opinion about the assessment and evaluation of the work
- possible **adjustments** in teacher directions and **support** for all/some of the students

Assessment Walls
Heather Clayton Kwit

One way to involve teachers in the ongoing collection and analyzing of student achievement data is through the use of assessment walls. Linda J. Dorn and Carla Soffos in their book **Shaping Literate Minds**, talk about the use of an "assessment wall" to make the data they are collecting visible. As cited in their book, the idea for the assessment wall was adapted from the work of David Kerbow and colleagues at the Center for School Improvement in Chicago. By making the data accessible, teachers can readily study learning trends among groups and analyze students' progression in learning relative to the established standards.

This assessment wall concept was adopted and modified to support teacher analysis of student learning data, specifically in the area of reading, in two schools in Greece Central School District, New York. These assessment walls (See below) had three pocket charts hanging side by side where there was a large section of wall space. Along the top row of the pocket charts were cards representing the various reading levels using Fountas and Pinnell's leveling system (A-Z). Each child in the school had an individual card, color-coded to match their current grade level. The students' reading level was written on their card, and their card was placed under the corresponding level in the charts. All students in a particular grade level were on the same rows, so trends could easily be seen. Bold letters (P, S, and V) represent the desired minimum performance levels for exiting grades 3, 4, and 5 respectively. The students' levels were updated frequently, and cards were then moved along the assessment wall.

Template for Our Assessment Walls

A	B	C	D	E	F	G	H	I	J	K	L	M	N	O	**P**	Q	R	**S**	T	U	**V**	W	X	Y	Z

Third grade cards placed along these rows

Fourth grade cards placed along these rows

Fifth grade cards placed along these rows

Assessment Walls

The first step in implementing assessment walls is ensuring that staff members understand the rationale for using assessment walls. Rationale for assessment walls include:

- Makes the data visible
- Allows teachers to see the trends within specific groups of students
- Allows teachers to see how students are progressing in reading in relation to the desired performance levels
- Becomes a tool for determining the root causes of specific students' difficulties with reading
- Provides information that can be used to effectively group students (i.e., into classes, or within classes, into specific reading groups)
- Allows staff to allocate resources where they are needed the most
- Serves as a record for individual student's reading progress

In addition, it is important for teachers to know that time will be dedicated to moving their students' cards along the wall and work within and across grade levels to analyze trends, problem solve, and decide how to allocate resources.

Preparing Student Cards for the Assessment Wall

Place student name on one side of each 2x3 card and the teacher's name of the other side of the card. When placing the cards on the assessment wall, the students' name should go inward, and the teacher's name should be on the outside. The purpose for this is two-fold. First, the teacher can readily find his/her cards when updating students' reading levels on the wall. Also, for anyone glancing at the assessment wall, it remains confidential as to which student is performing at which reading level.

On the side of the card that is facing outward, staff may choose to code certain subgroups of students, which will in turn assist with analyzing the trends for certain groups of students. Small colored dot labels, available at office supply stores, work well for this. For instance, you may want to code your English language learners, students with special needs, students who receive academic intervention services, or students who have just transferred into your school. The subgroups you choose to look at more closely is an individual decision, likely based on what your school's data is telling you about student performance in each of these subgroups.

As a staff, once you have determined the purpose for your assessment wall and what data you would like to gather, you need to establish benchmarks for students' performance. In this instance, the assessment wall was designed to show students' performance in reading; therefore, our staff needed to establish

Assessment Walls

the desired minimum performance levels for students exiting that grade level. Once we set these performance levels, we had to decide on a consistent way of gathering ongoing assessment data relative to your goals. In this instance, running reading records were used as the tool.

Establishing Benchmarks and Placing Cards on the Wall

At the first assessment wall meeting, teachers brought with them the most up-to-date assessment data on each of their students. We initially held grade level team meetings, then later we met with cross grade level groups. In this example, teachers filled out each student's card with the date and their current reading level near the top of the card to allow room for more dates and levels to be added throughout the year. Once all levels were filled in, students' cards were placed on the wall.

Analyzing and Updating the Data on the Assessment Wall

Once all data has been placed on the assessment wall, teachers then have the opportunity to reflect on what they see, and use this information to set goals for the future. In subsequent meetings, teachers would begin by pulling down all of their individual students' cards, updating the students' current reading levels, and placing students' cards back on the wall. Once the data has been reviewed, goals are set as well as timelines for updating the data on the assessment wall. It is important for teachers to know the dates the data will be updated, so that they can be prepared with current information about each student. Also, it shows them that time will be given to update and review trends in students' performance.

Questions to Anchor Discussions about Data

- Before we begin to analyze the data, what do you predict we will see? Why do you think that?
- What are some of our observations of the data?
- When looking across the data, what are some trends we see?
- What can we infer from looking at our data?
- What are some measurable goals we can set?
- What are some accountability measures we will include for ourselves to help us reach our goals?
- Are there important findings on our assessment wall that would inform how we are allocating both human and instructional resources?

Assessment Walls

- What moves did you make on the assessment wall today that you are especially proud of?
- Based on the data you see, which individual students will you target for support? How will this influence your instruction with these particular students? What specific actions will you take as a result?

Tips for Using Assessment Walls

Assessment walls can be used to measure any number of trends, based on what data you have used to decide what to study and improve. The key is for the assessment wall to be visible, and for it to be frequently updated and reflected on; you want your assessment wall to become a living representation of how your students are doing. To make that happen:

- Place your assessment wall in a location large enough to hold groups of teachers. You will need to be able to sit and view the wall in order to reflect on the data.
- If you do not have a space large enough, consider making your wall portable by hanging pocket charts on chart stands and then moving the charts to your meeting location.
- Have your goals and desired performance levels displayed in a prominent place near your wall. It is important to always keep your goals at the forefront.
- At the end of the school year, consider moving cards up to the next grade level (therefore changing your color coding). By doing so over subsequent years, you will have an excellent form of documentation of students' progress. Therefore, it is important to write small enough on the cards so that data over more than one year could be included.
- Just as it is important that teachers collaboratively decide on how they will collect their assessment data, it may be necessary to provide training so that everyone is using a consistent protocol. By doing so, your data will be more reliable.

Framework for Team Meeting
Establishing Reading Benchmarks

Timeframe	25 minutes
Preparation	• Bring the exiting reading standard or desired minimum performance level for that particular grade level as well as the grade level preceding it (i.e., for a third grade team meeting, bring the exiting standard in reading for second grade *and* for third grade)
Agenda	• Discuss the rationale for the meeting (1 minute) • Review the exiting standards for the current grade level and the previous grade level (1 minute) • Using exiting standards as a guide, identify benchmarks, or where students should be in November, January, and March, in relation to where they are expected to be in September and June (5 minutes) • Identify the formative assessment measures that will be used consistently across the grade level to determine if students have met the benchmark (i.e. running reading records) (5 minutes) • Identify how the data around the number of students not meeting, meeting, and exceeding the benchmarks will be shared in subsequent meetings (10 minutes) • Share the follow-up meeting date and what teachers are expected to bring to meeting (3 minutes)
Follow-up	• In subsequent meetings, teachers prepare to share in the agreed upon format the number of students not yet meeting the benchmark, meeting the benchmark, and exceeding the established benchmark • Teachers prepare to share instructional and learning strategies that have been effective • Teachers prepare to brainstorm new strategies and interventions for students who have not met established benchmarks

Framework for Team Meeting
Updating Data on the Assessment Wall

Timeframe	25 minutes
Preparation	• Teachers bring current reading levels for each child in their classroom based on results of a running reading record (ideally given in the week before updating the data)
Agenda	• Teachers pull down their students' cards and fill in the new date and students' new reading levels. Teachers should make a note as to which students have not been making progress so that information can inform their instructional planning (5 minutes) • Once data is on the wall, teachers reflect and discuss what they see in the data using some of the guiding questions (see pages 260-287) (15 minutes) • Based on the data, teachers set individual goals and actions they will take to support any students who are not making consistent and adequate progress (3 minutes)
Follow-up	• Share the follow-up meeting date and have teachers record their individual goals prior to that meeting date to take with them and use for instructional planning (2 minutes)

The next 15 pages feature a variety of tools for holding data-driven discussions and making data-driven decisions that translate into classroom and school-wide practice.

A Principal's Perspective
Key Data Sources
Heather Clayton Kwit

It is key to look at multiple measures of data, and to not focus on the results of only one measure, such as standardized test results. According to Douglas Reeves, examination of standardized test scores is not enough. Drawing inferences on multiple sources allows you to determine if it is truly an issue in student learning needing to be addressed, versus a misalignment of curriculum, standards, and state assessments. Similarly, it allows educators to determine the root cause of student learning issues. Looking at student achievement results within the context of the entire school will have a greater impact on improving the learning of students.

Reeves, in his book *Accountability in Action*, also stresses the importance of looking at cohort data, by comparing students to themselves rather than to different students. For instance, teachers analyzing data ask questions like "What percentage of our students have made gains of one or more grade levels in reading?" or "Of the number of students who weren't meeting standards in writing a year ago, what percentage are now meeting or exceeding the standards?" With so many rich data sources at our fingertips, one needs to be strategic about how to gather and organize the data so that it is easily accessible, understood, and analyzed.

When analyzing demographics consider:
- Number of students in school/per grade level
- Number of students moving in and out of the school/district (mobility rate)
- Class size/Ratio of student to teacher
- Absenteeism for students and teachers
- Tardies
- Gender
- Ethnicity/Race
- Free and reduced lunch rate
- Number of students with special needs
- Number of students who speak a second language
- Number of students attending preschool
- Social histories of students
- Truancy
- Number of suspensions
- Retention rates
- Dropout rates
- Graduation rates
- Post-graduation employment
- Number of students enrolled in extracurricular activities
- Number of students in advanced placement courses

A Principal's Perspective
Key Data Sources

- Number of students employed during high school

When analyzing student learning and achievement consider:
- Standardized tests
- Norm-referenced tests
- Criterion-referenced tests
- District tests
- Teacher-created tests
- Teacher-assigned report card grades
- Student portfolios
- Performance assessments

When analyzing perceptions consider:
- Survey results
- Questionnaires
- Interviews with staff, students, parents and community members
- Observations
- Meetings with focus groups

When analyzing school processes:
- Resources being used to implement curriculum
- Instructional programs being implemented
- Extracurricular and co-curricular programs being implemented
- Instructional strategies used by teachers
- Learning strategies used by students
- Assessment practices
- Allocation of human and financial resources
- Groupings of students
- Library/Media Center usage

Data Analysis for Instructional Decision Making
Heather Clayton Kwit

Much of the rest of this chapter is devoted to examples and tools you can use to analyze data for instructional decision making. You will find resources to:

- Identify and analyze general trends or patterns observed. These patterns might be:
  - Identify percentage or number of advanced proficient, proficient, and not proficient
  - Disaggregate data by demographics such as gender, ethnicity, time in district, English language proficiency, students on IEPs, and free and reduced lunch, etc. (required by No Child Left Behind Act of 2001)
  - Compare current data to data from past assessments at this grade level
  - Complete a longitudinal comparison of the work of individuals or groups of students over time
- Analyze data by subsets such as specific standards, benchmarks, or indicators
- Cause and effect analysis
  - Analyze how and when the assessed concepts, facts, and processes were taught
  - Consider which strategies were used
  - Consider what materials were used
  - Consider how much time was allocated
  - Consider the level of thinking the students/student groups now use and the level required by the assessment
  - Review the alignment of the learning experiences with the knowledge, skills, and level of thinking required by the assessment task
  - Ask what changes need to be made the next time these points are taught or to whom they should be retaught
- Compare classroom assessment data and external assessment data
- Do an item analysis
  - Which items were missed by most students
  - Which items were missed by highest performing students
  - Which items were missed by almost proficient students
  - Which items were missed by special needs students
  - Which items were missed by second language learners
- Create tables that show the data by students, by subgroup, by item, or broader categories such as benchmarks or standards

Following the data analysis, identify the baseline data for which targets will be set. Identify targets, and then make action plans based on what was learned from the data analysis.

Framework for Faculty Meeting Focused on Data Analysis
Heather Clayton Kwit

Timeframe	45 minutes
Preparation	• Distribute meeting agenda • Bring any charts co-constructed at previous meeting • Bring any necessary data and/or student work
Agenda	• Discuss the rationale for the meeting (1 minute) • Review previously identified goals or benchmarks for data being reviewed (1 minute) • Review previous observations from data analysis and strategies/interventions that were identified to support data-based needs (5 minutes) • In collaborative groups, analyze the data and/or student work brought to the meeting (20 minutes) • Brainstorm and chart additional strategies and interventions to address data-based needs, as well as identifying if there are any strategies/interventions that have been ineffective and should be changed (10 minutes) • Establish commitments for the next meeting (8 minutes)
Follow-up	• Publish the commitments that will be revisited at next meeting • Teachers prepare to bring necessary data to next meeting

Data-Driven Dialogue

Phase I

Before looking at the data, access background knowledge.

- I assume...

- I predict...

- I wonder...

Phase II

Study data privately. Record personal observations.

- I observe...

- Some patterns or trends I see...

- I can count...

- I'm surprised to see...

Phase III

Plan intervention and enrichment.

- I believe the data suggests...because...

- Additional data that would help me confirm/verify my explanation is...

- I think appropriate solutions/responses that address needs implied by the data are...

Meg Wagner, Instructional Coach, Fairfax County Public Schools, Virginia
Data-Driven Dialogue template is available online.

Data Reviews
Marcia Baldanza

What to Expect
- A meeting with teams to review progress on a regular basis based on **Data Review Questions**
- An honest conversation about student learning; what they've learned and what they need to learn
- A review for patterns and trends in performance

Why They Are Important
The regular review of student performance data helps us:
- Understand what students know and need to know
- Evaluate progress of school toward important initiatives; grade levels toward team goals; classrooms toward benchmarks by group, gender, and individual
- Communicate with greater accuracy to parents
- Design and assign interventions now before it is too late
- Look at the impact instruction is or is not having
- Provide data for student goal setting
- Look for patterns and trends in learning
- Regroup students for performance
- Reallocate school resources (money, people, and time)

Keep in Mind
Student learning is the goal. Control and compliance is not the goal. Seat time is not the goal. It is student learning for which we hold ourselves accountable. Data reviews are one way to use the body of evidence we collect to change the way we teach.

Analyzing the data is not optional and is not enough. It is the data-driven adjustment we make in our professional practice that must make a difference. We must, therefore, not be defensive about data and use it to inform our practice. It is the decision we make and the action we take as a result of the data analysis for which we are accountable.

> It is not acceptable for us to know a child is failing and not do something about it. Further, conflict avoidance in the face of poor performance is an act of moral neglect.
>
> Michael Fullan, *The Moral Imperative of School Leadership*

Data Review Questions
Marcia Baldanza

General

- What do we know from looking at this data?
- Do we know which students are learning and not learning?
- What patterns can we observe?
- What concerns are raised by a review of the data?
- What other data sources would clarify and inform our teaching practice?
- How do the programs we have in place connect with the concerns identified?
- What can we do about what the data reveal?
- What additional data should we collect?

Specific

- How well, overall, are our students doing on each benchmark?
- Do all of the items on each benchmark have a high percentage of correct answers?
- If not, which items under each benchmark have a high percentage of incorrect answers?
- On the incorrect test items, is there an incorrect answer that was picked by a high percentage of students?
- What kind of mistake is represented by this choice?
- What items do we need to disaggregate to find out if there is a pattern of students not doing well (boys/girls, free lunch, ESL, LD, etc.)?
- Write statements describing your findings using the template below:
  It seems that... because...

Data Review Questions template is available online.

Data Analysis Questions
Julie McVicker

What do these data tell us? What seems to "pop out"?	**What do they not tell us?**
What patterns or trends appear?	**How might we explain this data?**
In what other ways can this data be viewed?	**What's missing?** **Who will collect it- when?** **Who will evaluate it- when?**
What strengths are here to celebrate?	**How does this data compare with what we would hope to see in these areas?**

Data Analysis Questions template is available online.

Cause/Effect Analysis

Cause/Effect Analysis and Revision Planner for Family Unit

Standard: History 6 - Students know that religious and philosophical ideas have been powerful forces throughout history.

Benchmark: 6.1 Know the historical development of religions and philosophies:

Indicator: The student can recognize and describe family customs, traditions, and beliefs.

Desired Effect - What were the **desired** group and/or individual assessment results? Given 100% **Not Proficient** on narrative pre-assessment. At Least 75% of students scoring **Proficient**, or **Above Proficient** and none score **Not Proficient** on overall.

Effect - What were the **actual** group and/or individual assessment results? 88% **Proficient** or **Above Proficient** and 0% **Not Proficient** BUT on narrative post-assessment 28% **Proficient** or **Above Proficient** and 33% **Not Proficient** (structure and technology made a difference)

Cause: Methods

Methods used this time:
- Literature
- Class discussions
- Guest speaker
- Individual family inquiry
- Modeling/scaffolding

Potential changes for next time:
- Concentrate on origin & describing practice
- More modeling
- More peer sharing

Cause: People

People involved this time:
- Teacher
- Peer
- Family

Potential changes for next time:
- Have students interview family about specific family customs, traditions, or beliefs including origins
- Oral sharing with peers before post

Cause: Materials

Materials used this time:
- Paper and pencil
- Computer with KidPix program

Potential changes for next time:
- Better organizer for outlining presentation
- More fine-tuned naming & saving process
- Organization matrix to report responses on pre- and post-assessments

Cause: Time

Time used this time:
- 5 days planning
- 9 days designing
- One session

Potential changes for next time:
- Use timeline for how long to work on each page to help with time management
- Possibly more than one session

Cause/Effect Analysis template is available online.

The Five Whys
Sherri Stephens-Carter

Five Whys is the Japanese philosophy of repeatedly asking why to find not only the direct sources of your problems, but also the root of those sources. It is about thinking long-term and looking both ahead and behind, not just in the present.

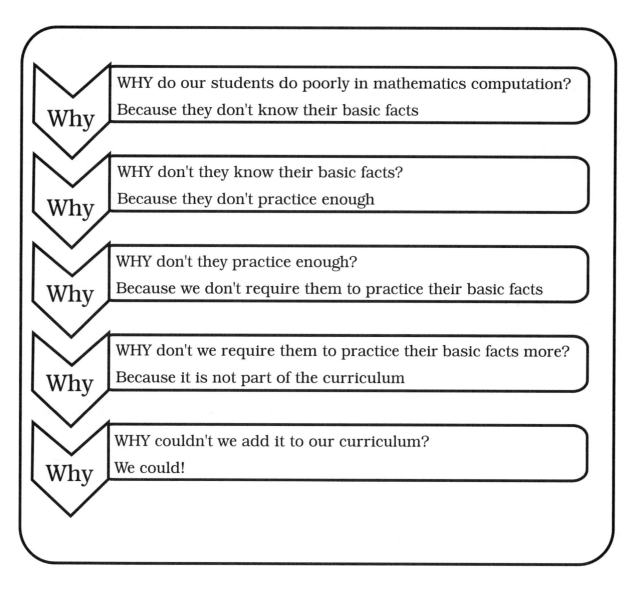

Why
WHY do our students do poorly in mathematics computation?
Because they don't know their basic facts

Why
WHY don't they know their basic facts?
Because they don't practice enough

Why
WHY don't they practice enough?
Because we don't require them to practice their basic facts

Why
WHY don't we require them to practice their basic facts more?
Because it is not part of the curriculum

Why
WHY couldn't we add it to our curriculum?
We could!

Five Whys
Sherri Stephens-Carter

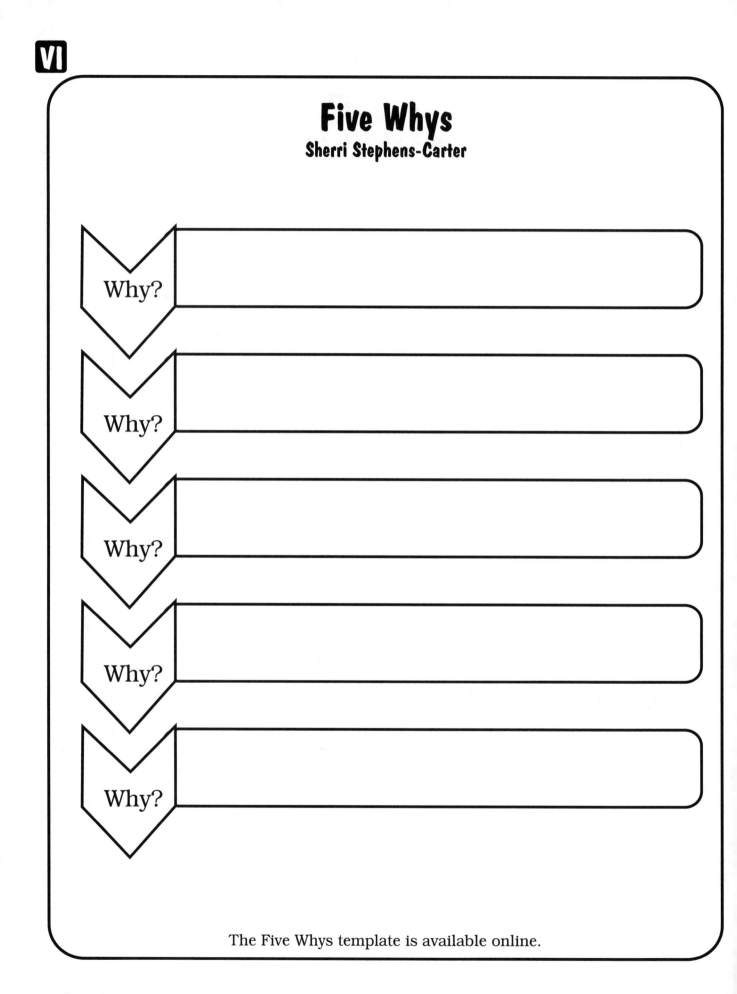

The Five Whys template is available online.

FHN with Data
Sherri Stephens-Carter

Just the Facts

- What do you notice about the data?
- What stands out?
- What surprises you? (Example: The overall trend for all students has been on a downward trend for the last 5 years but is slightly upward for the last 3 years.)
- What are the extremes in the data? Where are the highs and lows? (Example: ELL students had their highest performance in 2009.)

Make 7 factual statements about the data. Make sure to note both facts that we should celebrate and facts of concern.

Facts (F)	Hunches (H)	Next Steps (N)

FHN with Data

Hunches

- What do we think caused the successes or concerns? Consider both because we need to know what to continue and what to change.
- What do we remember about our instruction last year? What seemed to work and what didn't?
- What do we know about our students or our school that could explain the patterns in our data?

Consider the questions above and write down a hunch or two for each fact.

Next Steps

- What should we continue doing that was successful?
- What other information do we need to help us investigate our successes and our concerns?
- What part of this data is important as we set our goals for next year?
- What do we need to know about student achievement that is not apparent in this report? (Example: What is the performance of males and females?)
- Is this the right data for us to be examining? We may need more specific information than this provides or we may need different data completely. What other data or groups should we be looking at?

Now, considering the questions above, write a next step for each set of facts and hunches.

FHN with Data template is available online.

Table of Aggregated Data

English Language Arts 4 Performance Data	
Level of performance	Percentage of students scoring at that level
1	4.0%
2	4.8%
3	50.0%
4	41.2%

Table of Disaggregated Data

Student Subgroup	# Tested	% Proficieny
Total	127	71%
Disability		
General Education	111	71%
Students with disabilities	16	31%
Gender		
Male	69	65%
Female	58	78%
Ethnicity		
African American	6	33%
Hispanic	2	s
Asian or Pacific Islander	2	s
Caucasian	117	74%
American Indian/Alaskan Native	0	n/a
Income Level		
Low Income	26	58%
Not Low Income	101	74%

s = There were fewer than five students in subgroup so data was not reported.

Table of Individual Student Data for State Assessment

Student Name	Multiple Choice (out of 28)	Listening/ Writing (out of 4)	Independent Writing (out of 3)	Reading/ Writing (out of 4)	Mechanics (out of 3)	Holistic Level (3 & 4 proficiency)
Student A	27	3	3	4	3	4
Student B	23	4	3	3	2	3
Student C	20	3	3	2	3	2
Etc.						

Designing SMART Goals
Sherri Stephens-Carter

Specific: The more specific the goal, the more likely to have good results. Instead of improving reading, which part of reading do you want to improve? Instead of raising the reading scores of second language students, find out which sub-groups of second language students need which areas of reading the most.

Measureable: Large scale assessments like state tests provide a once-a-year opportunity to measure. To really see change you need to have ongoing measures (formative assessments) that let you know whether or not the strategies you are using are working.

Attainable: We all want 100% of our students to be proficient in reading, but for most schools, that is a long-term goal. What goal will stretch your current practices but you would still be able to reach?

Relevant: This is about picking the right goal. Have you looked at the root causes of student performance in enough detail to be confident that the goal you have chosen will give you the results you seek?

Time-bound: Be clear about when things need to happen. You need to have a goal for the end of the year and benchmark goals several times throughout the year.

	Nearing Proficient	**Proficient**	**Advanced**
Specific	Goal is general	Goal focuses on specific instructional needs	Goal focuses on specific instructional needs of specific groups
Measureable	There is a single stated measurement stated at the end of the goal	There is a stated measurement for the end of the goal and at least two checkpoints during the process	There is a stated measurement for the end of the goal and at least four checkpoints during the process
Attainable	The goal is either too high and is unlikely to be attained or so low that will not encourage meaningful change	The goal is reasonable for the time given to attain it	The goal will cause the school to stretch practices and/or beliefs
Relevant	No evidence of analysis of the cause of lack of achievement	It is apparent that data appropriate to the goal was analyzed and used to set the goal	It is apparent that multiple views of the data were analyzed in setting the goal. It is apparent that data has been disaggregated by group
Time-bound	There is a single stated time for the end of the goal	There is a stated time for the end of the goal and at least two checkpoints during the process	There is a stated time for the end of the goal and at least four checkpoints during the process

Indian Peaks 1st Grade 3rd Trimester Action Plan

School Goal: 60-63% of students will be reading at or above grade level

Student Names

Ariel	Paul
Derek	Sean
Jordan	Vanessa
Kai	
Luis	
Michael	
Marisa	
Nathaniel	

Alyssa
Chan
Chris
Tam
William

Don
Kelly
Sarah

Student Data

- Students still scoring at 2-3 level on Retelling Rubric (proficient basic/proficient)
- Focus: Verbal expression of ideas without prompting

- Reading/recognizing words at .50 level
- Goal: reading at .50-.75 fluently

- Reading/recognizing words at .25 level
- Identifying beginning sounds - "slide to the end of the word" (sound blending)
- Identifying when words/phrases do not make sense

Instructional Goals

Retell a story in logical, sequential order - including beginning, middle, and end (using the words first, then, next, last) Also, students will give details while recalling events.

Read at least 75 grade level words from Reading Words assessment, and demonstrate understanding of text by using words in sentences and discussing words read.

Recognize all lowercase and uppercase letters, and demonstrate phonemic awareness. Read at least 26 grade level words from Reading Words assessment and demonstrate understanding of text.

Strategies, Action, Resources, and Evidence

- Model through read-aloud; think-aloud
- Continued opportunities to retell stories
- Take-home reading comprehension activities
- Writing and sequencing activities
- Evaluation=Retelling Rubric
  - △ Work samples/completed activities

- "Right Start Reading" methods - small group/individualized instruction
- Phonological tasks
- Evaluation=Theme tests
  - △ Vocabulary Checklists
  - △ Spelling Sentences
  - △ Informal R.R.

- Word Wall activities
  - ▲ Daily review
  - ▲ Weekly word checklists
  - ▲ △ Spelling/writing/daily oral language

Action Plan template is available online.

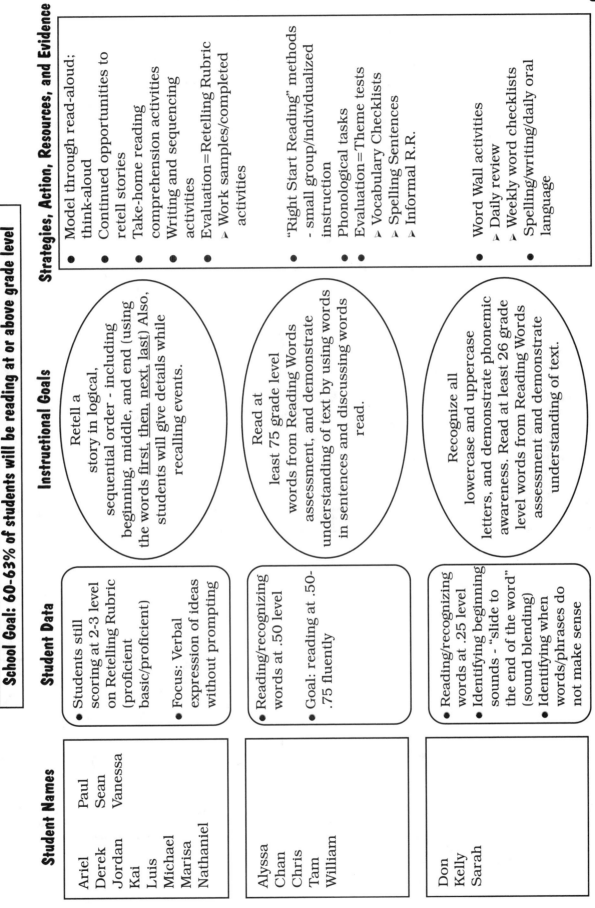

275

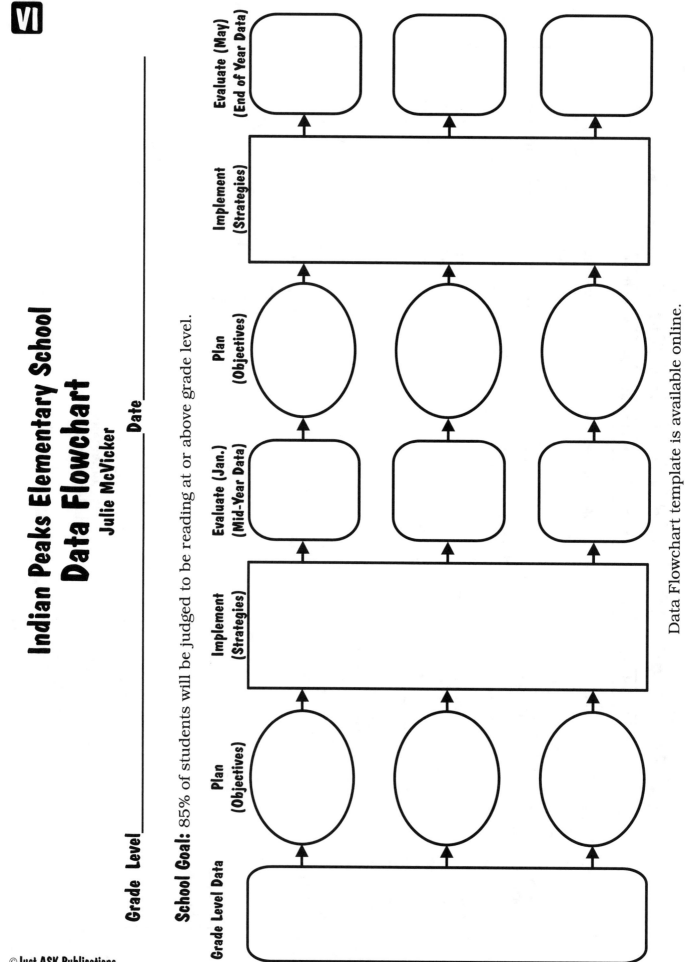

Indian Peaks Elementary School
Data Flowchart
Julie McVicker

Grade Level _____

Date _____

School Goal: 85% of students will be judged to be reading at or above grade level.

| Grade Level Data | Plan (Objectives) | Implement (Strategies) | Evaluate (Jan.) (Mid-Year Data) | Plan (Objectives) | Implement (Strategies) | Evaluate (May) (End of Year Data) |

Data Flowchart template is available online.

276

VI

Data Analysis

Indicators ↓ ↓ ↓	Struggling	Almost There	Proficient	Advanced Proficient

Data Analysis template is available online.

A Teacher's Perspctive
Analysis of Mid-Year Data
3rd Grade English Standards of Learning

Areas for Improvement and Focused Instruction
(Students Scoring Less Than 80%)

SOL/SWD Read-Aloud Students and Test Scores:
Philip (40), Eduardo (44), Daniel (67), Cristian (60), Ever (78)

Use Word Analysis Strategies	Use a Variety of Printed and Resource Materials	Understand Elements of Literature	Plan, Compose, and Revise Paragraphs, Stories, Letters	Edit for Grammar, Capitalization, Punctuation, and Spelling
Cristian Eduardo	Philip Eduardo	Ever Cristian Philip Eduardo	Cristian Philip Eduardo	Daniel Cristian Eduardo Philip

Independent Test Takers and Test Scores:
Ali (69), Mally (69), Kaisha (71), Juan (76), Brittany (76), Irene (79), Arwa (79)

Use Word Analysis Strategies	Use a Variety of Printed and Resource Materials	Understand Elements of Literature	Plan, Compose, and Revise Paragraphs, Stories, Letters	Edit for Grammar, Capitalization, Punctuation, and Spelling
Ali		Juan Kaisha	Arwa Brittany Juan Kaisha Mally Ali	Brittany Kaisha Mally

Richard Green, Glen Forest Elementary School, Fairfax County Public Schools, Virginia

A Teacher's Perspective: Translating Data into Areas of Focused Instruction

75% need support in planning, composing, and revising paragraphs, stories, letters, etc.: Major emphases: webbing, paragraph structure, combining sentences

- Most of the students had challenges identifying topic sentences on question 43, yet we had not focused on paragraph structure when the test was administered.
  Possible teaching strategies: Review topic sentence in writing workshop mini-lessons, review paragraph writing in writing workshop

- Most of the students, except for Eduardo and Philip, did NOT have problems identifying which sentences were in the wrong place or did not belong. A handful of students did have challenges on question 35, which asked them the best place to add a sentence.
  Possible teaching strategies: Giving cut-up paragraphs and having them order sentences and take out misplaced sentence, review paragraphing in writing workshop

- Questions 33 and 41 on joining or combining sentences were challenging, but only one of the students, Mally, missed both.
  Possible teaching strategies: Incorporating skill into daily oral language editing exercise to practice, using practice questions

- Three students had problems with question 39 on the purpose of a web, yet we had not focused on webbing as a planning tool when the test was administered. Three students also had problems identifying which sentences do not belong in a web on question 40.
  Possible teaching strategies: Review webbing and its purpose as a tool in writing workshop mini-lessons

58% of class needs support editing for grammar, capitalization, punctuation, and spelling: Major emphases: articles, contractions, editing for punctuation, irregular verbs

- Eduardo, Philip, Cristian, and Kaisha need help on contractions, according to the data. In class, the trend is toward misplacing the apostrophe in a number of contractions.
  Possible teaching strategies: Introduce review game to match contractions, incorporate into daily oral language editing, use multiple choice review activity to cross out incorrect contractions

Richard Green, Glen Forest Elementary School, Fairfax County Public Schools, Virginia

A Teacher's Perspective: Translating Data into Areas of Focused Instruction

- Daniel, Cristian, and Philip need help identifying correct end marks, according to question 30.
  Possible teaching strategies: Incorporating skill into daily oral language editing exercise to practice, having children look in their own writing

- There was a lot of confusion with articles (a, an) on question 44.
  Possible teaching strategies: Introduce during remediation time and incorporate into daily oral language editing

- Ever, Cristian, Philip, Mally, and Brittany need help editing for capital letters, specifically words surrounding those that require capitals (e.g., month of July) on question 37.
  Possible teaching strategies: Incorporating skill into daily oral language editing exercise to practice

- Juan, Cristian, Philip, Irene, and Daniel need help with irregular verbs, according to performance on question 45.
  Possible teaching strategies: Incorporating skill into daily oral language editing exercise to practice, review as grammar mini-lesson with whole class

50% need support understanding elements of literature: Major emphases: genre, making character inferences

- All six students needing improvement missed question 6 on inferring a character's trait. Another question, number 22 on how a speaker feels, was also challenging to the group.
  Possible teaching strategies: Using think/read-aloud to make character inferences and narrow choices, reinforcing crossing out wrong answers

- Only two of the students, Eduardo and Philip, had challenges categorizing qualities of a folktale on question 6. On a similar item, question 18, most of the students in this group had challenges determining why a story was a biography.
  Possible teaching strategies: Using open-ended questioning to discuss what makes a type of literature fit into a specific prose (e.g., Why is this NOT a folktale?), reinforcing crossing out wrong answers (i.e., students may have been confused by the word "lives" on letter F)

Richard Green, Glen Forest Elementary School, Fairfax County Public Schools, Virginia

A Teacher's Perspective: Analysis of Mid-Year Data
Math (Independent Test - Takers, B2 and SWD Read-Aloud Students*)

Challenging Skills* Items in which group scored 70 percent or below	Possible Instructional Review Strategies
Word form of six-digit numbers (Items 1, 3, 7) ● Using standard form to identify work form ● Identifying place value of digit ● Using word form to identify standard form	● Reviewed in EAR time in small groups in January-February ● Incorporate problem two-three times weekly as morning warm-up in April-May
Decimal subtraction with regrouping (Item 19)	● Reviewed in EAR time in small groups in January-February ● Incorporate problem two-three times weekly as morning warm-up in April-May, include decimal and money problem
Relative location forms and NOT (Item 27)	● Included questions with NOT on unit tests throughout year and in open-ended questioning ● Use Princeton Review activities as EAR activity with whole class ● Ask questions in bathroom line about relative location
Telling time to the nearest minute (Item 34)	● Reviewed in calendar in January-February, will continue in April-May ● Review with class throughout day when lining up in April-May
Use bar graph to interpret and compare data (Items 39, 43)	● Review with Christian and Eduardo in after-school coaching in April ● Provide pictograph and bar graph weekly to practice skills
Determining probability, using table (Item 40)	● Review material with tables as much as possible in April-May
Patterns (Item 50)	● Review patterns and related vocabulary in January ● Created patterns in February

* Skills not yet covered (i.e., fractions, decimals, division) at time of test not included in table.

Richard Green, Glen Forest Elementary School, Fairfax County Public Schools, Virgina

VI

281

©Just ASK Publications

A Principal's Perspective: Translating Data into School Improvement Planning
Heather Clayton Kwit

The key to having educators establish improvement priorities, and to use those goals to formatively measure progress, is to ensure that there is a simple template for a focused improvement plan with annual goals designed to improve student learning. As stated by Mike Schmoker, "This would go a long way towards solving the overload problem."

So how would a school improvement plan like this look? It could include annual goals for improving standardized testing scores, with strategies that take into account the various forms of data. According to Mike Schmoker, goals would be "measurable, focused on student achievement, and linked to effective assessments." Once goals have been established, a limited number of effective and targeted strategies to assist in meeting goals should be identified. Then, times throughout the year should be identified so that the progress towards the identified goals on the plan can be measured and strategies can be adjusted accordingly.

School Improvement Plan Template/Exemplar

Data-based Strengths
- Increase in the percent of all students meeting/exceeding standards in English Language Arts (ELA), Math, and Science 4.
- Increase in the percent of African-American and Hispanic students meeting/exceeding standards in ELA.

Data-based Improvement Opportunities
- Increase the percent of students with disabilities meeting/exceeding standards in ELA and Math.
- Increase the percent of Hispanic students meeting/exceeding standards on the Math 4.
- Increase the percent of all students meeting/exceeding standards on the Social Studies 5.

Strategies to Improve Student Performance
The following strategies are linked to next year's targets and will be implemented during the next school year to help all students meet or exceed the standards:
- Teachers will participate in district and school-based professional development and implement literacy-based instructional approaches in their daily work with students.

Translating Data into School Improvement Planning

- Teachers will participate in professional development on issues dealing with race, gender, socioeconomic status, demographic diversity, and the implications for improved academic achievement in the area of literacy.
- Administrators will participate in district and school-based professional development and monitor the implementation of literacy-based instructional approaches in the classroom.
- Principals will review student work weekly to analyze literacy integration, rigor, and alignment with curriculum. Student work will also be looked at in staff meetings and release sessions.
- Teachers will meet monthly with principals to review student literacy work and overall student progress utilizing the Corrective Action Plan.
- Teachers will meet bi-monthly in literacy team meetings in which they will discuss student progress, update data walls, look at student work, and receive professional development in the area of literacy.
- Teachers will implement a plan for individual students at risk of not meeting the standards in ELA or mathematics.
- Principals will meet monthly with the Deputy Superintendent and/or Director of Elementary/Secondary School Support to review student progress and evidence of actions to improve student achievement utilizing the Corrective Action Plan.
- School staff will continue to build students' assets to increase students' sense of belonging and knowledge of themselves as learners.

Our Collective Perspective
Data...Beyond THE Test
Bruce Oliver

When the analysis of standardized test scores became a constant focus of principal meetings, I became frustrated. Again and again, the same results from the previous year's tests were distributed in colored folders or packets and we were asked to pour over the data to determine how to improve scores the following year. We disaggregated the data from every possible angle including item analysis by question, student ethnicity and gender, special education designation, free and reduced lunch qualification, students for whom English was a second language, and history of student scores from previous testing. In turn, we passed the data on to our teachers who spent considerable time individually and collectively analyzing the results by question as well as by strand. The amount of time spent analyzing the data from one standardized test seemed excessive and inordinately time consuming.

School is so much more than a single test score on a reading or a math test given in the spring. I have seen teachers stress out and students reach unhealthy levels of anxiety. I do not mean to minimize the importance of standardized test results. However, educational leaders must help teachers understand that data should not be confined to a single event. Data are so much more.

> Bruce speaks for all of us at Just ASK because the overriding, essential question that provides the focus for our work is:
>
> **What do schools look like when they organize around a commitment to the achievement of high standards by all students?**
>
> In response to this question, we believe schools must use a standards-based planning process in which these questions are asked:
> - What should students know and be able to do?
> - How will they and I know when they are successful?
> - What does a task analysis tell me about the knowledge, skills, and levels of understanding required.
> - What learning experiences will facilitate their success? Which students will need scaffolding or extensions and what form will that scaffolding and those extensions take?
> - **Based on data, how do I design and refine the learning experiences?**

Data are everything that happens in the classroom.
Examples include the level and number of student responses to questions, how

Our Collective Perspective
Data...Beyond THE Test

students process their learning, questions that students pose in relation to their new learning, how students react to the lessons presented by the teacher, informal conversations with students, results from formative assessments, and teacher checks for understanding. Wise teachers ask students for feedback at the end of units by posing questions such as "What helped you learn best?" and "What types of learning experiences would help you in the future." To ignore these data is to overlook excellent sources of information that should guide future instructional decisions.

Data-driven instruction means that teachers use data to make instructional decisions on a daily, if not a moment-by-moment, basis.

Whether or not the level of learning meets expectations lets the teacher know when changes should be made in the implementation of the lesson. Apollo astronauts made over 20,000 mid-course adjustments on their trip to the moon. Researchers constantly re-evaluate the data they gather in order to determine the next steps to take. Madeline Hunter noted that there is only one thing that a teacher needs to do on a consistent basis and that is to think and make wise instructional decisions. The mid-course adjustments in lessons should be based on data and made in the interest of student learning.

Student learning is the goal.

Because of the pressures educators feel to make AYP, they sometimes lose sight of the real purpose of schools: student learning. Worksheets, drills, test preparation, remediation, pull-out programs, and double classes of reading and/or math are practices some schools have adopted. Additionally, an inordinate amount of school funds are spent annually on test prep materials which schools hope will produce the desired test scores. An important question to consider is: Are we neglecting student learning when we use valuable instructional time to prepare students for the test? We must not lose sight of the fact that focused, meaningful, engaging, and rigorous learning experiences promote student learning and lead to higher test scores.

An important source of data is how our students feel in our classrooms.

A teacher who provides a warm and inviting environment will get unimagined results from students. Brain research tells us that a safe, non-threatening environment is essential for student learning. **Mistakes are welcome here** is a great message to to see posted and acted upon in classrooms. There is no substitute for human kindness.

Data are much more than numbers.

We have participated in hundreds of parent conferences, both as teachers and as administrators. In so many instances, teachers came to conferences with grade

Our Collective Perspective
Data...Beyond THE Test

book in hand and reduced a student's performance to a number or a letter. The most successful teachers were the ones who could look directly at a parent and talk about the student's accomplishments as well as areas where a student could improve. They did not simply rely on numbers but used descriptors, work samples, and conversations they had with students to inform parents about their child's progress. Wise teachers get to know their students so well that they are able to talk about the academic growth they see in their students and not simply reduce them to missing homework assignments or poor quiz grades.

Data about student learning can be gathered by administrators talking to students during classroom visits.
Like teachers who are responsible for gathering assessment data on the achievement of their students, administrators have the responsibility of gathering data on the performance of the teachers they supervise. In the hectic life of an administrator, the data used to measure teacher effectiveness can often be reduced to one announced and one unannounced teacher observation per semester. When administrators carry out more frequent, informal visits to classrooms **with a focus on student learning instead of teacher behaviors**, the subsequent data provides powerful information about the impact of teacher behavior on student learning. As administrators interact with students, they can ask a variety of questions including:

- What are you supposed to be learning?
- How is what you are doing now helping you learn?
- How will you and your teacher measure your success?
- What are the next steps for you?
- How do you know what excellent work looks like?
- In what ways do you self-assess your efforts and your work?

How do we measure success?

The measure of a school's success should not be limited to data from standardized test scores. Good teachers teach compassion, kindness, and human decency, areas that cannot be measured by a pencil and paper test. Each of us remembers a favorite teacher not so much by what we were taught but how we were treated and encouraged. Although such behaviors are hard to quantify, teachers and administrators should set aside time to reflect on all the ways they touch students' lives. These are successes worthy of celebration.

The teaching-learning process is complicated and multi-layered. Reducing what happens in the classroom on a daily basis to a once-a-year test score is a real disservice to the art of teaching. If we are truly professionals, we must do what

Our Collective Perspective
Data...Beyond THE Test

other professionals do. Professionals are academically trained, they develop a high degree of knowledge and skill in their field, they immerse themselves in the continual study of their profession, they work collaboratively, and they use research findings and data to drive their decisions. If we want to be viewed as professionals, we must adhere to practices that provide continuous and valuable data that inform our practice and truly measure student learning on a regular basis.

Just ASK's Non-Negotiables for Creating a Culture for Learning

1. We believe and act on the belief that all students can learn!

2. We collectively develop clearly articulated norms that we adhere to in our work.

3. We accept learning as the fundamental purpose of the school and examine all our practices in light of their impact on learning.

4. We engage in, model, and promote collaborative practice.

5. All the students belong to all of us.

6. We establish and maintain an atmosphere of mutual respect.

7. Isolation is not an option. Collaboration is a right and responsibility.

8. All adults are committed to the success of all other adults.

9. We focus on results: That means we analyze student work and assessment results together, make data-driven decisions, establish goals for specific measurable skills and knowledge, identify improvement strategies, and adapt instruction to meet student needs.

Tools and Templates

Templates are available at www.justaskpublications.com/CCLtemplates

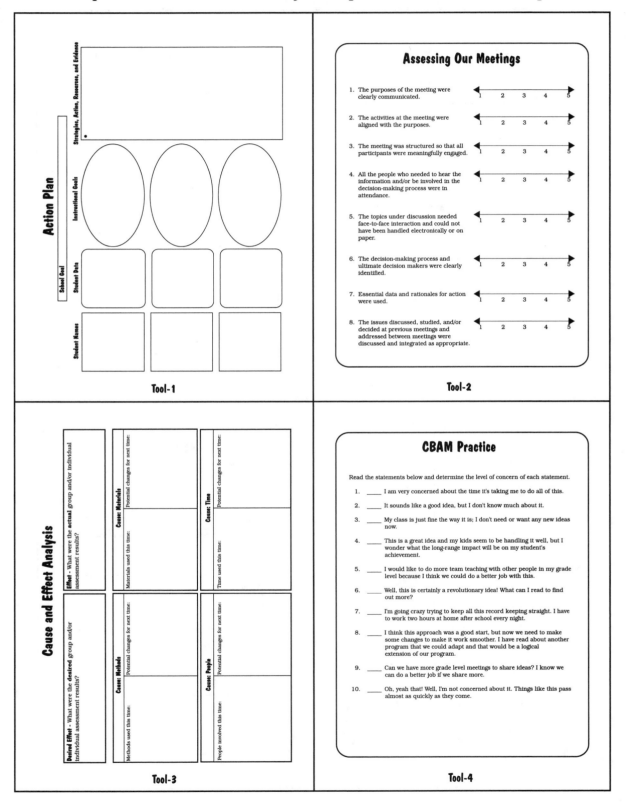

Action Plan — Tool-1

Strategies, Action, Resources, and Evidence

School Goal

Instructional Goals

Student Data

Student Names

Assessing Our Meetings — Tool-2

1. The purposes of the meeting were clearly communicated. 1 2 3 4 5
2. The activities at the meeting were aligned with the purposes. 1 2 3 4 5
3. The meeting was structured so that all participants were meaningfully engaged. 1 2 3 4 5
4. All the people who needed to hear the information and/or be involved in the decision-making process were in attendance. 1 2 3 4 5
5. The topics under discussion needed face-to-face interaction and could not have been handled electronically or on paper. 1 2 3 4 5
6. The decision-making process and ultimate decision makers were clearly identified. 1 2 3 4 5
7. Essential data and rationales for action were used. 1 2 3 4 5
8. The issues discussed, studied, and/or decided at previous meetings and addressed between meetings were discussed and integrated as appropriate. 1 2 3 4 5

Cause and Effect Analysis — Tool-3

Desired Effect - What were the desired group and/or individual assessment results?

Effect - What were the actual group and/or individual assessment results?

Cause: Methods
Methods used this time:
Potential changes for next time:

Cause: Materials
Materials used this time:
Potential changes for next time:

Cause: People
People involved this time:
Potential changes for next time:

Cause: Time
Time used this time:
Potential changes for next time:

CBAM Practice — Tool-4

Read the statements below and determine the level of concern of each statement.

1. _____ I am very concerned about the time it's taking me to do all of this.
2. _____ It sounds like a good idea, but I don't know much about it.
3. _____ My class is just fine the way it is; I don't need or want any new ideas now.
4. _____ This is a great idea and my kids seem to be handling it well, but I wonder what the long-range impact will be on my student's achievement.
5. _____ I would like to do more team teaching with other people in my grade level because I think we could do a better job with this.
6. _____ Well, this is certainly a revolutionary idea! What can I read to find out more?
7. _____ I'm going crazy trying to keep all this record keeping straight. I have to work two hours at home after school every night.
8. _____ I think this approach was a good start, but now we need to make some changes to make it work smoother. I have read about another program that we could adapt and that would be a logical extension of our program.
9. _____ Can we have more grade level meetings to share ideas? I know we can do a better job if we share more.
10. _____ Oh, yeah that! Well, I'm not concerned about it. Things like this pass almost as quickly as they come.

Tools and Templates

Templates are available at www.justaskpublications.com/CCLtemplates

The Collaborative Conference

Attendees _____

Date _____ Time _____

Purpose of Conference _____

How will we create a congenial beginning?

How will we identify the problem or issue? What data will be used?

How will we check for understanding and/or agreement on the area of focus?

What criteria will we use to weigh the alternatives?

What questions might we ask to facilitate the consideration of the alternatives?

Tool-5

The Collaborative Conference

How will we identify the acceptable action?

What data will be used to determine the success of the action?

When will a follow-up meeting be held to determine how the solution is working?

The Action Plan:

Tool-5a

Collaborative Team Agenda

Guiding Questions
- What do we want them to learn?
- How will we and they know when they've learned it?
- How will they learn it?
- What will we do when they haven't learned it?
- What will we do when they already know it?

Topic, I/D/A*, and Time *Information/Discussion/Action	Desired Outcomes	Person Responsible	Notes
Roundtable celebrations (1-2 minutes)			
EGART Data discussion (I/D/A-10 minutes)			
Lesson planning for Fractions (I/D/A-30 minutes)			
Parking Lot Items (1-1 minutes) Set agenda items for next meeting (1-2 minutes)			

Tool-6

Collegial Discussions

Use these questions to structure your discussions about what you did differently in your classroom as a result of your previous focus group, learning club, or workshop.

1. What You Tried

2. How It Went

Successes Experienced	Problems Encountered

3. What You Learned

Possible Revisions

Critical or Interesting Incidents

4. Next Steps

Tool-7

Tools and Templates

Templates are available at www.justaskpublications.com/CCLtemplates

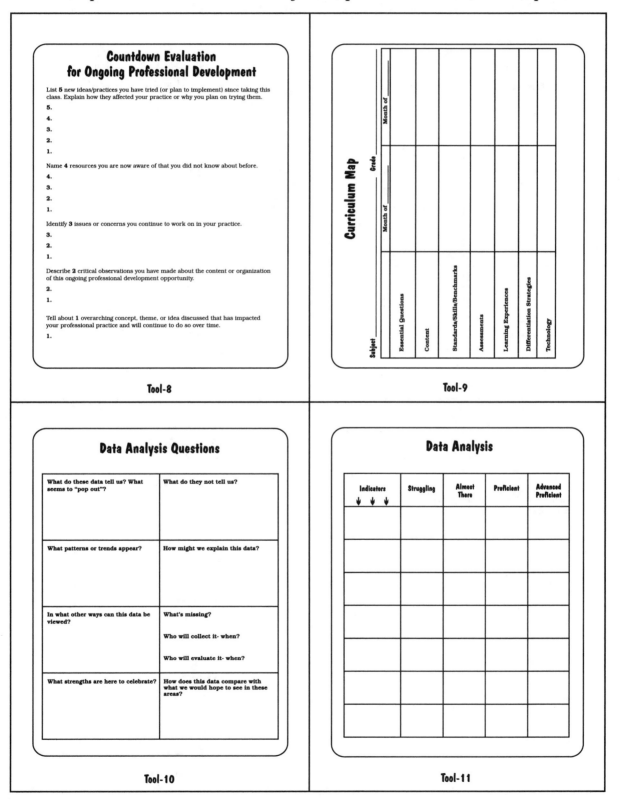

Countdown Evaluation for Ongoing Professional Development

List **5** new ideas/practices you have tried (or plan to implement) since taking this class. Explain how they affected your practice or why you plan on trying them.

5.

4.

3.

2.

1.

Name **4** resources you are now aware of that you did not know about before.

4.

3.

2.

1.

Identify **3** issues or concerns you continue to work on in your practice.

3.

2.

1.

Describe **2** critical observations you have made about the content or organization of this ongoing professional development opportunity.

2.

1.

Tell about **1** overarching concept, theme, or idea discussed that has impacted your professional practice and will continue to do so over time.

1.

Tool-8

Curriculum Map

Subject _____ Grade _____

Month of _____   Month of _____

- Essential Questions
- Content
- Standards/Skills/Benchmarks
- Assessments
- Learning Experiences
- Differentiation Strategies
- Technology

Tool-9

Data Analysis Questions

What do these data tell us? What seems to "pop out"?	What do they not tell us?
What patterns or trends appear?	How might we explain this data?
In what other ways can this data be viewed?	What's missing? Who will collect it- when? Who will evaluate it- when?
What strengths are here to celebrate?	How does this data compare with what we would hope to see in these areas?

Tool-10

Data Analysis

Indicators ↓ ↓ ↓	Struggling	Almost There	Proficient	Advanced Proficient

Tool-11

Tools and Templates

Templates are available at www.justaskpublications.com/CCLtemplates

Data Collection Tool
Use of Collaborative Norms

Behaviors			Participants				
Contributes ideas and opinions (puts ideas on the table)							
Models							
Presumes positive intent							
Clarifies/probes							
Paraphrases							
Summarizes							
Links							
Refocuses							
Checks perceptions							

Tool-12

Data Flowchart

Tool-13

Data Log for
Peer Observations and Learning Walks

Teacher's Name_____

Date _____

Subject/Grade _____

Focus of Observation/Learning Walk (Optional) _____

Standards/Indicators being addressed:

Students were:

Teacher was:

Evidence of rigor:

Evidence of positive and productive environment:

Points to ponder:

Tool-14

Data Review Questions

General

What do we know from looking at this data?

Do we know which students are learning and not learning?

What patterns can we observe?

What concerns are raised by a review of the data?

What other data sources would clarify and inform our teaching practice?

How do the programs we have in place connect with the concerns identified?

What can we do about what the data reveal?

Tool-15a

Tools and Templates

Templates are available at www.justaskpublications.com/CCLtemplates

Specific

How well, overall, are our students doing on each benchmark?

Do all of the items on each benchmark have a high percentage of correct answers?

If not, which items under each benchmark have a high percentage of incorrect answers?

On the incorrect test items, is there an incorrect answer that was picked by a high percentage of students?

What kind of mistake is represented by this choice?

What items do we need to disaggregate to find out if there is a pattern of students not doing well (boys/girls, free lunch, ESL, LD, etc.)?

Write statements describing your findings using the template below:
It seems that ......because......

Tool-15b

Data-Driven Dialogue

Phase I
Before looking at the data, access background knowledge
- I assume...

- I predict...

- I wonder...

Phase II
Study data privately. Record personal observations.
- I observe...

- Some patterns or trends I see...

- I can count...

- I'm surprised to see...

Phase III
Plan intervention and enrichment.
- I believe the data suggests...because...

- Additional data that would help me confirm/verify my explanation is...

- I think appropriate solutions/responses that address needs implied by the data are...

Tool-16

Using Knowledge of Self to
Develop Interpersonal Skills
Based on the Myers-Briggs Type Indicator

So you want to make things happen! You want to get things done! You want to convince someone else to walk beside you on a new or different adventure! Use your intrapersonal knowledge to be more interpersonally effective! Identify the three approaches you find most challenging.

_____ **Stop, look, and listen.** Extraverts always think they can talk their way through... and out of... most conflicts. The very thing they find most difficult is what may be needed most: listening to the other person's point of view. (Extraverts)

_____ **Express yourself.** As difficult as it often is, and sometimes seemingly redundant, it still is imperative to tell your side of the story... and maybe even tell it again until the other person has heard it. When conflict is concerned, a little overkill can help. Make sure you get a hearing. (Introverts)

_____ **There's more to conflicts than just the facts.** Sometimes, though it seems a waste of energy and may appear to cloud the issue, it is important to look at extenuating circumstances. If someone always disagrees with you no matter what you say, there may be issues involved that need attention other than just the situation of the moment. (Sensors)

_____ **Stick to the issues.** When conflict arises, intuitives want to relate it to the total picture. That's not always appropriate or helpful. It clouds the specifics and complicates resolution. Sometimes it helps just to gather the facts you need for the moment. (Intuitives)

_____ **Allow some genuine expression of emotions.** Thinkers become unglued when others cry at work; they act similarly when people hug or express warmth. But these emotions... at work or anywhere else... are integral with conflict resolution. Even if you're unable to express these things yourself, you should allow others the freedom to do so. (Thinkers)

Tool-17a

Using Knowledge of Self to
Develop Interpersonal Skills

_____ **Be direct and confrontive.** The world won't come to an end if you say something you really mean, even if it's negative. What sounds harsh to you as you say it probably won't be received as harshly by other types; if you are given to expressing a lot of emotion, don't apologize or feel guilty for doing so. Being upfront about your feelings facilitates moving to constructive resolution. (Feelers)

_____ **You're not always right.** It may be difficult to believe this, but you must if you want a conflict ever to be resolved. Judgers see the world as black and white, right and wrong, and have difficulty accepting opposing points of view. It's hard to negotiate with someone who thinks he or she is always right. (Judgers)

_____ **Take a clear position.** Perceivers can often argue both sides because they truly see both sides of an argument. Sometimes it comes in the form of playing devil's advocate. While flexible and adaptive, that's not always helpful to resolving a problem. It may even intensify the dispute. If you really feel strongly about something, better to take a stand and defend it. (Perceivers)

Tool-17b

Tools and Templates

Templates are available at www.justaskpublications.com/CCLtemplates

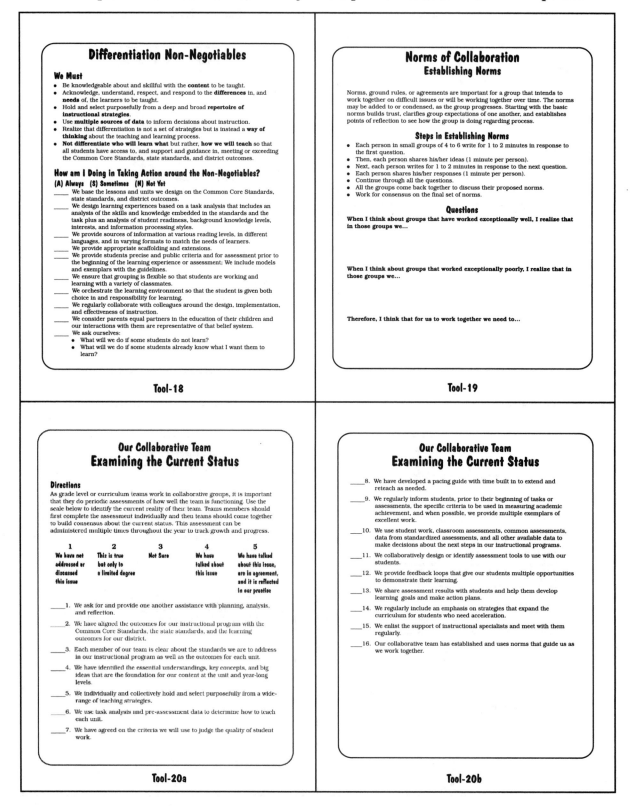

Differentiation Non-Negotiables

We Must
- Be knowledgeable about and skillful with the **content** to be taught.
- Acknowledge, understand, respect, and respond to the **differences** in, and **needs** of, the learners to be taught.
- Hold and select purposefully from a deep and broad **repertoire of instructional strategies**.
- Use **multiple sources of data** to inform decisions about instruction.
- Realize that differentiation is not a set of strategies but is instead a **way of thinking** about the teaching and learning process.
- **Not differentiate who will learn what** but rather, **how we will teach** so that all students have access to, and support and guidance in, meeting or exceeding the Common Core Standards, state standards, and district outcomes.

How am I Doing in Taking Action around the Non-Negotiables?
(A) Always   (S) Sometimes   (N) Not Yet

_____ We base the lessons and units we design on the Common Core Standards, state standards, and district outcomes.

_____ We design learning experiences based on a task analysis that includes an analysis of the skills and knowledge embedded in the standards and the task plus an analysis of student readiness, background knowledge levels, interests, and information processing styles.

_____ We provide sources of information at various reading levels, in different languages, and in varying formats to match the needs of learners.

_____ We provide appropriate scaffolding and extensions.

_____ We provide students precise and public criteria and for assessment prior to the beginning of the learning experience or assessment; We include models and exemplars with the guidelines.

_____ We ensure that grouping is flexible so that students are working and learning with a variety of classmates.

_____ We orchestrate the learning environment so that the student is given both choice in and responsibility for learning.

_____ We regularly collaborate with colleagues around the design, implementation, and effectiveness of instruction.

_____ We consider parents equal partners in the education of their children and our interactions with them are representative of that belief system.

_____ We ask ourselves:
- What will we do if some students do not learn?
- What will we do if some students already know what I want them to learn?

Tool-18

Norms of Collaboration
Establishing Norms

Norms, ground rules, or agreements are important for a group that intends to work together on difficult issues or will be working together over time. The norms may be added to or condensed, as the group progresses. Starting with the basic norms builds trust, clarifies group expectations of one another, and establishes points of reflection to see how the group is doing regarding process.

Steps in Establishing Norms
- Each person in small groups of 4 to 6 write for 1 to 2 minutes in response to the first question.
- Then, each person shares his/her ideas (1 minute per person).
- Next, each person writes for 1 to 2 minutes in response to the next question.
- Each person shares his/her responses (1 minute per person).
- Continue through all the questions.
- All the groups come back together to discuss their proposed norms.
- Work for consensus on the final set of norms.

Questions
When I think about groups that have worked exceptionally well, I realize that in those groups we...

When I think about groups that worked exceptionally poorly, I realize that in those groups we...

Therefore, I think that for us to work together we need to...

Tool-19

Our Collaborative Team
Examining the Current Status

Directions
As grade level or curriculum teams work in collaborative groups, it is important that they do periodic assessments of how well the team is functioning. Use the scale below to identify the current reality of their team. Teams members should first complete the assessment individually and then teams should come together to build consensus about the current status. This assessment can be administered multiple times throughout the year to track growth and progress.

1	2	3	4	5
We have not addressed or discussed this issue	This is true but only to a limited degree	Not Sure	We have talked about this issue	We have talked about this issue, are in agreement, and it is reflected in our practice

_____ 1. We ask for and provide one another assistance with planning, analysis, and reflection.

_____ 2. We have aligned the outcomes for our instructional program with the Common Core Standards, the state standards, and the learning outcomes for our district.

_____ 3. Each member of our team is clear about the standards we are to address in our instructional program as well as the outcomes for each unit.

_____ 4. We have identified the essential understandings, key concepts, and big ideas that are the foundation for our content at the unit and year-long levels.

_____ 5. We individually and collectively hold and select purposefully from a wide-range of teaching strategies.

_____ 6. We use task analysis and pre-assessment data to determine how to teach each unit.

_____ 7. We have agreed on the criteria we will use to judge the quality of student work.

Tool-20a

Our Collaborative Team
Examining the Current Status

_____ 8. We have developed a pacing guide with time built in to extend and reteach as needed.

_____ 9. We regularly inform students, prior to their beginning of tasks or assessments, the specific criteria to be used in measuring academic achievement, and when possible, we provide multiple exemplars of excellent work.

_____ 10. We use student work, classroom assessments, common assessments, data from standardized assessments, and all other available data to make decisions about the next steps in our instructional programs.

_____ 11. We collaboratively design or identify assessment tools to use with our students.

_____ 12. We provide feedback loops that give our students multiple opportunities to demonstrate their learning.

_____ 13. We share assessment results with students and help them develop learning goals and make action plans.

_____ 14. We regularly include an emphasis on strategies that expand the curriculum for students who need acceleration.

_____ 15. We enlist the support of instructional specialists and meet with them regularly.

_____ 16. Our collaborative team has established and uses norms that guide us as we work together.

Tool-20b

Tools and Templates

Templates are available at www.justaskpublications.com/CCLtemplates

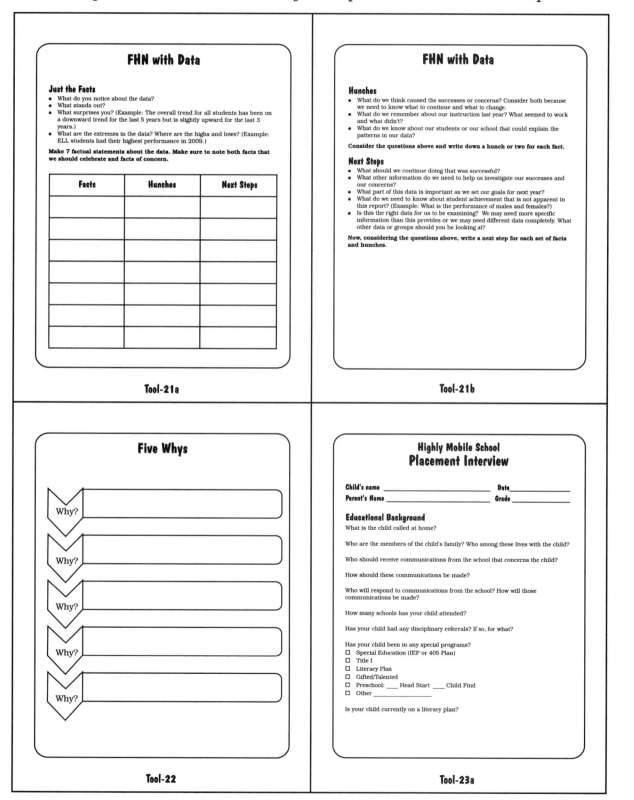

FHN with Data

Just the Facts
- What do you notice about the data?
- What stands out?
- What surprises you? (Example: The overall trend for all students has been on a downward trend for the last 5 years but is slightly upward for the last 3 years.)
- What are the extremes in the data? Where are the highs and lows? (Example: ELL students had their highest performance in 2009.)

Make 7 factual statements about the data. Make sure to note both facts that we should celebrate and facts of concern.

Facts	Hunches	Next Steps

Tool-21a

FHN with Data

Hunches
- What do we think caused the successes or concerns? Consider both because we need to know what to continue and what to change.
- What do we remember about our instruction last year? What seemed to work and what didn't?
- What do we know about our students or our school that could explain the patterns in our data?

Consider the questions above and write down a hunch or two for each fact.

Next Steps
- What should we continue doing that was successful?
- What other information do we need to help us investigate our successes and our concerns?
- What part of this data is important as we set our goals for next year?
- What do we need to know about student achievement that is not apparent in this report? (Example: What is the performance of males and females?)
- Is this the right data for us to be examining? We may need more specific information than this provides or we may need different data completely. What other data or groups should you be looking at?

Now, considering the questions above, write a next step for each set of facts and hunches.

Tool-21b

Five Whys

Why?

Why?

Why?

Why?

Why?

Tool-22

Highly Mobile School
Placement Interview

Child's name _____ **Date**_____
Parent's Name _____ **Grade** _____

Educational Background
What is the child called at home?

Who are the members of the child's family? Who among these lives with the child?

Who should receive communications from the school that concerns the child?

How should these communications be made?

Who will respond to communications from the school? How will those communications be made?

How many schools has your child attended?

Has your child had any disciplinary referrals? If so, for what?

Has your child been in any special programs?
- ☐ Special Education (IEP or 405 Plan)
- ☐ Title I
- ☐ Literacy Plan
- ☐ Gifted/Talented
- ☐ Preschool: ____ Head Start ____ Child Find
- ☐ Other _____

Is your child currently on a literacy plan?

Tool-23a

Tools and Templates

Templates are available at www.justaskpublications.com/CCLtemplates

Placement Interview

Language

What language did your child first speak?

What language was your child instructed in at their last school?

How much English does your child speak?

Learning Style

What would you like me to know about your child?

What do you see as areas of strength for your child?

What do you see as areas in need of improvement for your child?

Describe the teacher with whom your child has been the most successful.

How does your child learn best?

Health

Does your child have her immunizations?

Is your child on any medications? Will he be taking them at school?

Does your child have any severe allergies?

Has your child been hospitalized in the last 2 years? If so, for what?

Are there medical issues/concerns we should be aware of?

Does your child have insurance?
☐ Medicaid
☐ Child Health Plan Plus (CHP+)
☐ Private Insurance
☐ None

Tool-23b

Information Processing Styles Survey
Do you hear what I say? Do I hear what you say?

Complete the survey below by identifying your own preferences. Then compare your choices with a partner. Discuss how the similarities and differences you identify could impact the effectiveness and efficiency of your interactions if you were working together in a collegial relationship.

Me   You   Preferences in Processing Information

___   ___   **Are you more introverted or extroverted?** Do you prefer to respond to new information immediately and do your thinking out loud (extroverted) or do you prefer information in advance so that you have time to think about the issues before you have to respond (introverted)?

___   ___   **Are you more global or analytical?** Do you tend to see the big picture and like to have scaffolding on which to hang details (global) or do you prefer to see the bits and pieces and then put them into the whole (analytical)?

___   ___   **Are you more random or sequential?** Do you prefer to work through steps in sequence (sequential) or are you more inclined to jump around and deal with what interests you in the moment (random)?

___   ___   **Are you more concrete or abstract?** Do you want to see the real thing (concrete) rather than hear about the theory or the possibilities (abstract)?

___   ___   **Do you live more in the moment, in the past, or in the future?** Is what happened in the past, what is happening right now, or what the future will bring that matters most?

___   ___   **Are you inclined to be more decisive or open ended?** Do you tend to make quick decisions and stand by them (decisive) or do you prefer to continue to gather information and have several options (open ended)?

___   ___   **Do you lead with your heart or your head?** Do you most often say, "I think" (head) or are you more likely to say "I feel" (heart)?

Tool-24a

Information Processing Styles Survey

___   ___   **Do you ask why or how?** Which question is the first to come to your mind when someone presents information. Do you ask "Why is that a good idea?" (why) or do you more often ask "How would that look?" (how)?

___   ___   **Do you learn by observing or are you a hands-on active learner?** Do you learn best by observing from a distance (observer) or do you need to get into the action and mess around with the new ideas and processes (hands-on)?

___   ___   **Are you inclined to seek out research or focus on personal practical experience?** Are you interested in what the experts have to say about the information or strategy (research-based) or do you tend to rely more on what you have used in the past (personal practical experience)?

___   ___   **Do you prefer to plan ahead or wait until the last minute?** Do you finish projects well in advance and put them away until needed (plan ahead) or are you inclined to fill all available time no matter when you start (last minute)?

___   ___   **Do you make internal or external attributions?** Do you tend to question the effectiveness of your own efforts (internal) or do you attribute success or failure to variables that are beyond your control (external)?

___   ___   **Do you consider yourself more positive or pessimistic?** Do you view the world through a rose-colored lens (positive) or are you more likely to see problems just around the corner (pessimistic)?

___   ___   **Are you more logical or intuitive?** Do you prefer to measure and quantify things (logical) or are you comfortable knowing without knowing how you know (intuitive)?

___   ___   **Do you consider yourself a systems thinker or do you have more of a focused personal view?** Do you think more about how actions and information impact the complex organization around you (systems) or do you focus on the world right around you (personal view)?

___   ___   **Do you see power as based in position power or personal power?** Do you define authority primarily by the titles people hold (position)? or by the respect they have earned (personal)?

Tool-24b

Intervention and Enrichment Plan

Grade/Subject _____   Dates _____   Action Plan _____

SIP Goal:

Student Names	Student Data	Instructional Goals	Strategies, Actions, Resources, and Evidence		

Tool-25

© Just ASK Publications

Tools and Templates

Templates are available at www.justaskpublications.com/CCLtemplates

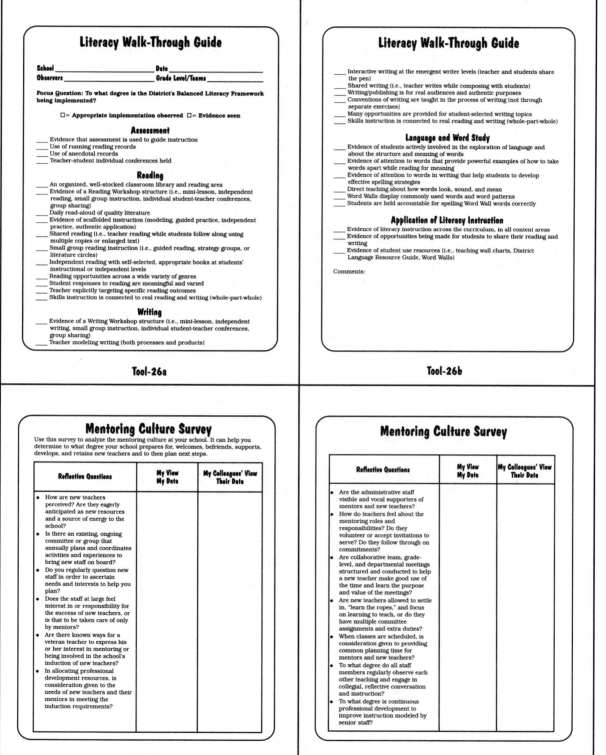

Literacy Walk-Through Guide

School _____ Date _____
Observers _____ Grade Level/Teams _____

Focus Question: To what degree is the District's Balanced Literacy Framework being implemented?

☐ = Appropriate implementation observed   ☐ = Evidence seen

Assessment
____ Evidence that assessment is used to guide instruction
____ Use of running reading records
____ Use of anecdotal records
____ Teacher-student individual conferences held

Reading
____ An organized, well-stocked classroom library and reading area
____ Evidence of a Reading Workshop structure (i.e., mini-lesson, independent reading, small group instruction, individual student-teacher conferences, group sharing)
____ Daily read-aloud of quality literature
____ Evidence of scaffolded instruction (modeling, guided practice, independent practice, authentic application)
____ Shared reading (i.e., teacher reading while students follow along using multiple copies or enlarged text)
____ Small group reading instruction (i.e., guided reading, strategy groups, or literature circles)
____ Independent reading with self-selected, appropriate books at students' instructional or independent levels
____ Reading opportunities across a wide variety of genres
____ Student responses to reading are meaningful and varied
____ Teacher explicitly targeting specific reading outcomes
____ Skills instruction is connected to real reading and writing (whole-part-whole)

Writing
____ Evidence of a Writing Workshop structure (i.e., mini-lesson, independent writing, small group instruction, individual student-teacher conferences, group sharing)
____ Teacher modeling writing (both processes and products)

Tool-26a

Literacy Walk-Through Guide

____ Interactive writing at the emergent writer levels (teacher and students share the pen)
____ Shared writing (i.e., teacher writes while composing with students)
____ Writing/publishing is for real audiences and authentic purposes
____ Conventions of writing are taught in the process of writing (not through separate exercises)
____ Many opportunities are provided for student-selected writing topics
____ Skills instruction is connected to real reading and writing (whole-part-whole)

Language and Word Study
____ Evidence of students actively involved in the exploration of language and about the structure and meaning of words
____ Evidence of attention to words that provide powerful examples of how to take words apart while reading for meaning
____ Evidence of attention to words in writing that help students to develop effective spelling strategies
____ Direct teaching about how words look, sound, and mean
____ Word Walls display commonly used words and word patterns
____ Students are held accountable for spelling Word Wall words correctly

Application of Literacy Instruction
____ Evidence of literacy instruction across the curriculum, in all content areas
____ Evidence of opportunities being made for students to share their reading and writing
____ Evidence of student use resources (i.e., teaching wall charts, District Language Resource Guide, Word Walls)

Comments:

Tool-26b

Mentoring Culture Survey

Use this survey to analyze the mentoring culture at your school. It can help you determine to what degree your school prepares for, welcomes, befriends, supports, develops, and retains new teachers and to then plan next steps.

Reflective Questions	My View My Data	My Colleagues' View Their Data
• How are new teachers perceived? Are they eagerly anticipated as new resources and a source of energy to the school? • Is there an existing, ongoing committee or group that annually plans and coordinates activities and experiences to bring new staff on board? • Do you regularly question new staff in order to ascertain needs and interests to help you plan? • Does the staff at large feel interest in or responsibility for the success of new teachers, or is that to be taken care of only by mentors? • Are there known ways for a veteran teacher to express his or her interest in mentoring or being involved in the school's induction of new teachers? • In allocating professional development resources, is consideration given to the needs of new teachers and their mentors in meeting the induction requirements?		

Tool-27a

Mentoring Culture Survey

Reflective Questions	My View My Data	My Colleagues' View Their Data
• Are the administrative staff visible and vocal supporters of mentors and new teachers? • How do teachers feel about the mentoring roles and responsibilities? Do they volunteer or accept invitations to serve? Do they follow through on commitments? • Are collaborative team, grade-level, and departmental meetings structured and conducted to help a new teacher make good use of the time and learn the purpose and value of the meetings? • Are new teachers allowed to settle in, "learn the ropes," and focus on learning to teach, or do they have multiple committee assignments and extra duties? • When classes are scheduled, is consideration given to providing common planning time for mentors and new teachers? • To what degree do all staff members regularly observe each other teaching and engage in collegial, reflective conversation and instruction? • To what degree is continuous professional development to improve instruction modeled by senior staff?		

Tool-27b

Tools and Templates

Templates are available at www.justaskpublications.com/CCLtemplates

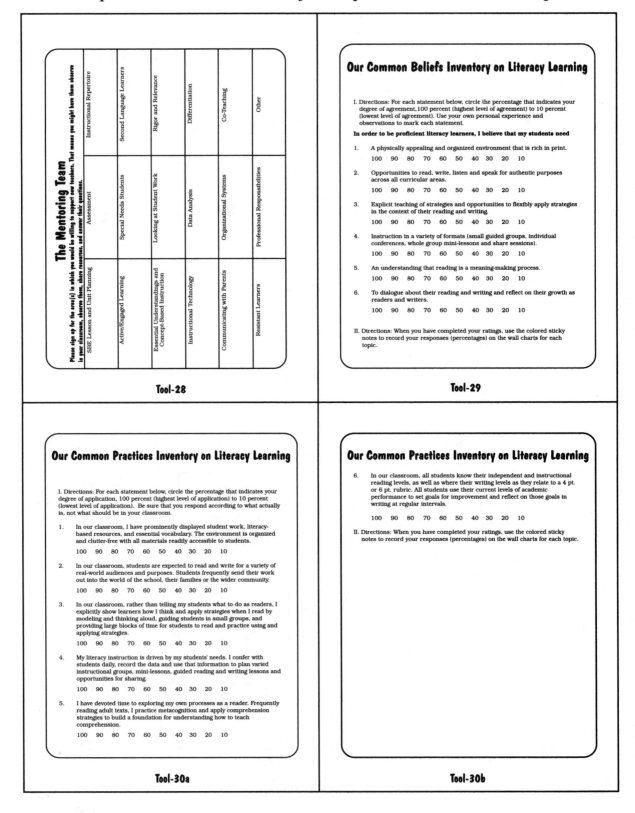

The Mentoring Team

Please sign up for the area(s) in which you would be willing to support new teachers. That means you might have them observe in your classroom, observe them, share resources, and answer their questions.

SBE Lesson and Unit Planning	Assessment	Instructional Repertoire
Active/Engaged Learning	Special Needs Students	Second Language Learners
Essential Understandings and Concept-Based Instruction	Looking at Student Work	Rigor and Relevance
Instructional Technology	Data Analysis	Differentiation
Communicating with Parents	Organizational Systems	Co-Teaching
Resistant Learners	Professional Responsibilities	Other

Tool-28

Our Common Beliefs Inventory on Literacy Learning

I. Directions: For each statement below, circle the percentage that indicates your degree of agreement, 100 percent (highest level of agreement) to 10 percent (lowest level of agreement). Use your own personal experience and observations to mark each statement.

In order to be proficient literacy learners, I believe that my students need

1. A physically appealing and organized environment that is rich in print.
    100 90 80 70 60 50 40 30 20 10

2. Opportunities to read, write, listen and speak for authentic purposes across all curricular areas.
    100 90 80 70 60 50 40 30 20 10

3. Explicit teaching of strategies and opportunities to flexibly apply strategies in the context of their reading and writing.
    100 90 80 70 60 50 40 30 20 10

4. Instruction in a variety of formats (small guided groups, individual conferences, whole group mini-lessons and share sessions).
    100 90 80 70 60 50 40 30 20 10

5. An understanding that reading is a meaning-making process.
    100 90 80 70 60 50 40 30 20 10

6. To dialogue about their reading and writing and reflect on their growth as readers and writers.
    100 90 80 70 60 50 40 30 20 10

II. Directions: When you have completed your ratings, use the colored sticky notes to record your responses (percentages) on the wall charts for each topic.

Tool-29

Our Common Practices Inventory on Literacy Learning

I. Directions: For each statement below, circle the percentage that indicates your degree of application, 100 percent (highest level of application) to 10 percent (lowest level of application). Be sure that you respond according to what actually is, not what should be in your classroom.

1. In our classroom, I have prominently displayed student work, literacy-based resources, and essential vocabulary. The environment is organized and clutter-free with all materials readily accessible to students.
    100 90 80 70 60 50 40 30 20 10

2. In our classroom, students are expected to read and write for a variety of real-world audiences and purposes. Students frequently send their work out into the world of the school, their families or the wider community.
    100 90 80 70 60 50 40 30 20 10

3. In our classroom, rather than telling my students what to do as readers, I explicitly show learners how I think and apply strategies when I read by modeling and thinking aloud, guiding students in small groups, and providing large blocks of time for students to read and practice using and applying strategies.
    100 90 80 70 60 50 40 30 20 10

4. My literacy instruction is driven by my students' needs. I confer with students daily, record the data and use that information to plan varied instructional groups, mini-lessons, guided reading and writing lessons and opportunities for sharing.
    100 90 80 70 60 50 40 30 20 10

5. I have devoted time to exploring my own processes as a reader. Frequently reading adult texts, I practice metacognition and apply comprehension strategies to build a foundation for understanding how to teach comprehension.
    100 90 80 70 60 50 40 30 20 10

Tool-30a

Our Common Practices Inventory on Literacy Learning

6. In our classroom, all students know their independent and instructional reading levels, as well as where their writing levels are as they relate to a 4 pt. or 6 pt. rubric. All students use their current levels of academic performance to set goals for improvement and reflect on those goals in writing at regular intervals.
    100 90 80 70 60 50 40 30 20 10

II. Directions: When you have completed your ratings, use the colored sticky notes to record your responses (percentages) on the wall charts for each topic.

Tool-30b

Tools and Templates

Templates are available at www.justaskpublications.com/CCLtemplates

Peer Poaching Pass!

_____ visited my class on
_____ so that she/he could
learn how to further the learning of more
students more of the time.

Signed _____

Peer Poaching Pass!

_____ visited my class on
_____ so that she/he could
learn how to further the learning of more
students more of the time.

Signed _____

Peer Poaching Pass!

_____ visited my class on
_____ so that she/he could
learn how to further the learning of more
students more of the time.

Signed _____

Peer Poaching Pass!

_____ visited my class on
_____ so that she/he could
learn how to further the learning of more
students more of the time.

Signed _____

Peer Poaching Pass!

_____ visited my class on
_____ so that she/he could
learn how to further the learning of more
students more of the time.

Signed _____

Peer Poaching Pass!

_____ visited my class on
_____ so that she/he could
learn how to further the learning of more
students more of the time.

Signed _____

Peer Poaching Pass!

_____ visited my class on
_____ so that she/he could
learn how to further the learning of more
students more of the time.

Signed _____

Peer Poaching Pass!

_____ visited my class on
_____ so that she/he could
learn how to further the learning of more
students more of the time.

Signed _____

Tool-31

Planning Professional Development

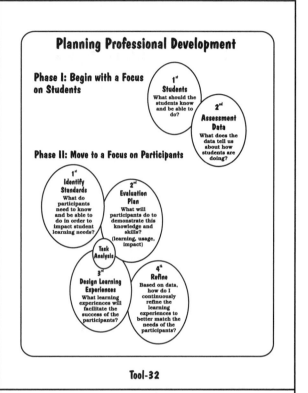

Phase I: Begin with a Focus on Students

1st **Students** What should the students know and be able to do?

2nd **Assessment Data** What does the data tell us about how students are doing?

Phase II: Move to a Focus on Participants

1st **Identify Standards** What do participants need to know and be able to do in order to impact student learning needs?

2nd **Evaluation Plan** What will participants do to demonstrate this knowledge and skills? (learning, usage, impact)

Task Analysis

3rd **Design Learning Experiences** What learning experiences will facilitate the success of the participants?

4th **Refine** Based on data, how do I continuously refine the learning experiences to better match the needs of the participants?

Tool-32

Professional Development Evaluation

Please evaluate the professional development opportunity with the following scale:
5= always, 4= usually, 3= sometimes, 2= rarely, 1= never

Should you rank an item 3, 2, or 1 please indicate in the comments section how this variable could have been, from your perspective, more positive.

____ 1. The content and processes learned are relevant and will be of practical use to me.
____ 2. There were opportunities for me to be involved in hands-on learning.
____ 3. There were opportunities for me to apply what I already knew.
____ 4. I was able to integrate new knowledge and skills in my own bank of knowledge and skills.
____ 5 I understood why the particular knowledge and skills were emphasized.
____ 6. The learning environment offered multiple opportunities to work with a partner or group.
____ 7. There were options and/or flexibility in the assignments.
____ 8. The amount of work was reasonable for the amount of time.
____ 9. Active participation was allowed and encouraged.
____ 10. Effective two-way communication was established and maintained.
____ 11. The furniture, equipment, etc. were sufficient for my needs.
____ 12. The facilitators offered expertise, both in knowledge and preparation.
____ 13. The facilitators conducted the sessions with understanding and consideration towards the participants.
____ 14. The facilitators showed enthusiasm for the course, the content, the participants, and the profession of teaching.
____ 15. The facilitators showed clarity in their teaching, their explanations of assignments, and the workshop discussions.

Comments (List item number and suggestions.)

I would have liked more _____

I would have liked less _____

There was just the right amount of _____

Tool-33

Professional Dialogue Tool
Learning Together, Achieving Together

School _____

Indicator	Next Steps
Data- Evidence of proactive analysis of student data (i.e. formative and summative) in effort to predict areas of instructional strengths and weaknesses. Comments:	
PLC- Evidence of a professional, instructional culture that is focused on learning as the fundamental purpose, building a collaborative culture through high performing teams, and analyzing results. Master schedule provides embedded collaborative team time. Comments:	
Intervention- System of monitoring students for instructional intervention. Master schedule provides time for embedded review, remediation, and enrichment for students. Comments:	
Communication- Evidence of ongoing internal and external communication of School Improvement Plan for all staff and community members. Comments:	

Tool-34a

Tools and Templates

Templates are available at www.justaskpublications.com/CCLtemplates

Professional Dialogue Tool
Learning Together, Achieving Together

Indicator	Next Steps
Classroom Visits- Evidence of student learning through implementation of Best Practices that include a focus on the following: checking for understanding, relationships, and engagement. Comments:	
Goals- Evidence of implementing goals specific to School Improvement Plan Comments:	

_____   _____
Visitor   Date

Tool-34b

Professional Learning Goals Worksheet

Teacher _____ Grade/Subject Area _____

Personal Learning Goal(s)
Reflect on your instructional strengths and potential areas of growth. Identify one or more skills or practices you plan to improve or acquire that relate specifically to the act of improving your teaching (e.g., differentiation of instruction, student performance assessments, lesson pacing) and, by extension, the performance of your students. Consider ways that you can participate in workshops, tap into the expertise of colleagues, and/or locate relevant readings or reference materials. Identify each personal learning goal and respond to the listed questions to complete your plan.

1. How does this goal support our school's student achievement objectives in math and reading?

2. Identify activities you will participate in and/or methods you will use to acquire/improve the skill.

3. How will you build opportunities for repeated practice of the skill into your plan?

4. What methods will you use to get feedback on your performance (from other professionals and from students)?

5. What data will you collect to demonstrate your progress?

6. What indicators will demonstrate that you have achieved (or made progress toward) your goal?

Tool-35

Professional Learning Reflections

Please take a few moments and reflect on the outcomes for today's session. Your feedback is important to us.

List three concepts/processes we discussed today that were meaningful to you. Please explain why?
-
-
-

Describe one way the key concepts we learned today connect to what you do in your current position.

Name one process strategy introduced today that you will use in your classroom.

What questions do you have about topics discussed today?

Turn to a table partner and discuss ways we might adjust our strategies for providing you with feedback on your work/performance. List 2-3 ideas you come up with together.
-
-
-

Look ahead three months. What processes or content ideas do you think you will be continuing to implement and why?

Tool-36

SBE and Multiple Pathways to Learning

Differentiation of instruction does not mean that you individualize instruction or provide something "different" from the normal lesson for struggling or advanced students. It means that you think proactively and, from the beginning, the "normal" lesson includes more than one avenue for success. It means that you think about the diversity of your learners when you are planning and don't fall into the trap of thinking that "one size fits all." Use what you know about the **SBE Planning Process** and the needs of your diverse learners to answer the following questions.

1. Identify a standard/benchmark/indicator you will be addressing in the near future.

2. What assessment opportunities might you give students to demonstrate what they have learned about the above concept?

3. Given the task analysis, what information and skills should all students experience? List a few instructional strategies and practice and/or processing activities that would facilitate that learning.

Tool-37a

Tools and Templates

Templates are available at www.justaskpublications.com/CCLtemplates

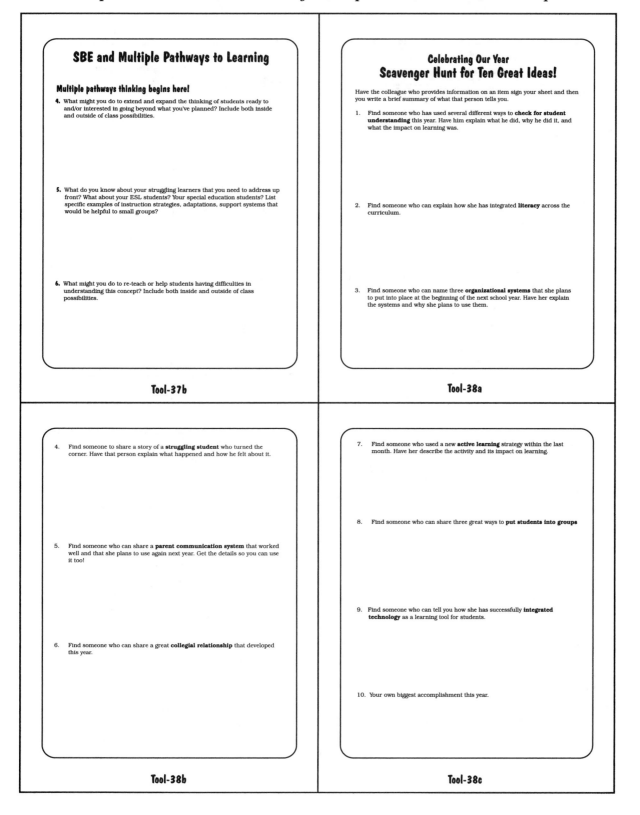

SBE and Multiple Pathways to Learning

Multiple pathways thinking begins here!

4. What might you do to extend and expand the thinking of students ready to and/or interested in going beyond what you've planned? Include both inside and outside of class possibilities.

5. What do you know about your struggling learners that you need to address up front? What about your ESL students? Your special education students? List specific examples of instruction strategies, adaptations, support systems that would be helpful to small groups?

6. What might you do to re-teach or help students having difficulties in understanding this concept? Include both inside and outside of class possibilities.

Tool-37b

Celebrating Our Year
Scavenger Hunt for Ten Great Ideas!

Have the colleague who provides information on an item sign your sheet and then you write a brief summary of what that person tells you.

1. Find someone who has used several different ways to **check for student understanding** this year. Have him explain what he did, why he did it, and what the impact on learning was.

2. Find someone who can explain how she has integrated **literacy** across the curriculum.

3. Find someone who can name three **organizational systems** that she plans to put into place at the beginning of the next school year. Have her explain the systems and why she plans to use them.

Tool-38a

4. Find someone to share a story of a **struggling student** who turned the corner. Have that person explain what happened and how he felt about it.

5. Find someone who can share a **parent communication system** that worked well and that she plans to use again next year. Get the details so you can use it too!

6. Find someone who can share a great **collegial relationship** that developed this year.

Tool-38b

7. Find someone who used a new **active learning** strategy within the last month. Have her describe the activity and its impact on learning.

8. Find someone who can share three great ways to **put students into groups**

9. Find someone who can tell you how she has successfully **integrated technology** as a learning tool for students.

10. Your own biggest accomplishment this year.

Tool-38c

Tools and Templates

Templates are available at www.justaskpublications.com/CCLtemplates

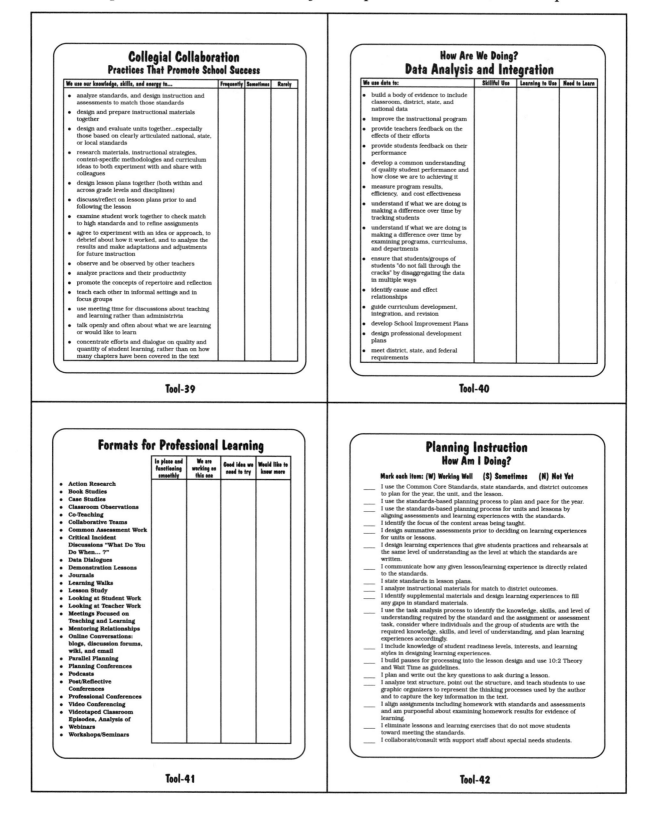

Collegial Collaboration
Practices That Promote School Success

We use our knowledge, skills, and energy to...	Frequently	Sometimes	Rarely
• analyze standards, and design instruction and assessments to match those standards			
• design and prepare instructional materials together			
• design and evaluate units together...especially those based on clearly articulated national, state, or local standards			
• research materials, instructional strategies, content-specific methodologies and curriculum ideas to both experiment with and share with colleagues			
• design lesson plans together (both within and across grade levels and disciplines)			
• discuss/reflect on lesson plans prior to and following the lesson			
• examine student work together to check match to high standards and to refine assignments			
• agree to experiment with an idea or approach, to debrief about how it worked, and to analyze the results and make adaptations and adjustments for future instruction			
• observe and be observed by other teachers			
• analyze practices and their productivity			
• promote the concepts of repertoire and reflection			
• teach each other in informal settings and in focus groups			
• use meeting time for discussions about teaching and learning rather than administrivia			
• talk openly and often about what we are learning or would like to learn			
• concentrate efforts and dialogue on quality and quantity of student learning, rather than on how many chapters have been covered in the text			

Tool-39

How Are We Doing?
Data Analysis and Integration

We use data to:	Skillful Use	Learning to Use	Need to Learn
• build a body of evidence to include classroom, district, state, and national data			
• improve the instructional program			
• provide teachers feedback on the effects of their efforts			
• provide students feedback on their performance			
• develop a common understanding of quality student performance and how close we are to achieving it			
• measure program results, efficiency, and cost effectiveness			
• understand if what we are doing is making a difference over time by tracking students			
• understand if what we are doing is making a difference over time by examining programs, curriculums, and departments			
• ensure that students/groups of students "do not fall through the cracks" by disaggregating the data in multiple ways			
• identify cause and effect relationships			
• guide curriculum development, integration, and revision			
• develop School Improvement Plans			
• design professional development plans			
• meet district, state, and federal requirements			

Tool-40

Formats for Professional Learning

	In place and functioning smoothly	We are working on this one	Good idea we need to try	Would like to know more
• Action Research				
• Book Studies				
• Case Studies				
• Classroom Observations				
• Co-Teaching				
• Collaborative Teams				
• Common Assessment Work				
• Critical Incident Discussions "What Do You Do When... ?"				
• Data Dialogues				
• Demonstration Lessons				
• Journals				
• Learning Walks				
• Lesson Study				
• Looking at Student Work				
• Looking at Teacher Work				
• Meetings Focused on Teaching and Learning				
• Mentoring Relationships				
• Online Conversations: blogs, discussion forums, wiki, and email				
• Parallel Planning				
• Planning Conferences				
• Podcasts				
• Post/Reflective Conferences				
• Professional Conferences				
• Video Conferencing				
• Videotaped Classroom Episodes, Analysis of				
• Webinars				
• Workshops/Seminars				

Tool-41

Planning Instruction
How Am I Doing?

Mark each item: (W) Working Well   (S) Sometimes   (N) Not Yet

____ I use the Common Core Standards, state standards, and district outcomes to plan for the year, the unit, and the lesson.
____ I use the standards-based planning process to plan and pace for the year.
____ I use the standards-based planning process for units and lessons by aligning assessments and learning experiences with the standards.
____ I identify the focus of the content areas being taught.
____ I design summative assessments prior to deciding on learning experiences for units or lessons.
____ I design learning experiences that give students practices and rehearsals at the same level of understanding as the level at which the standards are written.
____ I communicate how any given lesson/learning experience is directly related to the standards.
____ I state standards in lesson plans.
____ I analyze instructional materials for match to district outcomes.
____ I identify supplemental materials and design learning experiences to fill any gaps in standard materials.
____ I use the task analysis process to identify the knowledge, skills, and level of understanding required by the standard and the assignment or assessment task, consider where individuals and the group of students are with the required knowledge, skills, and level of understanding, and plan learning experiences accordingly.
____ I include knowledge of student readiness levels, interests, and learning styles in designing learning experiences.
____ I build pauses for processing into the lesson design and use 10:2 Theory and Wait Time as guidelines.
____ I plan and write out the key questions to ask during a lesson.
____ I analyze text structure, point out the structure, and teach students to use graphic organizers to represent the thinking processes used by the author and to capture the key information in the text.
____ I align assignments including homework with standards and assessments and am purposeful about examining homework results for evidence of learning.
____ I eliminate lessons and learning exercises that do not move students toward meeting the standards.
____ I collaborate/consult with support staff about special needs students.

Tool-42

Tools and Templates

Templates are available at www.justaskpublications.com/CCLtemplates

Self-Assessment
Ways to Scaffold and Extend Instruction

We base our planning on the key concepts/essential understandings of our curriculum. To provide additional challenges, or additional support, we move from those understandings to deciding what support systems students need to master those essential understandings as well as what we will need to do to provide rigorous and challenging learning experiences for those who can easily demonstrate mastery of those understandings.

Read through the statements below, mark with an X those that you already consider in your planning, and reflect on those that you need to use to guide your thinking as you plan future instruction.

- ☐ I design lessons and units based on the essential understandings, key concepts, big ideas, and level of understanding required by the Common Core Standards, state standards, and district curriculum.
- ☐ I make abstract concepts more accessible through semi-abstract (pictures or graphs) or concrete (realia/props/exemplars) representations.
- ☐ I promote learning by linking new concepts and ideas to familiar concepts or experiences.
- ☐ I purposefully learn about my students readiness levels, interests, and learning strengths and design standards-based learning experiences that build on their current status.
- ☐ I increase/decrease accessibility by providing alternative resources, by giving more/less guidance, or by supplying resources.
- ☐ I ensure that students working at all skill levels constantly build expertise at accessing resources for increasingly independent learning.
- ☐ I break the task or goal into simpler parts...such as chunking the task, providing check-in points and time guidelines, or having advanced students do more independent investigations.
- ☐ I provide more/less structure as needed.
- ☐ I adjust the level of independence to ensure success without enabling.
- ☐ I adjust the frequency of feedback so that students can adjust their learning efforts.
- ☐ I adjust the time for input of new information, the meaning making, and the demonstrations of understanding as needed.
- ☐ I extend and enrich the learning experiences for those who are able to do complex quality work and demonstrate understanding in a short time.

Tool-43

Session Planning Worksheet

Getting Started
- **Essential and Focus Questions**

- **Agenda**

- **Community Builder**

- **Collegial Discussions**

New Learning Focus*
- **Accessing Prior Knowledge**

*Repeat the **New Learning Focus** sequence as many times as the schedule allows.

Tool-44a

- **Input of New Information**

- **Processing/Applying New Information/Skills**

- **Summarizing**

Professional Practice and/or Planning Next Steps

Tool-44b

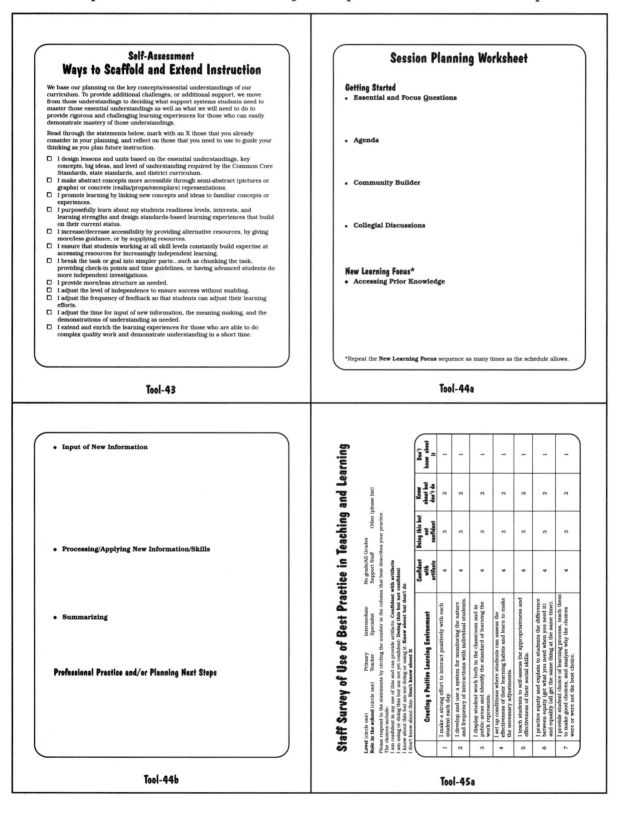

Staff Survey of Use of Best Practice in Teaching and Learning

Level (circle one): Primary Teacher / Intermediate Specialist / No grade/All Grades Support Staff / Other (please list)
Role in the school (circle one)

Please respond to the statements by circling the number in the column that best describes your practice.
The choices include:
I am confident in my use of this and can provide artifacts: **Confident with artifacts**
I am using or doing this but am not yet confident: **Doing this but not confident**
I know about this but am not doing or using it: **Know about but don't do**
I don't know about this: **Don't know about it**

	Creating a Positive Learning Environment	Confident with artifacts	Doing this but not confident	Know about but don't do	Don't know about it
1	I make a strong effort to interact positively with each student each day.	4	3	2	1
2	I develop and use a system for monitoring the nature and frequency of interactions with individual students.	4	3	2	1
3	I display student work both in the classroom and in public areas and identify the standard of learning the work represents.	4	3	2	1
4	I set up conditions where students can assess the effectiveness of their learning habits and learn to make the necessary adjustments.	4	3	2	1
5	I teach students to self-assess the appropriateness and effectiveness of their social skills.	4	3	2	1
6	I practice equity and explain to students the difference between equity (get what you need when you need it) and equality (all get the same thing at the same time).	4	3	2	1
7	I provide student choice of learning process, teach them to make good choices, and analyze why the choices were or were not the best choice.	4	3	2	1

Tool-45a

Tools and Templates

Templates are available at www.justaskpublications.com/CCLtemplates

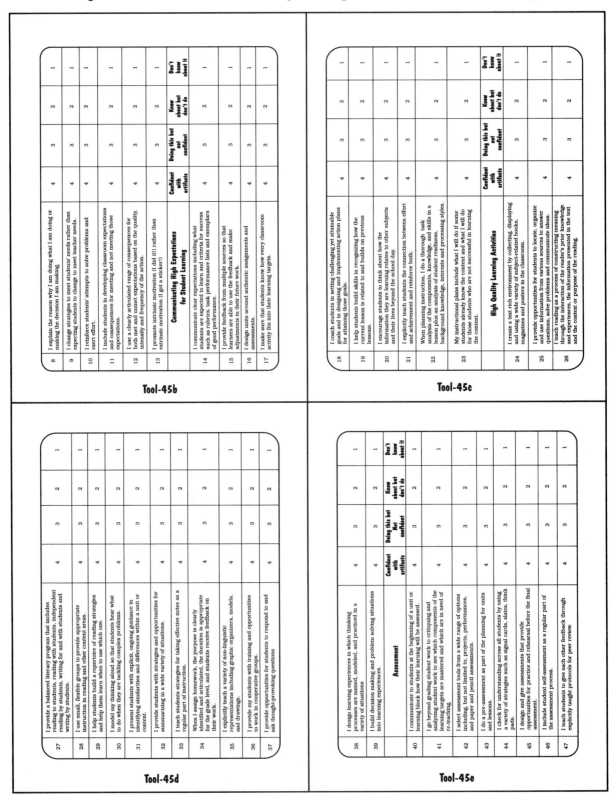

Tool-45b

		Confident with artifacts	Doing this but not confident	Know about but don't do	Don't know about it
8	I explain the reason why I am doing what I am doing or making the decision I am making.	4	3	2	1
9	I change strategies to meet students' needs rather than expecting students to change to meet teacher needs.	4	3	2	1
10	I reinforce students' attempts to solve problems and exert effort.	4	3	2	1
11	I include students in developing classroom expectations and consequences for meeting and not meeting those expectations.	4	3	2	1
12	I use a clearly articulated range of consequences for both met and unmet expectations based on the quality, intensity and frequency of the action.	4	3	2	1
13	I promote intrinsic motivation (I did it!) rather than extrinsic motivation (I got a sticker!)	4	3	2	1
	Communicating High Expectations for Student Learning	Confident with artifacts	Doing this but not confident	Know about but don't do	Don't know about it
14	I communicate clear expectations including what students are expected to learn and criteria for success such as rubrics, task performance lists and exemplars of good performance.	4	3	2	1
15	I provide feedback from multiple sources so that learners are able to use the feedback and make adjustments in their future work.	4	3	2	1
16	I design units around authentic assignments and assessments.	4	3	2	1
17	I make sure that students know how every classroom activity fits into their learning targets.	4	3	2	1

Tool-45c

		Confident with artifacts	Doing this but not confident	Know about but don't do	Don't know about it
18	I coach students in setting challenging yet attainable goals and in designing and implementing action plans for attaining those goals.	4	3	2	1
19	I help students build skills in recognizing how the current lesson is related to and builds on previous lessons.	4	3	2	1
20	I encourage students to think about how the information they are learning relates to other subjects and their lives beyond the school day.	4	3	2	1
21	I explicitly teach students the connection between effort and achievement and reinforce both.	4	3	2	1
22	When planning instruction, I do a thorough task analysis of the components, knowledge, and skills in a lesson plus an analysis of student readiness, background knowledge, interests and processing styles.	4	3	2	1
23	My instructional plans include what I will do if some students already know the content and what I will do for those students who are not successful in learning the content.	4	3	2	1
	High Quality Learning Activities	Confident with artifacts	Doing this but not confident	Know about but don't do	Don't know about it
24	I create a text rich environment by collecting, displaying and using a wide variety of subject-related books, magazines and posters in the classroom.	4	3	2	1
25	I provide opportunities for students to locate, organize and use information from various sources to answer questions, solve problems and communicate ideas.	4	3	2	1
26	I teach reading as a process of constructing meaning through the interaction of the reader's prior knowledge and experiences, the information presented in the text and the context or purpose of the reading.	4	3	2	1

Tool-45d

		4	3	2	1
27	I provide a balanced literacy program that includes reading to students, reading with students, independent reading by students, writing for and with students and writing by students.	4	3	2	1
28	I use small, flexible groups to provide appropriate instruction in reading and other content areas.	4	3	2	1
29	I help students build a repertoire of reading strategies and help them learn when to use which one.	4	3	2	1
30	I model my thinking aloud so that students hear what to do when they are tackling complex problems.	4	3	2	1
31	I present students with explicit, ongoing guidance in identifying similarities and differences within a unit or content.	4	3	2	1
32	I provide students with strategies and opportunities for summarizing in a wide variety of situations.	4	3	2	1
33	I teach students strategies for taking effective notes as a regular part of instruction.	4	3	2	1
34	When I assign homework, the purpose is clearly identified and articulated, the duration is appropriate for the grade level, and students receive feedback on their work.	4	3	2	1
35	I explicitly teach a variety of non-linguistic representations including graphic organizers, models, and drawings.	4	3	2	1
36	I provide my students with training and opportunities to work in cooperative groups.	4	3	2	1
37	I provide opportunities for students to respond to and ask thought-provoking questions	4	3	2	1

Tool-45e

		Confident with artifacts	Doing this but not confident	Know about but don't do	Don't know about it
38	I design learning experiences in which thinking processes are named, modeled, and practiced in a variety of situations.	4	3	2	1
39	I build decision making and problem solving situations into learning experiences.	4	3	2	1
	Assessment	Confident with artifacts	Doing this but not confident	Know about but don't do	Don't know about it
40	I communicate to students at the beginning of a unit or learning block how their learning will be assessed.	4	3	2	1
41	I go beyond grading student work to critiquing and analyzing student work to assess which components of the learning targets are mastered and which are in need of re-teaching.	4	3	2	1
42	I select assessment tools from a wide range of options including, but not limited to, projects, performances, and paper and pencil assessments.	4	3	2	1
43	I do a pre-assessment as part of the planning for units and lessons.	4	3	2	1
44	I check for understanding across all students by using a variety of strategies such as signal cards, slates, think pads.	4	3	2	1
45	I design and give assessments that provide opportunities for practice and rehearsal before the final assessment.	4	3	2	1
46	I include student self-assessment as a regular part of the assessment process.	4	3	2	1
47	I teach students to give each other feedback through explicitly taught protocols for peer review.	4	3	2	1

Tools and Templates

Templates are available at www.justaskpublications.com/CCLtemplates

	4	3	2	1
48	I engage students in the creation and use of rubrics.			
49	I have students score work to help them understand how the scoring criteria are used to evaluate student work.			
50	When I have students work in groups, I structure the assignments to assure individual accountability for the work.			
51	I regularly look at the progress my students are making in their attainment of the learning targets and adjust my teaching to their needs.			

Tool-45f

Standards-Based Education Learning Walk

School_____   Date _____
Observers_____   Grade Level/Teams_____

Focus Question: To what extent is the SBE Planning Process being implemented?

+ = Appropriate implementation observed
X = Evidence seen
# = Did not observe

1st Oval: What should students know and be able to do?
____ Standards drive curriculum planning and classroom decisions.
____ Learning outcomes and agenda for the lesson are communicated to the students before the lesson begins.
____ Lessons are linked to essential understandings, key concepts, or big ideas.
____ Students can articulate what they are expected to know and be able to do as a result of the lesson or unit.

2nd Oval: How will the students and I know when they are successful?
____ Public and precise criteria are communicated to students prior to the beginning of the lesson or unit.
____ Exemplars, where appropriate, are provided for processes and products.
____ Students can explain how they are going to be evaluated.

3rd Oval: What learning experiences will facilitate student success?
____ The teacher has planned the lesson/unit with the end in mind.
____ A task analysis is used to determine the required skills and knowledge and the level of understanding demanded, (writing, small group instruction, individual student-teacher conferences, group sharing)
____ Students are provided an opportunity to access prior knowledge and/or experiences about the topic to be studied.
____ Misconceptions and naive understandings are identified and addressed.
____ The learning experiences are aligned with lesson and outcomes and information revealed by the task analysis.
____ Accommodations are made for different readiness levels and learning styles of students.

Tool-46a

Standards-Based Education Learning Walk

____ Scaffolding is provided so that students have appropriate levels of support and structure to be successful as learners.
____ Scaffolding is withdrawn as the students become more independent in their learning.
____ Extensions are provided for accelerated learners.
____ Pauses for processing and summarizing new information are built into the lesson.
____ Clear explanations of assignments are provided so students know exactly what they are supposed to do.

4th Oval: Based on data, how are learning experiences refined?
____ On-the-spot adjustments are made based on how well the lesson is meeting the needs of students.
____ Teacher decisions are guided by formative and summative assessments.
____ The results of formative and summative assessments are used to inform students of their learning and next steps in their own learning.

Comments:

Tool-46b

Points to Note in the Review of a Standards-Based Lesson or Unit

Analyze the lesson or unit plan using the following criteria. Note strengths and consider what changes, if made, might make the most difference in student learning.

Addresses district **standards, benchmarks,** and **indicators** at the appropriate grade level
Data:

Focuses on **essential understandings, key concepts,** and **big ideas**
Data:

Incorporates **formative** and **summative assessment** components with a feedback loop clearly articulated
Data:

Uses **assessment strategies** that allow students to demonstrate what they know in **different ways**
Data:

Provides public and precise **assessment criteria** communicated to the learners prior to beginning the work (If possible, exemplars are provided.)
Data:

Tool-47a

Tools and Templates

Templates are available at www.justaskpublications.com/CCLtemplates

Tool-47b

Includes a thorough and detailed **task analysis** of the standards and the assessment task
Data:

Includes instructional strategies which address **required knowledge and skills** identified in the task analysis as necessary for mastery
Data

Includes strategies that **Frame the Learning** by accessing prior knowledge, providing opportunities for meaning making and real world connections, and having students summarize their learning to promote retention and transfer
Data:

Requires **rigor** and **complex thinking skills**
Data

Provides **scaffolding** and **extensions** to meet the needs of a wide range of learners
Data:

Includes an emphasis on **literacy** across the curriculum
Data:

Tool-47b

Tool-48

Task Analysis

Knowledge | Skills

- Is there background knowledge or a level of understanding the entire group is lacking? How about individual students?
- Are there academic or social skills the entire group is lacking? How about the skill level of individuals?
- What shall I do in a proactive way to prevent frustrations and problems with learning?
- What shall I do with students who already know and can apply this information?

Students	Potential Problem	Possible Intervention

Tool-48

Tool-49

Tier 1 Math (Grades K-5)
Teacher Self-Assessment

The following is a list of the essential components of a **Math Workshop**. Identify your level of use of the activities and structures that need to occur if your students are ultimately to achieve math success. **This reflection tool is a starting point for ongoing collaboration, practice, and continual learning school wide and in your grade level.**

Essential Component	Frequency	Always: 95%+ / Usually: 75%-90% / Sometimes: 40%-75% / Rarely: 0%-40%	If unable to mark Always, my plan for reaching the goal of this Math Workshop component is:
1. I have a **daily** math workshop of at least 60 minutes (Monday-Friday).			
2. I start my math block with an engaging **opening** (that focuses on a specific strategy, i.e. counting, vocabulary development, test-taking strategy, etc.)			
3. I launch students into a discovery of certain standards/concepts through a focus lesson.			
4. I plan for and provide guided math groups with explicit instruction based on students' needs.			
5. I prepare meaningful math tasks for small groups and/or individual students (i.e. centers, targeted games, math journals, other investigations).			
6. I dedicate time at the end of the math block for students to reflect on the math concept through whole group discussion, exit tickets, journal writing or think-pair-share.			

Tool-49

Tool-50

Tier 1 Reading Instruction (Grades K-2)
Teacher Self-Assessment

The following is a list of the essential components of a **Primary Reading Workshop**. Identify your level of use of the activities and structures that are ultimately to achieve reading success. This reflection tool is a starting point for ongoing collaboration, practice, and continual learning school wide and in your grade level.

Essential Component	Frequency	Always: 95%+ / Usually: 75%-90% / Sometimes: 40%-75% / Rarely: 0%-40%	If unable to mark Always, my plan for reaching the goal of this Reading Workshop component is:
1. I **read aloud** to the class each day allowing time for discussion among the students.			
2. During **interactive read-aloud** I ask questions to elicit higher level thinking and stimulate rich discussion.			
3. I use **shared reading** to teach students reading strategies. Children can all see the text and can read along.			
4. I plan for and provide **guided reading** groups for each student reading below grade level using appropriate leveled text; small group explicit instruction based on students' needs.			
5. I plan for and provide **guided reading** groups for each student reading on/above grade level using appropriate leveled text; small group explicit instruction based on students' needs.			
6. I provide each student with an individual book box with texts at each student's appropriate level (e.g. guided reading books) for **independent reading**. I provide time for independent reading.			

Tool-50

©Just ASK Publications

306

Tools and Templates

Templates are available at www.justaskpublications.com/CCLtemplates

Tier 1 Reading Instruction (Grades 3-5)
Teacher Self-Assessment

The following is a list of the essential components of a **Intermediate Reading Workshop.** Identify your level of use of the activities and structures that need to occur if your students are ultimately to achieve reading success. **This reflection tool is a starting point for ongoing collaboration, practice, and continual learning school wide and in your grade level.**

Essential Component	Frequency	Always: 95%+ Usually: 75%-90% Sometimes: 40%-75% Rarely: 0%-40%	If unable to mark Always, my plan for reaching the goal of this Reading Workshop component is:
1. I **read aloud** to the class each day allowing time for discussion among the students.			
2. I plan for and provide **guided reading** groups for each student below grade level using appropriate leveled text; small group explicit instruction based on students' needs and reading level.			
3. I plan for and provide guided reading groups for each student on/above grade level using appropriate leveled text; small group explicit instruction based on students' needs and reading level.			
4. I provide each student with an individual book box with texts at each student's appropriate level (e.g. guided reading books) for independent reading. I provide time for independent reading.			
5. I provide students with the opportunity to participate in in-depth analysis of one or more aspects of literature study-author study, genre study, picture book study.			
6. I provide small groups of students the opportunity to participate in literature discussion groups around a text-picture books, nonfiction texts, poetry.			
7. Each student in my class keeps a Reader's Notebook where he/she articulates thoughts, questions, comments and predictions about texts and I respond on a regular basis. Each of my students also keeps a reading log			

Tool-51

Whole School Observation Form

Use this form to capture data about the implementation of the best practices you see across the school or throughout a department or grade level. Use the district's performance criteria or strategies the staff is studying together as the focus of the data gathering. You can provide feedback electronically or in a newsletter.

Teacher Name	A	B	C	D	Data

In the areas designated A, B, C, and D insert the specific behaviors for which you are observing on a given day. You may choose to observe for only one or two at a time. In the Data column include teacher actions, student actions, and artifacts.

Tool-52

Resources and References

Albritton, Rick, Terry Morganti-Fisher, Jan O'Neil, and Sigrid Yates. "SMART Partners." **JSD**. Learning Forward, June 2011, pp 55-58.

Armstrong, Anthony. "Lesson Study Puts a Collaborative Lens on Student Learning." **Tools for Schools**. Learning Forward, Summer 2011, pp 1-4.

Baker, William. "The Seven Norms of Collaborative Work." **Collaborative Cutlures Tools and Skills Workshop**. Berkeley, CA: Group Dynamics Associates, 2008.

Blythe, Tina, David Allen and Barbara Powell. **Looking Together at Student Work**. New York: Teachers College Press, 1999.

Bernhardt, Victoria. **Translating Data into Information to Improve Teaching and Learning**. Larchmont, NY: Eye on Education, 2007.

_____ **Data, Data Everywhere: Bringing All the Data Together for Continuous School Improvement**. Larchmont, NY: Eye on Education, 2009.

_____ "Measuring School Success." **Instructional Leader**. Texas Elementary Principals and Supervisors Association. January 2011, pp 1-8.

Bolton, Robert. **People Skills**. New York, NY: Simon & Schuster, 1979.

Brown Easton, Lois, Editor. **Powerful Designs for Professional Learning**. Oxford, OH: Learning Forward, 2008.

Chadwick, Bob. Facilitation Ideas. Access at www.coloradocfg.org

Collins, Jim. **Good to Great**. New York: Harper Collins, 2001.

Colorado Deportment of Education. "Colorado Educators Study Homeless and Highly Mobile Students." Denver, CO: Colorado Department of Education, 2005. Available at http://www.cde.state.co.us/cdeprevention/download/pdf/COPAR %20Book%20Final%204-25-05.pdf

Conzemius, Anne and O'Neill, Jen. **The Power of SMART Goals**. Bloomington, IN: Solution Tree, 2005.

Costa, Art and Robert Garmston. **Cognitive Coaching: A Foundation for Renaissance Schools**. Norwood, MA: Christopher Gordon, 2002.

Darling-Hammond, Linda. "The Quiet Revolution: Rethinking Teacher Development." **Educational Leadership**. March 1996.

Darling-Hammond, Linda, and Diane Friedlaender. "Creating Excellent and Equitable Schools." **Educational Leadership**. May 2008, pp 14-21.

Davidson-Taylor, Carolyn. "Is Instruction Working? Students Have the Answer." **Principal Leadership**. November 2002, pp 30-34.

Deal, Jennifer. **Retiring the Generation Gap: How Employees Young and Old Can Find Common Ground**. Hoboken, NJ: John Wiley & Sons, Inc., 2007.

Resources and References

Deal, Terry and Kent Peterson. *Shaping School Culture: The Heart of Leadership*. Hoboken, NJ: John Wiley & Sons, Inc., 1999.

DeJarnette-Caldwell, Sara. *Professional Development in Learning-Centered Schools*. Oxford, OH: Learning Forward (National Staff Development Council), 1997.

Delbecq, Andre , David Gustafson, and Andrew Van de Ven. *Group Techniques for Program Planning: A Guide to Nominal Group and Delphi Processes*. Chicago, IL: Scott Foresman and Company, 1975.

Dorn, Linda and Carla Soffos. *Shaping Literate Minds*. Portland, ME: Stenhouse Publishers, 2001.

DuFour, Richard. "Work Together: But Only If You Want To." *Phi Delta Kappan*, September 2010, pp 54-66.

DuFour, Richard and Robert Eaker. *Professional Learning Communities at Work: Best Practices for Enhancing Student Achievement*. Bloomington, IN: Solution Tree Press, 1998.

DuFour, Richard, Rebecca DuFour, Robert Eaker, and Thomas Many. *Learning by Doing: A Handbook for Professional Learning Communities at Work Second Edition*. Bloomington, IN: Solution Tree Press, 2010.

Easton, Lois Brown. *Powerful Designs for Professional Learning Second Edition*: Oxford, OH: Learning Forward, 2008.

Erickson, Lynn. *Concept-Based Curriculum and Instruction for the Thinking Classroom*. Thousand Oaks, CA: Corwin Press, 2007.

"Essential Roles and Responsibilities within a Standards-Based Education System." SBE Design Team. Longmont, CO: Centennial BOCES, 1998.

Facilitator's Guide for Common Ground in the Standards-Based Educations Classroom. Longmont, CO: Centennial BOCES. 2002.

Fountas, Irene and Gay Su Pinnell. *Matching Books to Readers: Using Leveled Books in Guided Reading, K–3*. Portsmouth, NH: Heinemann,1999.

Fullan, Michael. *Leadership and Sustainability: System Thinkers in Action*. Thousand Oaks, CA: Corwin Press, 2005.

_____ *Leading in a Culture of Change*. San Francisco, CA: Jossey-Bass, 2001.

_____ *The Moral Imperative of School Leadership*. Thousand Oaks, CA: Corwin Press, 2003.

Fullan, Michael and Andy Hargreaves. *What's Worth Fighting for in Your School*. New York: Teacher College Press, 1996.

Resources and References

Garmston, Robert and Bruce Wellman. ***The Adaptive School***. Norwood, MA: Christopher-Gordon Publishers, 1999.

Glickman, Carl. ***Renewing America's Schools***. Hoboken, NJ: John Wiley & Sons, Inc., 1998.

Gordon, Thomas. ***T.E.T. Teacher Effectiveness Training***. New York: David McKay Company, Inc, 1974.

Graham, Parry. "The Role of Conversation, Contention, and Commitment in a Professional Learning Community: Connections Module m14270." Accessed at http://cnx.org/content/m14270/1.1

Guskey, Thomas. ***Evaluating Professional Development***. Thousand Oaks, CA: Corwin Press, 2000.

Hanson, Robert, Patricia Schwartz, Harvey Sliver, and Richard Strong. ***Teaching Styles and Strategies: Interventions to Enrich Instructional Decision-Making***. Ho Ho Kus, NJ: Thoughtful Education Press, 1994.

Harrison, Cindy and Chris Bryan. "Data Dialogue." ***JSD***. Fall 2008, pp 15-18.

Hord, Shirley. Professional Learning Communities: Communities of Continuous Inquiry and Improvement. Southwest Educational Development Laboratory, 1997, pp 18-19. Access at http://www.sedl.org/pubs/change34/

Hord, Shirley, William Rutherford, Leslie Huling-Austin, and Gene Hall. ***Taking Charge of Change Third Edition***. Southwest Educational Development Laboratory, 1998.

Ingersoll, Richard and Michael Strong. "The Impact of Induction and Mentoring Programs for Beginning Teachers: A Critical Review of the Literature." Review of Educational Research, June 2011.

Jamentz, Kate. ***Standards: From Document to Dialogue***. San Francisco, CA: West Ed, 1998.

James, Jennifer. ***Thinking in the Future Tense***. New York, NY: Simon and Schuster, 1997.

Joyce, Bruce and Beverly Showers. ***Student Achievement Through Staff Development***. Alexandria, VA: ASCD, 2002.

Kaylor, Brenda, Editor. ***Results-Based Professional Development Models***. Longmont, CO: Office of Professional Development, St. Vrain Valley School District, 2002.

Kerbow, David, Julia Gwynne, and Brian Jacob. "Implementation of a Balanced Literacy Framework and Student Learning: Implications for Program Development." Chicago, IL: University of Chicago Center for School Improvement, 2001.

Kilgore, Sally and Karen Reynolds. ***From Silos to Systems: Reframing Schools for Success***. Thousand Oaks, CA: Corwin, 2011.

Resources and References

Killion, Joellen and Cindy Harrison. *Taking the Lead: New Roles for Teachers and School-Based Coaches*. Oxford, OH: Learning Forward, 2006.

Kirkpatrick, Donald. *A Practical Guide for Supervisory Training and Development*. Boston, MA: Addison-Wesley, 1983.

Krupp, Judy-Arin. *The Adult Learner: A Unique Entity*. Manchester, CT: Adult Development and Learning, 1982.

Kruse, Sharon and Karen Louis. *Building Strong School Cultures: A Guide to Leading Change*. Thousand Oaks, CA: Corwin Press. 2009.

Kruse, Sharon, Karen Louis, and Anthony Bryk. "Building Professional Community in Schools." *Issues in Restructuring Schools*. Spring 1994, pp 3-6.

Lambert, Linda. "How to Build Leadership Capacity." *Educational Leadership*. April 1998, pp 17-19.

Lancaster, Lynne and David Stillman. *When Generations Collide: Who They Are. Why They Clash. How to Solve the Generational Puzzle at Work*. New York: Harper Business, February 4, 2002.

Lewis, Catherine. *Lesson Study: A Handbook of Teacher-Led Instructional Change*. Philadelphia, PA: Research for Better Schools, Inc., 2002.

Lieberman, Ann. *Building a Professional Culture in Schools*. New York, NY: Teachers College Press, Teachers College, Columbia University, 1988.

Lightfoot, Sara Lawrence. *The Good High School: Portraits of Character and Culture*. New York: Basic Books, 1983.

Lipton, Laura and Bruce Wellman. *Mentoring Matters: A Practical Guide to Learning*. Sherman, CT: MiraVia, 2002.

Little, Judith Warren. "Norms of Collegiality and Experimentation: Workplace Conditions of School Success." *American Educational Research Journal*. Fall 1982, pp 325-340.

Louis, Karen, Helen Marks, and Sharon Kruse. "Teachers' Professional Community in Restructuring Schools." *American Educational Research Journal*. 1996, pp 757-798.

MacDonald, Elisa. "When Nice Won't Suffice." *JSD*. June 2011, 45-47, 51.

Mangan, Melinda and Sara Ray Stoelinga. "Peer? Expert?" *JSD*. June 2011, 48-51.

Marzano, Robert, Deborah Pickering, and Jane Pollack. *Classroom Instruction That Works: Research-Based Strategies for Increasing Student Achievement*. Denver, CO: McREL, 2011.

McLaughlin, Milbrey and Joan Talbert. "Contexts That Matter for Teaching and Learning: Strategic Opportunities for Meeting the Nation's Educational Goals." Stanford University: Center for Research On The Context of Secondary School Teaching, 1993.

Resources and References

Miles, Matthew. *Learning to Work in Groups: A Program Guide for Educational Leaders*. New York: Columbia Teachers College, 1959.

Murphy, Michael. *Tools & Talk: Data, Conversation, and Action for Classroom and School Improvement*, Oxford, OH: Learning Forward, 2009.

Oliver, Bruce. *Just for the ASKing! e-newsletters*. Archive of all issues is available at www.justaskpublications.com/jfta.htm.

Peterson, Kent and Terrence Deal. "How Leaders Influence the Culture of Schools." *Educational Leadership*. September 1998, pp 28-30.

Purnell, Susanna and Paul Hill. *Time for Reform*. Santa Monica, CA: RAND Corporation, 1991.

Richardson, Joan. "Applause! Applause!" *Tools for Schools*. National Staff Development Council. April/May 1998.

Raywid, Mary Ann. "Finding Time for Collaboration." *Educational Leadership*. September 1993, pp 30-34.

Reeves, Douglas. *Accountability in Action*. Englewood, CO: Lead + Learn Press, 2004.

Resnick, Lauren. "Learning Walk-Through." University of Pittsburgh, PA: The Institute for Learning, 2001.

Rosenholtz, Susan. "The Formation of Ability Conceptions: Developmental Trend or Social Construction?" *Review of Educational Research*. Spring 1984, pp 31-63.

Rutherford, Paula. *Instruction for All Students, Second Edition*. Alexandria, VA: Just ASK Publications, 2008.

_____ *Meeting the Needs of Diverse Learners*. Alexandria, VA: Just ASK Publications, 2010.

_____ *Leading the Learning*. Alexandria, VA: Just ASK Publications, 2005.

_____ *The 21st Century Mentor's Handbook*. Alexandria, VA: Just ASK Publications, 2008.

_____ *Why Didn't I Learn This in College? Second Edition*. Alexandria, VA: Just ASK Publications, 2009.

Sagor, Richard. *Guiding School Improvement with Action Research*. Alexandria, VA: ASCD, 2000.

Saphier, Jon and Matthew King. "Good Seeds Grow in Strong Cultures." *Educational Leadership*. March, 1985.

Schlechty, Phillip. *Schools for the 21st Century: Leadership Imperatives for Educational Reform*. San Francisco, CA: Jossey-Bass Publishers, 1990.

Resources and References

Schmoker, Mike. *Results: The Key to Continuous School Improvement*. Alexandria, VA: ASCD, 1996.

_____ *Results Now: How We Can Achieve Unprecedented Improvements in Teaching and Learning*. Alexandria, VA: ASCD, 2006.

_____ *Focus: Elevating the Essentials to Radically Improve Student Learning*. Alexandria, VA: ASCD, 2011.

_____ *Results Field Book*. Alexandria, VA: ASCD, 2001.

_____ "First Things First: Demystifying Data Analysis." *Educational Leadership*. February 2003, pp 22-24.

Senge, Peter. *The Fifth Discipline: The Art and Practice of the Learning Organization*. New York: Currency Doubleday, 1990.

Singleton, Glenn and Curtis Linton. *Courageous Conversations about Race: A Field Guide for Achieving Equity in Schools*. Thousand Oaks, CA: Corwin Press, 2006.

Standards-Based Classroom Operator's Manual, 3rd Edition. Longmont, CO: Centennial BOCES, 2002.

Stiggins, Rick. "From Formative Assessment to Assessment FOR Learning." *Phi Delta Kappan*. December 2005, pp 324-328.

Wellman, Bruce and Laura Lipton. *Data-Driven Dialogue: A Facilitator's Guide to Collaborative Inquiry*. Sherman, CT: MiraVia, LLC, 2004.

Welsh, Sue Wells. *Peer Coaching Skills*. San Fransico, CA: ASCD, March 1991.

Wood, Fred, Frank McQuarrie, and Steven Thompson. "Practitioners and Professors Agree on Effective Staff Development Practices." *Educational Leadership*. October 1982, pp 28-31.

Wood, Fred and Steven Thompson. "Assumptions about Staff Development Based on Research and Best Practice." *Journal of Staff Development*. Fall 1993, pp 52-57.

Index

"**T**" indicates that there is a template available online at
www.justaskpublications.com/CCLtemplates

Index

"**T**" indicates that there is a template available online at
www.justaskpublications.com/CCLtemplates

Index

"**T**" indicates that there is a template available online at
www.justaskpublications.com/CCLtemplates

Index

"**T**" indicates that there is a template available online at
www.justaskpublications.com/CCLtemplates

Index

"**T**" indicates that there is a template available online at
www.justaskpublications.com/CCLtemplates

Index

"**T**" indicates that there is a template available online at
www.justaskpublications.com/CCLtemplates

Index

Index

"**T**" indicates that there is a template available online at
www.justaskpublications.com/CCLtemplates

Index

"**T**" indicates that there is a template available online at
www.justaskpublications.com/CCLtemplates

About the Authors

Paula Rutherford

Paula lives in the Washington, D.C. area and consults with school districts and educational organizations around the world. Her publications include *Why Didn't I Learn This in College?*, *The 21ˢᵗ Century Mentor's Handbook*, *Instruction for All Students*, *Leading the Learning: A Field Guide for Supervision and Evaluation*, and *Meeting the Needs of Diverse Learners*.

She has been a history and social studies teacher, a physical education teacher, a kindergarten teacher, a special education teacher, coordinator of special education programs, a school administrator, and professional development specialist in school districts across the country.

Brenda Kaylor

Brenda lives in Northglenn, Colorado, a suburb of Denver, and works with school districts to design and implement long term, multifaceted professional development programs. Brenda is the editor of *Results-Based Professional Development Models* and the director of Just ASK's **TL21 DVD Series** featuring exemplary teaching and learning episodes and the **Collegial Conversations DVD**. She was the project coordinator and a presenter for the 2010 and the 2011 Las Cruces **Creating a Culture for Learning**™ Summits.

Brenda is an active member of Learning Forward and served most recently as the Director of Professional Development for St. Vrain Valley School District, Longmont, Colorado and Brighton Public Schools, Colorado.

The depth of her knowledge is revealed in her contributions to this book. Those contributions include her adaptation of the RPLIM model, exemplars of collaborative teams in action, guidelines for attending professional conferences as a team, the CBAM case study, and many other tools for collaboration.

Heather Clayton Kwit

Heather lives in Webster, New York, a suburb of Rochester. She is the principal of Mendon Center Elementary School in Pittsford Central School District, New York. Previous principalships include two schools in the Greece Central School District, New York. In 2005 Longridge Elementary School where she was principal was recognized by the NY State Department of Education as a high performing/gap closing school and as a high achieving school for

English Language Learners. Earlier Heather was a teacher and curriculum leader for English Language Arts in the award-winning West Irondequoit Central School District where she did extensive professional development work in the areas of standards-based planning, differentiation, and ongoing assessment. Her book *Great Mini-Lessons for Teaching Genre Writing* was published by Scholastic in 2001.

Heather's contributions to this book include the great segment on **Waving Your Priorities from the Flag Pole** in Chapter I plus explicit ways to use assessment walls and straight-forward information about how to gather and analyze data to inform instruction and school improvement planning in Chapter VI.

Julie McVicker

Julie helps school districts across the country develop long-term, multifaceted professional development plans that include our **Mentoring in the 21ˢᵗ Century**® Institute and our workshops **Why Didn't I Learn This in College?**®, **Instruction for All Students**™, and **Meeting the Needs of Diverse Learners**®.

Julie was most recently the Director of Priority Schools in St. Vrain Valley School District, Longmont, Colorado, during which time her responsibilities included coordinating the K-5 Literacy Department, supervising elementary principals, working with schools on closing the achievement gap, and leading systemic change. Earlier, she was principal of multiple elementary schools and served as a District Migrant/ELPA Education Coordinator, Gifted and Talented Coordinator, and staff developer. Her action research is published online in the Colorado State Department of Education's report: **Colorado Educators Study Homeless and Highly Mobile Students**.

Exemplars from Indian Peaks Elementary School are examples of Julie's work in a bilingual school. Her action research and the **Placement Interview** she developed as a result of that research are included in Chapter VI.

Bruce Oliver

Bruce lives in Northern Virginia. He is the author of *Just for the ASKing!*, the highly acclaimed monthly e-Newsletter published on the Just ASK website. Over 15,000 educators subscribe to this e-Newsletter.

Bruce uses the knowledge, skills, and experience he acquired as a teacher, professional developer, mentor, and middle school principal in his work with school districts across the country. He works at the district and school level with leadership on establishing professional learning communities and leading in a standards-based environment. Areas of focus for instructional staff include making assessment a learning experience, meeting the

Exemplars from and references to Thoreau Middle School are provided by Bruce from his 16 year tenure as principal of that school. Additionally, multiple issues of *Just for the ASKing!* are included in many chapters because he has emphasized creating a culture for learning in many issues.

Sherri Stephens-Carter

Sherri lives in the Denver, Colorado area. She is a member of the **Just ASK Colorado Turnaround Schools Team** and she led multiple sessions at the 2010 and 2011 Las Cruces **Creating a Culture for Learning**™ **Summit**. Most recently Sherri was Executive Director, Assessment and Curriculum in St. Vrain Valley School District, Colorado. In her "retirement" Sherri continues to coordinate the work of charter schools for St. Vrain and has crazily enough agreed on two occasions to be acting principal at two different charter schools.

Sherri's professional experiences include not only extensive leadership in assessment but eight years as a mathematics coordinator. Additionally, she served as President of the Colorado Association of Educational Evaluators and on the Colorado Standards Committee that developed the math standards for Colorado.

The Staff Survey of Best Practices along with multiple data analysis tools are products of Sherri's work in St. Vrain and her consulting work with schools in Colorado.

Theresa West

Theresa lives in the Washington, D. C. metropolitan area. She retired from Fairfax County Public Schools (FCPS) June 2011. Her most recent position in FCPS was the principalship of McNair Elementary School. Prior to that, she was the Director of Cluster III and Principal of Glen Forest Elementary School, another FCPS school. Under Theresa's leadership, both McNair and Glen Forest made AYP after having failed to do so in previous years.

Besides her work as a school and district level administrator, a teacher of Spanish, ESL, civics, math, and a professional developer, Theresa brings to her work many years of experience working with children of poverty, extensive cross-cultural experience including eleven years living overseas, and bilingual Spanish/English fluency. She has also served as a principal mentor for NAESP.

Theresa and Maria Eck, former assistant principal and now principal at McNair Elementary School, are the chief architects of the **McNair Elementary Case Study** embedded in all chapters of this book.

Ordering Information

Books

	Order #	Price
Active Learning and Engagement Strategies	11060	$ 29.95
Creating a Culture for Learning	11055	$ 34.95
Instruction for All Students Second Edition	11027	$ 34.95
Instruction for All Students Facilitator's Handbook Second Edition	11061	$ 74.95
Leading the Learning	11005	$ 34.95
Meeting the Needs of Diverse Learners	11033	$ 34.95
Meeting the Needs of Diverse Learners Facilitator's Handbook	11056	$ 74.95
Standards-Based Classroom Operator's Manual	11012	$ 24.95
Strategies in Action: A Collection of Classroom Applications - Volume I	11049	$ 19.95
Strategies in Action: Applications in Today's Diverse Classrooms - Volume II	11054	$ 19.95
The 21st Century Mentor's Handbook	11003	$ 34.95
Why Didn't I Learn This in College? Second Edition	11002	$ 29.95
Why Didn't I Learn This in College? and *The 21st Century Mentor's Handbook* Save 20%	11029	$ 50.00

DVDs

	Order #	Price
Collegial Conversations	11031	$ 195.00
Helping New Teachers Succeed	11021	$ 60.00
Lesson Collection: Biology Visual Learning Tools (ASCD)	11026	$ 95.00
Lesson Collection: HS Geometry Surface Area and Volume (ASCD)	11034	$ 95.00
Lesson Collection: HS Reciprocal Teaching (ASCD)	11035	$ 95.00
Lesson Collection: Primary Math (ASCD)	11025	$ 95.00
Points to Ponder	11016	$ 29.95
Principles in Action	11019	$ 19.95
Success Factors in a Standards-Based Classroom	11017	$ 75.00
Teaching and Learning in the 21st Century: 2nd Grade Writer's Workshop	11053	$ 95.00
Teaching and Learning in the 21st Century: 3rd Grade Science	11047	$ 95.00
Teaching and Learning in the 21st Century: 4th/5th Grade Writer's Workshop	11048	$ 95.00

Other Products

	Order #	Price
Mentoring in the 21st Century® Resource Kit	11028	$ 985.00
New Teacher Professional Development Kit	11046	$ 795.00
Instruction for All Students PLC Pack	11051	$ 799.00
Meeting the Needs of Diverse Learners PLC Pack	11052	$ 799.00
Poster Pack	11006	$ 16.95
Visual Tools: The Complete Collection CD-ROM	11041	$ 375.00
Visual Tools: Meeting the Needs of Diverse Learners™ CD-ROM	11040	$ 100.00
Visual Tools: Instruction for All Students™ CD-ROM	11036	$ 100.00
Visual Tools: Leading the Learning® CD-ROM	11039	$ 100.00
Visual Tools: The 21st Century Mentor's Handbook™ CD-ROM	11038	$ 100.00
Visual Tools: Why Didn't I Learn This in College?® CD-ROM	11037	$ 100.00
What Do You Do When... Cards: Mentoring and Supervision Scenarios	11032	$ 49.95
What Do You Do When... Cards: New Teacher Challenges and Concerns	11050	$ 49.95
Scavenger Hunt Cards: *Instruction for All Students*™	11044	$ 10.00
Scavenger Hunt Cards: *Why Didn't I Learn This in College?*®	11045	$ 10.00
Meeting the Needs of Diverse Learners Sort Cards	11059	$ 49.95

To Order

Prices subject to change without notice

Call
800-940-5434

Fax
703-535-8502

Online
www.justaskpublications.com

Mail
2214 King Street, Alexandria, VA 22301

Order Form

Just ASK Publications & Professional Development

Ship To	Bill To (If different)
Name _____	Name _____
Title _____	Title _____
School/District _____	School/District _____
_____	
Address _____	Address _____
City_____ State_____ ZIP_____	City_____ State_____ ZIP_____
Email _____	Email _____
Telephone _____	Telephone _____
Fax _____	Fax _____

Order #	Title	Quantity	Unit Price	Total Price

Please attach a sheet of paper for additional products ordered

Subtotal	
Shipping and Handling	
TOTAL	

$6 S&H minimum per order
15% on orders under 10 units, 10% on orders 10 units or more
$49 S&H for each resource kit

Contact us for quantity discounts and special offers Call 800-940-5434

Payment Method (Select One)

☐ Check (Please make checks or purchase orders payable to Just ASK Publications)

☐ Purchase Order   Purchase Order Number_____

☐ Credit Card   ☐ Visa   ☐ MasterCard   ☐ AMEX

Name as it appears on the card _____

Credit Card # _____

Expiration Date ☐☐ / ☐☐
               Month   Year

**Mail or Fax to:
Just ASK Publications
2214 King Street
Alexandria, VA 22301
Fax: 703-535-8502**

☐ Check here to receive information about Just ASK workshops, institutes, and train-the-trainer opportunities.

Creating a Culture for Learning